D1604135

4-4-74

NATURE AND NECESSITY

An Essay in Physical Ontology

Milton Fisk

NATURE AND NECESSITY

AN ESSAY IN PHYSICAL ONTOLOGY

INDIANA UNIVERSITY PRESS
Bloomington and London

Published in Canada by Fitzhenry & Whiteside Limited, Don Mills, Ontario
Library of Congress catalog card number: 72–85605
ISBN: 0–253–33980–4

This volume is No. 73 in the Indiana University Humanities Series.

Manufactured in the United States of America

For my mother

LUCY YOUNG FISK

CONTENTS

PREFACE

An ontology aims at more than a catalogue of categories of entities. It also aspires to be a system. The way things and properties or things and events fit together is as important for an ontology that admits such entities as the considerations requiring their existence. Two matters are central to any system of categories and in particular to this one that as a system of categories for physical reality I have called a physical ontology. First, the ontologist needs to ask whether entities of one category depend on those of another. Are things and properties independent in the way dogs and cats are, and if they are, is there still some other way that there is dependency between them? Second, there is a question about sameness. People and their coats are surely distinct, but can this model be applied to things and their properties, to things and their actions, and to things and their physical parts?

Certain chronic philosophical infirmities can be traced to a familiar view about dependence and sameness. On the one hand, this view limits dependencies between entities to causal dependencies of the familiar sort. One entity may wound, convince, or beget a second, and then the second is dependent in some respect on the first. But this causal dependence is supposed to be the only kind. There is no ontological dependence of entities of one category on those of a second whereby the former become secondary or derivative and the later primary or fundamental. On the other hand, this view treats entities of different categories as distinct. For a property, action, or part of a thing is quite naturally taken to be distinct from the thing since none of the former is ontologically dependent on the latter. This amounts to an extension of the principle that discernibly different things are not the same. A property, action, or part of a thing must, in this view, be distinct from the thing because of a discernible difference between them. The principle is extended here to apply not just to things but to entities in different categories.

This view of the independence and distinctness of entities of different categories turns certain seemingly harmless dualisms into untenable ones. The dualisms between things and properties, agents and their actions, stuffs and their constituent atoms, and persons and minds become similar in all important respects to the dualisms between cats and dogs, persons and coats, and pilots and ships. As a result, the dualisms between entities of different categories call for a reduction of the entities of one kind to those of the other kind in each pair. For the strict independence and distinctness attributed to entities of the different kinds in these pairs generate undesirable consequences. It is immaterial here which way the reduction goes—things to properties, or properties to things; things to events, or events to things. The important matter is that reductionism does not challenge but is in fact a consequence of the claim that entities of different categories are related by independence and distinctness. Reductionism also has its problems, however. As the inadequacy of reductionism to cope with all the facts becomes more evident, an anti-reductionist reaction starts the cycle over again by positing the original dualisms in their untenable form.

One way to break out of this cycle of dualism and reductionism is to change the view of dependence and sameness that is integral to it. Yet, at least on the matter of sameness, opinion is so conservative that any attempt to tamper with it merely to avoid difficulties on the seemingly quite different matter of traditional dualisms will fail to gather much support. A more direct argument must be attempted here. The crucial claim in this argument concerns both sameness and necessity. It is that unless things can have components not distinct from them, there are no necessities for these things to be and to behave in certain ways. There are entities, commonly called natures, that are inherent in the sense that they both depend on the things with them and are not distinct from those things. Otherwise, there are no necessities for these things to be and to behave in certain ways. With this exception established, strict independence and distinctness are easily seen to fail in other cases as well.

The necessities requiring inherent natures are not offshoots of concepts or language. But it is easy to see why, if entities in different categories are always distinct, there can be no real, as opposed to intentional, necessity. If a thing is distinct from its nature, its properties, its actions, and its parts, it is a simple entity. There is then nothing about it alone that influences what it is or does. The necessity of a thing to be or to behave in a certain way cannot be due to what it is, if it is a simple. It can be due only to the concept or term under which we place it.

Unfortunately for any conceptualist or linguistic view of necessity, the need for real necessities is evident from an examination of the requirements of a coherent inductive practice. Such an examination is, thus, a crucial part of my argument. As noted, a conceptualist or linguistic view of necessity is implied by distinctness between entities of all categories. The inadequacy of this intentionalist view of necessity in respect to inductive practice means that entities from certain different categories are not distinct. This, in turn, will imply that there are dependencies between entities of certain categories. With these results, we are able to break out of the cycle of dualism and reductionism.

The shift to the unorthodox view that entities of different categories need not be independent and distinct has interesting consequences for a number of philosophical issues. Relations, actions, time, capacities, and events are surveyed below from the new point of view. A work with such a broad scope is inevitably programmatic. It shares with other programmatic work a drawback for the reader seeking solutions to problems formulated in terms of principles current in the profession. It attempts to give reasons for formulating those problems on a different base.

The treatment of temporal asymmetry, for example, adds nothing toward the solution of the problem of temporal asymmetry conceived as a problem in scientific ontology. It attempts to justify alternative principles, and it suggests how one may advance if the same problems are formulated in terms of these principles. One principle behind the treatment of temporal asymmetry in scientific ontology is that actions are sequences of states. This view of action is shown to lead to difficulties. An alternative view is developed in terms of which it is possible to solve the problem of temporal asymmetry without the scientific ontologist's reliance on scientific results. The difficulties raised for this and other current ontological principles may not turn out to be sufficiently damaging to make the general program adopted here a compelling one. Still, the attempt will have been amply rewarding if only it occasions the formulation of stronger defenses for the accepted principles.

Anticipations of some of the specific themes, but not of the general plan, have already appeared. Chapters IV and V take a different approach to the conclusion already argued for in "Are There Necessary Connections in Nature?" from *Philosophy of Science* (*37,* 1970, pp. 385–404). Chapter X is a development of an essay with the same title, "Capacities and Natures," appearing in *Boston Studies in Philosophy of Science,* VIII (R. C. Buck and R. S. Cohen, eds., Reidel, Dordrecht, 1972, pp. 49–62). A very early version of Chapter I appeared as "Naturphilosophie" in *Sowjetsystem und Demokratische Gesellschaft,* VI (C. D. Kernig, ed., Herder, Freiburg, pp. 40–46, 1972). The thesis of Chapter VI was argued for in less convincing ways in "Analyticity and Conceptual Revision" from *The Journal of Philosophy* (*63,* 1966, pp. 627–37) and in "A Modal Analogue of Free Logic" from *The Logical Way of Doing Things* (K. Lambert, ed., Yale, New Haven, 1969, pp. 147–84). Chapter VII is simply a fuller version of "Relatedness Without Relations" appearing in *Nous* (*6,* 1972, pp. 139–51).

My first serious questioning in the field of physical ontology was influenced in different ways by a number of post-phenomenalist contemporaries, notably Grünbaum, Wilfrid Sellars, and Strawson. While welcoming their realism, I felt the need of extending it to provide a realistic account of necessity. In regard to necessity, post-phenomenalist realists are, regrettably, still the disciples of Hume. Gradually then the central issues in physical ontology took shape for me in the context of the contrast, not between phenomenalism and realism, but between ontologies that prohibit and those that allow a realistic account of modalities. This contrast came to be identified for me with that between ontologies in which the primary entities are simples, in the way that Hume's impressions are simples, and ontologies in which the primary entities are complexes, as they were for Aristotle. This polarity provides the stage for the major events in what follows.

Most Anglo-American contemporaries rely on an ontology of simples. Thus I have been able to rely on them for little more than technical props, and I have had to look generally to earlier traditions for suggestions about an ontology of complexes. Once the need for a realistic account of necessity is established, the general methodology adopted in what follows is to look for those ontological principles that are required by such an account.

I am grateful to students from seminars both at Yale and Indiana who, between 1963 and 1970, advanced many useful criticisms of this book in the various stages of its development. To my friends James Bogen, Ernan McMullin, Richard Rorty, and Angus Ross I owe thanks for suggestions on certain of the chapters and for encouragement on the entire project. I am indebted to my colleague Reinhardt Grossmann for having communicated something of his belief in the purity of ontology in the sense of its independence of linguistic and logical concerns, and, posthumously, to my teacher Arthur Pap for having generated an abiding philosophical interest in problems of necessity. For assistance in readying the manuscript for publication I am grateful to Walter Albee and Wanda Lee Smith. In writing this book I received constant encouragement from my wife, Ruth, who endured many sacrifices for it.

M.F.

Bloomington, Indiana
February, 1972

NATURE AND NECESSITY

An Essay in Physical Ontology

CHAPTER I

Empiricism and Ontology

§1. *Consequences of Necessity.* From beginning to end the concept of necessity is the crucial one in this book. Stress will be laid on two facts about necessity. The first concerns its existence: there are compelling reasons for recognizing that there are objectively based physical necessities. The second concerns its consequences: a number of important features of an ontology of the physical world are determined in view of there being such necessities.

Opposed to the view that the necessity of a proton to attract an electron or of salt to dissolve in pure water is objectively based is the view that it is psychologically, conceptually, or linguistically based. What necessity adds beyond truth is found in us, not in things. This rejection of an objectively based physical necessity results more from the adoption of an ontology that is inadequate to support such a necessity than from a direct attack on it. The ontology called for by objectively based necessity will then be a rich one indeed. In it there will be natures, and not just properties had either by nature or accidentally; there will be actions, and not just strings of conditions; and there will be things, and not just collections of conditions. The kind of necessity that can be accounted for when one or another of these factors has been rejected is a kind that can be accounted for only by appeal to psychological, conceptual, or linguistic factors.

An ontology that rejects things, for example, but retains conditions will quite naturally lead to a rejection of an objective base for necessity. If we carefully remove the dog's conditions of being a quadruped, of being brown, of being overfed, and so on from the dog itself, we are left with such a thin layer of reality when we collect these conditions together that it is no wonder none of them has any necessary consequences in time. These excised conditions simply are what they are and thus they possess no powers to determine anything else.

The discussion of objectively based physical necessity would be clarified if it were recognized that many arguments against it have served only to conceal the fact that an ontology has already been adopted that is incompatible with it. The classical empiricist argument—the one used by Hume—is that we do not know what we are talking about when we affirm or deny the necessity, in the sense of the objectively based necessity, of a physical connection, since there is no way of getting an idea of this necessity. It may be suggested that the impossibility of forming such an idea has to do with some limitation of our receptive faculties, but in fact these are not in question. Rather, hidden behind the talk about what ideas can be formed is an ontological principle that by itself eliminates this necessity from the world of entities accessible to knowledge.

The ontological principle is that in this knowable world "impressions" are the primary entities; but impressions share with conditions excised from things the kind of thinness of reality that prompted Hume's famous maxim: whatever is distinct is separable. For if the primary entities (impressions) are like conditions excised from things, then any one of them could exist without the other—that is, they are separable. So, in the context of an empiricist view of the source of ideas, the rejection of the idea of necessity is based on an ontology whose entities are quite clearly incompatible with necessary connections.[1] Hume's form of the rejection of necessity thus requires an ontology which restricts the knowable world to impressions and to entities that are dependent on impressions. Conversely, once we have established the need for an objectively based necessity in a world that is accessible to knowledge, Hume's argument can be inverted to show that his ontology for this world is impoverished.

Granting the connection between necessity and ontology, what broad factors appear decisive in accepting ontologies that exclude necessity? My conjecture is that they have been epistemological factors. One of them is surely the high priority set on the avoidance of error. This priority favors those entities about which, for a given amount of sense experience, one is less likely to be in error, and is thus thought to favor impressions over things. Another factor is the high priority set on the avoidance of dogmatism about the physical world. One should, in view of this preference, reject any ontology that tends to slacken inquiry and to transform hypotheses into dogmas. Allegedly, natures, so conceived that they differ from empirical properties, are such that commitment to them has this negative (dogmatic) effect.

The cogency of both these reasons for an anti-necessitarian ontology is questionable. Why, after all, suppose that the direction of certainty is the direction of being? Perhaps being less likely to be in error about something is an index of its derivative entitative status. I see no reason to adopt either point of view: that entities must be in the domain of the certain or that they must be so hidden that we remain most uncertain about them. Whether entities of some category exist is independent of how much or how little a given amount of experience supports claims about them.

Also, I fail to see the connection between the dogma-inducing powers of belief in entities of a given category and their nonexistence. If indeed believing in natures induces dogmatic slumbers, then this means only that special efforts are needed to reinforce the attitude of inquiry. It can hardly mean that natures do not exist. The bogey of dogmatism will, for some time to come, afflict the upholders of natures. But it will eventually be clear that in an epoch of developed scientific thought the doctrine of natures has an important role, even though it must be denied the pretensions that it had in an epoch of less developed science.

Questioning the cogency of these reasons is not enough. What is needed in addition is some positive reason for accepting a necessitarian ontology. By far the most economical way to support it is to find a defense for necessity itself. Then merely unfolding the requirements of necessity would reveal the special elements of the ontology. These elements would not have to be defended one by one on their own quite apart from the support given them from the defense for necessity. The defense for all of them is contained in the defense of necessity. The concept of necessity is a crucial one throughout, not because necessity is seen as important by itself, but because it provides a window onto ontology. Necessity itself is, of course, not an entity, and it is, thus, not part of the ontology developed here. If a grain of salt necessarily dissolves in pure water, there is no entity, necessity, alongside the grain of salt and the dissolving. Rather, it is precisely because the objective base for the necessity of the salt's dissolving belongs to the ontology that it is a "necessitarian ontology."

It is important to emphasize again the kind of necessity that is to be defended here. It is a necessity that has a sufficient basis in the world quite apart from the mind. There is, then, no obvious connection, either way, between necessity and analyticity.* Assume, for the moment, that there is a viable notion of a rule of meaning, and let being analytic mean having a denial that violates a rule of meaning. Then, for the analytic and the necessary to be co-extensive, there would have to be a miraculous correspondence between rules of meaning and the objective factors grounding necessity. As it is, where there is an objective basis for something's being necessarily a certain way, there may well not have developed, at the intentional level, a corresponding rule of meaning. Thus there would be no analytic sentence corresponding to the necessity. And, conversely, a rule of meaning may mislead us as to the way things are, with the result that there is an analytic sentence corresponding to no necessity. Of course, in a non-necessitarian ontology, the surrogate for necessity will doubtless be analyticity, but analyticity gains little of the philosophical importance of necessity in this way.

§2. *Practice and Ontology.* What is there to go on in formulating an ontology of the physical world? There are many things that ought to be taken into account. But not all of them will play an equally basic role. For example, we do not want to ignore current scientific theory. But its suggestions are only as strong as its inductive warrant. A philosophical ontology gets its support elsewhere.

*Hence, it is not to be objected that we have begun to speak freely of necessity without having bothered to clear up the numerous troubles that are associated with analyticity.

For the ontologist, current scientific theory is limited to the role of a reminder. For an explicit conflict with current scientific theory would, at least initially, support the suspicion that there had been a failure to achieve the full generality required of an ontology. Of course, it does not follow that the ontologist realizes the aim of generality by looking for entities that are common to many—past and present—scientific theories. Rather, the aim of generality may lead to entities that are not explicitly part of any scientific theory.

Where, then, does ontology look for its content and its support? Limiting ourselves to the suggestions of the content of scientific theory requires us to limit ourselves to the suggestions of a propositional rendering of the physical world. Such a rendering does not exist in isolation from but in conjunction with human practices. At the very least, the content of scientific theories is that of judgments; not only is judging a human practice but it is also a facet of inferential practice. By a practice I mean something more than a type of activity. For a practice involves criteria for determining whether actions of the given type are warranted. (There is no need for the criteria to be the same for the practice to be the same.) So a human practice is a type of human activity subject to criteria of warrantability. The conjunction of theory—i.e., the content of theory—with practices is not just accidental. We cannot then proceed as though the propositional content of theories were altogether isolated from certain practices.

This suggests the possibility of looking to practice for at least some of the content of and perhaps even the support for an ontology. But do practices have ontological suggestions? There are certain familiar cases where they do. The practice of praising and blaming would seem to require that other people be treated as responsible agents. The practice of counting distinct objects would seem to require belief in something other than undivided stuffs. That these practices have ontological suggestions is clear from the fact that it would be incoherent of anyone who engages in them not to grant the existence of certain entities. There are, of course, changes in practices, and, in view of the requirement of generality, we want more from a philosophical ontology than a recapitulation of the practices of a given culture. Moreover, provincial practices could not provide the support needed for an ontology held to be universally valid.

Are there, perhaps, practices without which it would be difficult to conceive of any other practices? If there are, then since the content of scientific theory is never completely separated from practices, these "basic practices" would transcend differences in the content of theories. Their ontological import would provide not only a framework for practice but also for theory. Should there be a theoretical content common to every scientific theory and without which no such theory would be conceivable, this content would, in general, be additional to and not part of the ontology drawn from such a basic practice. The ontological import of a basic practice need not be part of the content of any theory.

The practice of acting on the basis of, that is, in the light of, prior sense experience has a solid claim to being essential to any battery of practices and will be used as the basis for a later defense of physical necessity. We shall agree that actions based on prior experience concern possible combinations of features in new situations that would be similar to features that were the objects of prior experiences. I act on the basis of prior unpleasant experiences when I insist on having a commitment of management in writing. Similarly, I act on the basis of prior experiences of Jones when I accept as true the proposition that his new venture will succeed. I may or may not remember, when I act, prior experiences of broken commitments or of Jones. So remembrance cannot be appealed to in order to distinguish such action from action on habit.

Though a habit is developed by prior experience, to act on habit is not to act on the basis of (that is, not to act in the light of) prior experience. One does something on the basis of prior experience voluntarily, but if the same thing is done purely out of habit the action is removed from the realm of the voluntary. Also, flexibility of response is important if one is acting on the basis of prior experience, whereas action on habit tends to be invariant under what might otherwise be important differences in the agent's situation. Nonetheless, in acting on the basis of prior experience, the agent need not be propositionally aware of the subtle factors in the situation that influence the choice of the action. Suppose there were no practice of action on the basis of prior sense experience. Prior experience could be utilized only in action on habit. Could there then be any human practices at all?

A consideration of the broadest categories of human practice reveals ways in which practices in these categories are dependent on the practice of acting on the basis of prior sense experience.

(1) The practice of communication shows such a dependence. One communicates with an interlocutor on the basis of certain assumptions made about the interlocutor. The assumptions are quite different for different interlocutors. So the flexibility required is not supplied entirely by a single habit applied to all interlocutors. Yet there is normally not a special habit for each case. One is then acting on the basis of prior experience with interlocutors in making certain of these assumptions. Of course, as familiarity with a stable set of interlocutors grows, the assumptions about each may become habitual. But if one is to communicate and not merely make noises in a less familiar situation, then one needs to estimate what means will be appropriate, on the basis of one's own or on the basis of someone else's prior experience. That an entity like the straw scarecrow in Oz was, at first, unable to communicate because it did not know how to work its mouth, rather than because of its limited experience with interlocutors, is an entertaining reversal of the priorities.[2]

(2) There is a like dependence in the practice of making judgments. The genesis of this practice is bound up with the need to make our responses (at least those that are based on prior experience) to troublesome situations more discriminating through the resources of propositional thought. The point is not simply that judgment is occasioned by problems. If this were all, action based on prior experience would not necessarily play a role. Rather, judgment refines responses that are already based on prior experience. It enters at a point at which the unlearned and habitual responses have already been added to by the more flexible responses based on prior experience. The flight of thought to abstract matters from its role in guiding concrete responses in no way establishes the possibility of judgment apart from having an origin in this concrete role.

(3) Social regimentation, discipline, and punishment clearly

belong to a category of practices that involve action on prior experience. One regiments where prior experience indicates that behavior would otherwise take a different course from the one desired. Even regimentation by so-called *a priori* standards is to be understood in terms of this dependence. For standards come to be called *a priori* when their long entrenchment obscures the fact that they were originally thought to be warranted in the light of still earlier experience.

(4) Ceremony and art are sometimes held to transcend calculations serving material interests and thus to be independent of action on prior experience. Yet it is obvious that ceremony and art are possible only in an environment in which, if it has not been won, the struggle for survival has at least achieved a temporary freedom from immediate needs for some few individuals. Labor practices are then presupposed. The techniques needed for any labor practices will have been developed by actions based on prior experience.

In all these cases and in any others, I suggest that the possibility of the practice in question rests on the general possibility of the practice of acting on prior experience. The notion of possibility here is not systematized in the ontology that follows. It is a notion of "practical" possibility in the sense that it concerns the interrelations of practices. These practical possibilities, I contend, do not rest on any special scientific assumptions. Nothing is assumed about the make-up of brains, the nature of sound waves, or the nature of matter in the environment that labor struggles with. Thus these possibilities are not undercut by scientific thought experiments. But of course it is assumed that the agents engaging in these practices are physical persons and have a material environment, for it is human practices we are talking about, not those of angels.

An ontology based on a fundamental practice has certain advantages over other ontologies. For example, an epistemological ontology—one whose entities are chosen because we are less likely to make mistakes about them—can at most reveal what is involved in the practice of looking for the experiential bases of claims that go beyond experience. Such a practice is clearly not one that is needed to make all others possible. It is limited to a concern with the grounding of propositional thinking in experience, and many human practices have no dependence on propositional thinking. Still there are those who, without explicitly considering wider alternatives, erect the epistemological criterion into a norm of philosophical conscience.[3]

A scientific ontology is also limited. This will be so whether we conceive a scientific ontology as one whose entities are required by the content of *current* science, or by some conception of what the content of science *will* ultimately be, or even by the content of *any* science. For, the ontological requirements coming from practice, rather than deriving from a theoretical content, may be missed by a scientific ontology. This will be true even for the last of the above forms of scientific ontology, which is the most general one. Moreover, those features of the world that make practice such that it can be carried on without illusion will be the context for those features, if any, that are implied by the content of a wide variety of scientific theories. This is not to deny that one is doing philosophy when one does scientific ontology in that most general form. The Kantian study of the requirements of the content of any science—of the conditions of the make-up of empirical knowledge—is undoubtedly philosophical. But the undertaking is more special than the one envisaged here since it is concerned exclusively with the content of propositional thought. Even so, our undertaking is limited also, for it considers the implications of only one of possibly many basic human practices.

§3. *Moderate Empiricism.* The practice of action on prior experience covers very disparate actions. On the one extreme there are actions satisfying physical needs. On the other there are the relatively detached acts of judging to be true certain propositions that claim for as-yet unobserved entities what has been noted for observed entities. Making such a judgment is making an induction, and the canons of induction are relevant to its evaluation. It seems clear that there are prudential considerations involved in evaluating non-judgmental actions that are not relevant to evaluating judgments. I may, for example, warrantedly believe something even though it would be foolish of me to bet my last dollar on it.

Still, for our purposes, there are common factors that are quite important. If the judgment that a proposition is true is an acceptable induction, then the experience on which it is based *supports* to a certain degree, *confirms* to a certain degree, or increases by a certain amount the *probability* of that proposition. Similarly, a non-judgmental action based on prior experience is warranted in view of that experience only if that experience supports, confirms, or increases the probability of its success. The notion of support by experience is, then, integral to the notion of the practice of action on prior experience. Support, of course, is not itself an action, as accepting a proposition is. Still, support is something that a proposition or a project should have in order to be accepted or to be undertaken. But support is only a necessary condition for warranted action. This is obvious when conflicting propositions or projects are equally well supported.

Even though action based on prior experience is warranted only if supported by experience, it does not follow directly that "extreme rationalism" is wrong. For the extreme rationalist, the act of accepting a proposition does not require, for the acceptance to be warranted, that the proposition have support from sense experience. There may be other ways of accepting any proposition than that of proceeding on the basis of prior sense experience. However, once we consider that the practice of action based on prior experience is a fundamental practice, it turns out that extreme rationalism cannot be accepted. There are two steps to the argument for this conclusion.

First, judgment, like other practices, is dependent on the practice of action based on prior experience. There would not be judgments unless some judgments made responses based on prior experience more discriminating. Judgments in this role are an integral part of the more discriminating responses, and they are not things outside those responses. Thus since the responses that are guided by judgment are based on prior experience, the judgments will be based, in part at least, on the prior experience that the responses are based on. It *must* then be the case that some judgments are based on prior experience.

Second, it has still to be shown that some specific judgments *must* be made on the basis of prior experience. Could not each judgment that is actually based on prior experience also be made warrantedly on some *a priori* grounds without any change in the basis of judgments actually made on *a priori* grounds? If each one of them could be made *a priori,* would there be any constraint that would make it impossible for all of them to be made *a priori?* If there is no constraint of this kind, then the practice of judgment would, contrary to fact, be independent of the practice of action on prior experience. In an economy of a given kind, there may be no individual who must be poor, even though in that economy it must be the case that there are poor. Such an economy provides the constraint needed to guarantee poverty despite the possibility of individual betterment. In our case, there is no comparable constraint. If each proposition could be supported for acceptance in an *a priori* fashion, then all of them could be accepted in an *a priori* way. This forces us to conclude that some judgments can be supported only in an empirical way. Otherwise, the result of the first step would be false; it would be possible that no judgment would be made on the basis of prior experience. Thus extreme rationalism is false.

It is not necessary to accept the strong empiricist standard that any proposition pertaining to the as-yet unexperienced can be accepted only if supported by, among other things, previous sense experience. The practice of action on prior experience can be fundamental even though *some* propositions about the as-yet unexperienced are acceptable on the basis of support from *a priori* considerations. However, the fundamental nature of this practice does require at least a "moderate empiricist" standard. This standard asserts that some propositions about combinations of features in the as-yet unexperienced are acceptable only if they are supported by, among other things, previous sense experience of similar features.

Accepting propositions in a way that accords with moderate empiricism is a practice of a judgmental sort and is therefore limited. We have seen, however, that even non-judgmental action on prior experience requires that there be support, from such experience, for the proposition that the project will succeed. So any ontological requirements resulting from the adoption of moderate empiricism as a standard for accepting propositions about the as-yet unexperienced will also be requirements for the practice of action based on prior experience. Accordingly, I shall attempt to find ontological consequences of moderate empiricism and treat them as parts of an ontology of the practice of action based on prior experience.

This claim of generality for the standard of moderate empiricism might appear unjustified in view of the debated nature of the inductive status of science. Science, of all things, seems to be inductive in nature. Its propositions seem to require empirical support for acceptance. But if science is in fact not inductive, then to take seriously the idea of acceptance based on empirical support as the starting point for an ontology is to risk building the ontology on sand. Popper has argued vigorously that induction has no place in the logic of theoretical science. As an explanatory hypothesis, a theory can be characterized as having passed the text of experience so far, but as an explanatory hypothesis, it is irrelevant to characterize it as judged true or accepted in the light of experience.[4] Hence it is irrelevant to characterize it as being strongly enough supported or confirmed to be judged true. As explanatory hypotheses, theories are corroborated, not supported or confirmed.

The position I have taken would not be undercut if Popper were right. There is then no call to argue with him. For Popper, the theorist, as theorist, is a contemplative in regard to his theory, so long as it is unrefuted. The theorist will act, on the one hand, to accept simple experiential claims and, on the other hand, to reject a theory conflicting with such claims. But the theorist will not act to judge a theory true. Even if theorizing proceeds on this contemplative level, there are other occupations within the domain of science itself that do involve the act of accepting claims that go beyond previous experience. In this very regard, Popper himself recognizes the difference between theory and technology.[5]

Before the atomic bomb was exploded, scientists were asked if exploding it would destroy the face of the globe. Their report was a negative judgment on the global destructiveness of the bomb, and not merely an appraisal of the past performance of a theory. So even if induction is not deemed relevant to science as limited to the contemplation of a set of explanatory hypotheses, it is relevant to science in other respects. It is even relevant to science as a world-view, for a scientific world-view is a judgment as to how things are, and the judgment is made on the basis of collective experience. There is, then, no reason to suppose we were wrong in taking action based on prior experience as a fundamental practice. And hence no reason to suppose that an ontology based on moderate empiricism is insecurely founded.

When rationalism is so conceived that pure reason is called on to secure only basic principles, rationalism need not conflict with moderate empiricism. Descartes seems to have thought that basic laws could be both discovered and justified *a priori*. Still, he thought there were many different worlds compatible with these laws. Experience was to play the role of deciding which among these is the actual world.[6] Any true general proposition not derived from laws alone would have support from experience. That the amino acid alanine occurs most commonly in higher life forms only in the configuration that rotates light to the right would not be *a priori* since it rests in part on the boundary conditions of the evolving world. This is not to say that general propositions can be empirically supported when all the factors involved are assumed to be contingent. There would be no empirical support, according to the view I shall develop, for the generalization about the configuration of alanine unless the boundary conditions were assumed to unfold their consequences according to laws.

But there are forms of rationalism that do conflict with moderate empiricism. To that extent they give a misleading picture of human practice. Platonic rationalism extends both to the study of physical nature and to the affairs of the citizen. A theoretical claim about physical nature is not, for Plato, capable of being supported by experience. He thought that experiments of the fundamental sort needed to give support to theoretical hypotheses were humanly impossible.[7] So a physical claim is acceptable, in the sense of being plausible, on the basis of its agreement with some mathematical construction. The Platonic theory of the elements, for example, derives its plausibility from being based on Theaetetus' construction of the five regular polyhedra. There is no reason to suppose that human practice in general could not adjust to this Platonic practice, in science, of relying on *a priori* considerations.

But for Plato reliance on the *a priori* is extended to the concrete affairs of the citizen. The citizen obtains a modicum of assurance about the future because there are "wise" men in the state.[8] And the wise man is one whose proposals are supported by a vision of the moral forms. No room is made for the experienced man as a moral leader, that is, for the man whose ideas are warranted by his rich experience. Between wisdom, as intellectual vision, and skill, as inflexible habit, there is no place for the competence of experience. There is either action informed by moral patterns or the rigid response of good or bad habit. But can action informed by moral patterns be deemed possible apart from action based on prior experience? Such action would be conceivable in the context of human practice only if at some point the adoption of some moral pattern seemed warranted in terms of certain prior experiences. The over-all scientific and moral rationalism of Plato's thinking is at odds with the fundamental nature of the practice of action on prior experience, and hence with moderate empiricism.

We have noted that the practice of making judgments about the world on the basis of prior experience is only one aspect of the practice of acting on the basis of prior experience. One can act on the basis of prior experience without affirming the proposition that something will happen or that things are generally of a certain kind. Suppose there are, or were, cultures with no activity of affirming propositions about the world. The notion of support by prior experience would still be relevant so long as there remained action on prior experience. It has been argued that, in the mythopoeic thought of ancient Egypt and Mesopotamia, there was no affirming of propositions about the world.[9] Whatever was present to awareness was so as part of the emotional context of myth. On this interpretation, descriptive propositions were not among the intellectual components of mythopoeic thought. But even when awareness of nature has this mythopoeic character, it does not follow that action in response to immediate problems is based on myth alone. It may still be appropriate to say that some action is based on prior experience, and hence to say that the notion of support is relevant to an analysis of the evaluation of actions.

A specific concept of experience is needed to prevent this discussion of action based on prior experience and of moderate empiricism from being purely schematic. Certain views of experience are so limiting that the practice of action based on prior experience could not be a fundamental practice. I shall review three of these briefly. But beyond rejecting these views, I shall add nothing that will make the concept of experience more specific.

First, the view that experiences are indubitable is not accepted here. Experiences are indubitable if they must be experiences of just what they seem to be experiences of. If the objects of experience are sufficiently restricted—for example, to what philosophers call sense data—then one might seriously argue that they are indubitable. But then there would be no justification for claiming that the practice of action on prior experience of such objects is basic to all action. So here an experience may seem to be an experience of a certain condition when it is not an experience of that condition. An experience of the condition of being hot—for example, the condition of a sample of water of being hot—may seem to be an experience of the condition of being cold of the sample of water.

This is equally true of the experiences that I may refer to in support of a hypothesis. They may well support the hypothesis if they are the experiences that I take them to be. But they may not be experiences of what I take them to be experiences of. Without assuming that experiences are indubitable, we must assume that they are experiences of what we take them to be experiences of when we say that they support an hypothesis. Hence, to say that some propositions are acceptable only if they are supported by experience is not to imply that experience is indubitable.

Second, the view that experiences are invariably propositional is not accepted here. That is, it need not be the case that when I have an experience I judge or in any way entertain a proposition. Otherwise, the entertaining of propositions would be basic to all practices, which it clearly is not. Still, non-propositional experiences can play a role in supporting propositions. For example, the condition of a vixen behaving slyly can, of course, be experienced, and this experience can be appealed to in support of a general hypothesis which implies, among other things, that a condition of this type obtains in the given circumstances.

Now seeing the vixen behaving slyly and seeing it having a bushy tail are perceptions of distinct conditions and thus have distinct objects, even though the same fox has both conditions. Similarly, seeing *that* the vixen behaves slyly and seeing *that* the vixen is bushy tailed are perceptions that involve, in some way, distinct propositions. But from this similarity it does not in any way follow that experiencing conditions is the same as the entertaining of propositions. Conditions—such as the water being hot and the vixen behaving slyly—are, as I shall argue below, extra-mental entities, whereas propositions are intentional. So even if experiencing-*that* is universally judgmental, it in no way follows that experiencing a condition involves making a judgment.

Still, experience is not to be distinguished from thinking by excluding propositions from experience. Many experiences may well involve the entertaining of propositions. A discussion of the distinction between sense experience and propositional thought would involve an elaboration of the notion of an "affect" as that indispensable component of experience that involves the body in experience and that stimulates sense awareness.

Third, the view that experience, when it is of physical things or their conditions, must be of middle-sized, everyday things or their conditions is not accepted here. Moderate empiricism does not then mean that certain propositions are acceptable only if supported by reference to data about middle-sized, everyday things. The important factor in delimiting experience is not the size or familiarity of its object, but the fact that an affect is involved in becoming aware of that object. The affective element can accompany, at least in principle, awareness of entities that are quite disparate. The philosopher's sense-data and the scientist's microsystems might also be objects of experience, depending on how the relation between the sources of affectivity and the content of experience is ultimately defined.

§4. *Realism and Materialism.* The ontology derived by setting out from necessity is put forth as a realistic one. Its elements are to be mind-independent components of the physical world. They are not categories of a mind that organizes nature. The emphasis on practice and experience might seem to suggest, however, that the conclusions must be about the structure of consciousness. Now, in respect to our basic practice, there are two related but distinct questions that could have been asked. First, what must a conscious being be like for the practice of acting on prior experience to be one of its practices? Second, what general views of the physical world would it be reasonable for someone adopting the practice of acting on prior experience to hold? It is the second question that interests us, and although answering it involves setting out from a consideration of practice, it involves ending up with claims about the physical world.

But is it not entirely possible that the world is other than what it is made to seem to be by the practice of acting on the basis of prior experience? Must we not then abandon any categorical commitment to realism for the merely conditional claim that, *if* the world conforms to the presuppositions of the practice of acting on prior experience, *then* such and such entities are in the world? To make this retreat would be to ignore the serious consequences of asserting the possibility of a split between this practice and the world. If this practice were of minor importance, if we could limit the number of practices dependent on it, then we might well admit that the world could conflict with the beliefs that this practice makes undeniable. In fact, however, the practice of acting on prior experience is fundamental in respect to other practices. Without it they would be left in the air. Yet to affirm its basic role is to grant the beliefs about the world that are made undeniable by this practice. Nothing in the vast cultural superstructure of practices dependent on it can make legitimate the possibility of conditions conflicting with those beliefs.

The view that this practice cannot be relied on to determine ontology faces a clear dilemma. Suppose there is the possibility of a conflict between the world and the beliefs that are made undeniable by the practice of action on prior experience. Then this possibility can be derived either from considerations arrived at by practices that are independent of the practice of acting on the basis of prior experience or from those arrived at by practices that are dependent on it. In the former case, it is assumed that there are practices that could go on if there were no practice of acting on the basis of prior experience. And this assumption we have denied above. In the latter case, we are asked to grant that by speculative reasoning, for example, the possibility could be derived and warrantedly asserted as a possibility, even when it is recognized that speculative reasoning is a practice that is not independent of its role in guiding action based on prior experience. Thus, since it is limited by the context of action on prior experience, speculative reasoning cannot coherently challenge the beliefs made undeniable by such a practice. Of course, a theory based on a given practice may predict a change, in the world, to conditions that are incompatible with that practice. But then these conditions are not alleged to have existed when the practice was current. More generally, theory may project conditions in which no human practice of any kind is possible. But all that is denied here is that theory can justifiably say that such conditions might hold while there is human practice, of which it itself is an instance. In sum, the possibility of a conflict between the world and a basic practice cannot be justified. There is then no reason to modify the categorical character of our realism based on practice.

Our ontology is not intended as a complete list of all the categories of entities there are. It is thus not offered as a "full" ontology. It is not even intended as a list of all the categories of entities in the physical world, and so it is not offered as a full physical ontology. It can, however, be called a "required" physical ontology in that it is the physical ontology of a practice required by all other practices.

The standpoint from which a required ontology is written can be called "critical." It is not based on a cultural *status quo,* be it commonsense or scientific. It involves the assumption that the ontological suggestions of a fundamental practice are more reliable than those of either common sense or current science. The world-view of common sense needs to be scrutinized in the light of other approaches to the world. And speculative alternatives need to be viewed not just in the context of the content of current science but in the context of practices basic to both science and common sense.

The required ontology—that is, the one that is the physical ontology of the practice of action based on prior experience—is distinct from both materialism and idealism. Let us think of materialism here as an ontology that (1) recognizes only those entities that the propositions of physical theory could be true of,

(2) interprets these propositions as true or false of entities that the propositions are standardly taken to be about, rather than of the sense data that the positivist takes them to be about, and (3) treats these propositions as incapable of being true or false of minds, actions, and middle-sized (ordinary) things. Thus the entities that the materialist puts in the domain of physical theory are non-mental, connected by relations rather than involved in actions, and devoid of sense qualities.

But the practice of action based on prior experience, and hence the ontology that is required by this practice, is compatible with, even if it does not contain, many entities excluded by materialism. Thus one might consistently hold the required ontology while agreeing with C. S. Lewis that each of the entities that are parts of the myths we make here on earth has actuality somewhere else in the universe. For the benefit of materialists, Lewis conceived of a rational being, the eldil, that inhabited outer space.[10] It had no body in the gross sense, but was a mere luminous presence. The point is that even if there are no eldila, a fully critical ontology does not busy itself with showing that there are none.

On the other hand, idealism, as the ontological negation of physical things, their components, and their conditions, is incompatible with the existence of human practices. These practices are carried out by physical persons in physical settings. The idealist asks us to perform an act of speculative thought resulting in the judgment that there are no human practices but only practices of entities that not only, like eldila, lack ordinary bodies but are completely disembodied. Yet speculative thought itself is a practice that depends on human practices in physical settings. Any judgment arrived at by speculative thought that rejects the physical setting is unwarranted.

Ironically, although idealism prides itself on being critical, it is critical only in a limited epistemological sense; it gives high priority to making only those commitments that, for a given amount of data, are least likely to be in error. If we accept this priority, we may well be trapped in our own minds. But setting this priority is itself uncritical. It is a priority having to do with the practice of making judgments about what is. And this practice exists only in a context of practices that clearly involve a physical setting. The priority is set without regard to dependence on this context.

Materialism is, to an extent, a critical ontology in that it has gotten where it is by going behind the superficially plausible claims of a commonsense ontology. But it exhausts its critical animus with this first step. Its subsequent lapse into dogmatism leaves it with little or no advantage over commonsense ontology. For at least what common sense lacks in theoretical sophistication it makes up by containing practices widely different from the merely descriptive ones of physical theory. It is open to the commonsense ontologist to emphasize both the implications of these practices and those of the merely descriptive apparatus of common sense.

If materialism, as a critique of common sense, based itself exclusively on the deliverances of current physics, it would be clear what the source and strength of the critique are. But as often as not the source of the critique is an idealized extension of current physics. When confronted with the question of whether current quantum theory, with its systems characterized by superpositions of apparently non-actual states, really supports the materialist's conception of objectively existing material entities, the materialist is apt to wave a hand at the "inelegant mess" of quantum theory and speak about the possibility of new developments in microphysics.[11] Those principles that determine how science will come out are, then, just the ontological ones that science was to justify. The ontology turns out to be a dogma, and the critical attitude toward common sense reduces to pretense.

In the writing of Wilfrid Sellars, for example, the critical attitude toward common sense is, he strongly suggests, supported by science. But a closer look leaves one unclear from what quarter it is supported. After seemingly defending the commonsense view of time as involving the perspectival characters of past, present, and future, Sellars advances the higher wisdom of science. "The non-perspectival structure which, as realists, we conceive to underlie and support perspectival temporal discourse is, as yet, a partially covered promissory note the cash for which is to be provided not by metaphysics (McTaggart's C-series), but by the advance of science (physical theory of time)."[12] If the realist issues promissory notes that are to be made good by science, where does he get his authorization? Not from science, since science makes no predictions on where it will come out. But we are not told where else. Also, Sellars recognizes an event ontology, in distinction from an ontology of physical things, as a regulative ideal. This, however, is only an ideal and not an established belief partly because "science has not yet achieved the very concepts in terms of which such a picture might be formulated."[13] To say that science *will* justify an ontology that undercuts commonsense amounts to nothing unless some authorization outside contemporary science is forthcoming for this statement.

In a required ontology the claims can be traced back to a fundamental practice. They are not left as unsupported dogmas. A materialist ontology can, when it is taken from current physical theory, also claim support from certain practices, as well as from the content of current theory. But these practices will not all be basic. Thus arises the possibility that ontological claims that do receive support in relation to such limited practices might have to be rejected when the context is broadened to include basic practices. Consider, for example, the following claim. "*Speaking as a philosopher,* I am quite prepared to say that the commonsense world of physical objects in Space and Time is unreal . . . ."[14] What Sellars takes as support for this view is the greater descriptive and explanatory power of current microtheory in comparison with common sense and the fact that in principle the theoretical expressions of this microtheory could replace commensense expressions in an observation language.[15]

It is assumed by Sellars that what is not required by the practices of making descriptions and explanations in terms that can be observational, when these practices are considered by themselves, is not required by anything. But one can make this assumption only by systematically ignoring the fact that description and explanation have a setting amidst other practices and that they are dependent on other practices. Perhaps commonsense objects do not belong to a full physical ontology, but all the relevant considerations should be in before they are excluded.

CHAPTER II

The Ground of Necessity

§1. *The Identity of Physical with Logical Necessity.* Ultimately, I shall show that the practice of action based on prior experience is incompatible with the view that there are no physical necessities, that is, no physical necessities whose necessity is objectively based. That proof will be postponed until it is made reasonably clear what physical necessity is. In making this clarification, I shall be led to introduce natures as the objective basis for physical necessity. And so the kind of necessity called for by practice is a "natural" necessity, that is, a necessity grounded by natures. In view of its etymology, 'physical' should mean what 'natural' means. However, let us agree to mean by a "physical" feature one that any entity has only if it is a spatio-temporal entity. Correspondingly, a necessity will be physical if it is a necessity of an entity having certain physical, and not merely logical or other non-physical, features. It is no mere tautology, then, that the necessity of a physical necessity is based on natures.

It is crucial here that a distinction be made between a necessity and necessity itself. A necessity is some condition of entities; if the condition of this gas to expand when heated under constant pressure is a condition that obtains with necessity, then this condition is a necessity. Sometimes, though, it is more convenient to call propositions necessities. This is the procedure I shall follow in the present chapter. Propositional necessities are necessities only if the conditions making them true are necessities. Action based on prior experience does not require propositions, and so requires only necessities as conditions. Further, the necessity of a necessity, in either sense, is a modality of a condition's obtaining or of a proposition, but is neither a condition nor a proposition.

There is surely a need to clarify the modality of physical necessity. For it is often wrongly believed that the necessity called in by an appeal to physical necessities is something totally unexplained and unfamiliar. Behind this belief is the following train of thought.

The appeal to physical necessities is not reducible to an appeal to mere regularities. So the necessity involved is not to be explicated in terms of regularities. Further, the appeal to physical necessities is not an appeal to logical necessities. So the necessity involved is not to be identified with that of logical truths. There is nothing else with which it could plausibly be identified. Hence the modality of physical necessity is totally unexplained and unfamiliar. In Hume's terms, there is no idea of physical necessity, and thus an appeal to it is meaningless.

The flaw here is not hard to find. For the distinction between a necessity and necessity itself has been overlooked. Physical necessities are not the same propositions as logical necessities. The proposition that this gas expands when heated under constant pressure is not a logical necessity, though the proposition that this gas expands when it expands is a logical necessity. All that follows, however, is that there are two sets of necessities. It in no way follows that the necessity itself—the modality—of a physical necessity differs from that of a logical truth.

To make it follow, two additional premisses might be added. The first premiss is that logical truths unlike physical truths have contradictory denials; the second is that having a contradictory denial is their necessity. Thus not only are logical and physical necessities different propositions but their very necessity is different. Caution should be exercised here lest one confuse a characteristic of logical truths with an analysis of their necessity. Granting that logical truths have contradictory denials, can we safely assert that saying that they are necessary amounts to no more than saying that they have contradictory denials? If so, then saying that a contradiction cannot be true is merely saying that a contradiction is a contradiction. But this is manifestly not the case. A contradiction affirms and denies the same thing, and it is an important, even if familiar, fact that such a claim cannot be true. So its impossibility does not consist in its being contradictory.

Physical and logical necessity are distinguished not by distinguishing two species of necessity but by distinguishing the physical from the logical truths to which the necessity applies. Thus, to say *A* is "physically" necessary is to make the conjunctive claim (i) that *A* is a physical truth and (ii) that necessarily *A*. Even when (ii) here is a so-called *de re* modal proposition, the claim that *A* is physically necessary will not be a purely *de re* modal proposition, since (i) has a *de dicto* character (cf. §5, following). Similarly, to say *A* is "logically" necessary is to say (i) that *A* is a logical truth and (ii) that necessarily *A*.

By a physical (logical) truth I mean a truth whose truth conditions require that appropriate entities have certain physical (logical) features. Having the property of igniting if struck would be to have a physical feature; whereas, having the property of lacking and possessing a certain property would be to have a logical feature. There will doubtless be difficulties in delimiting the classes of physical and logical features, but my task here is merely to indicate that this is where the difficulties lie, rather than with distinguishing two species of necessity.

Since the necessity is identical in both cases, physical and logical necessities may well be alike in being natural necessities. That Jones does not both have and lack a nose may be necessary for the reason that it is Jones's nature not to have and lack the same part. A logical truth would not then be necessary because its denial is contradictory or because its truth is invariant under changes in non-logical content. Rather, the logical truth would be necessary because it is the nature of the entities covered by the truth to support truths of that sort. This is not to rest the thesis of the univocity of necessity on the view that both physical and logical necessities are natural necessities. The present discussion merely illustrates the point that the univocity thesis allows both necessities to be viewed as natural. Moreover, forms of the univocity thesis that try to avoid natures are, as I shall show in §2 and §3, less than satisfying.

The univocity thesis is not a new one. Kneale said that "since men undoubtedly speak of necessity in nature, we find ourselves driven to say that the word 'necessity' must have a special meaning in this context and cudgel our brains to give an analysis. In fact, the word 'necessity' is the least troublesome of those with which we have to deal in this part of philosophy. For it has the same sense here as elsewhere."[1] Kneale's view did not go unchallenged. Popper said in reply that, "Compared with logical tautologies, laws of nature have a contingent, an accidental character. . . . For there may be *structurally different worlds*—worlds with different natural laws."[2]

The intuitive substance of Kneale's view, as of my own, is that necessities restrict alternatives and that one should not confuse the restriction of alternatives with the different sources of restriction. A restriction is a restriction whether it comes from the logic or the physics of the world. It is misleading to speak of one source as giving rise to a weaker or looser restricton than another. For a restriction on alternatives either closes down alternatives or it does not. If being weaker means leaving an alternative partly open, then a weaker restriction is just not a restriction on alternatives. If it means that a restriction genuinely eliminates an alternative, then it is just misleading to call the restriction weak.

Popper's argument patently begs the question. Grant that among the logically possible worlds there are worlds in which different physical laws hold. Popper first identifies the logically possible worlds with the possible worlds. He then validly concludes that physical laws are contingent since they do not hold in all possible worlds. But the identification is precisely what is in question. For consider what it is based on. A logically possible world is one in which logical necessities hold. We can identify a logically possible world with a possible world only if we assume that the logical necessities are the only necessities, or at least the only necessities in the sense in which Popper here speaks of necessity. Thus the identification rests either on denying that there are physical necessities in any sense or on affirming that physical necessities are necessities in a different sense. Popper is not willing to deny that there are physical necessities in any sense, so his argument assumes its conclusion that a physical necessity is a necessity in a different sense, and is hence contingent in the sense of the word as he originally used it.

In sum, there is nothing for the equivocity thesis to stand on. In the remainder of this chapter, I shall provide a foundation for the univocity thesis. Once univocity is accepted, the appeal to physical necessities can be rejected as meaningless only if one is prepared to call the notion of logical necessity meaningless. Moreover, it will be seen in Chapter VI that the identity of necessity in the two cases is compatible with the allegation that logical necessities are analytic and *a priori,* whereas physical necessities are neither. For even if logical necessities were analytic and *a priori,* their being so would not follow from their necessity.

§2. *Laws in Ontological Perspective.* Even while holding that the necessity of physical and logical necessities is identical, there is no obstacle to thinking of necessity simply as lawfulness. For, there are both physical and logical laws, and what holds under each is said to hold necessarily. But what makes something a law? The answer to this question requires us to take a route that is no shorter than the one that we would have had to take in answering a similar question about necessity, and the two routes end at the same place. So, switching to lawfulness gets us no closer to the goal of finding an objective basis for necessity. Moreover, there are necessities which turn out to be crucial, that cannot be treated as laws or derivatives from laws. For example, the necessity that an individual has of belonging to a certain natural kind is not a matter of laws. No law is the basis for its membership in that kind. Rather, a law always tells us what is characteristic of individuals of a given natural kind.

Nonetheless, there is a reason for talking about laws. The route commonly followed in saying what makes something a law leads to the intentional rather than to the real. Taking this "flight to intentions" for the lawfulness of laws will, accordingly, lead to an intentional basis for the necessity of corresponding necessities. Something is to be gained by pointing out that this intentional account will not do for necessity and hence not for lawfulness.

The kind of necessity needed if experience is to support propositions about the as-yet unexperienced has an objective basis and is thus real rather than intentional. The necessity of *A* would be "intentional" if all it implied, beyond the truth of *A*, were that the proposition *A* had a certain place in a system of thought, that the mind was conditioned to believe it, that it was promulgated by a high authority as true, or that linguistic propriety would not admit an expression of its negation. In broadest terms, the necessity of *A* would be intentional if its being necessary meant, beyond the truth of *A*, a certification of *A* indicating *A* stands in a certain relation to consciousness. The necessity of *A* would be "real" not just if *A* were true but only if there were in the entities that *A* is about a basis that were sufficient for their having the features that makes *A* true of them. Such a basis might be a material stuff, microparticles, capacities, or natures. Why it cannot be some of these will become clear only gradually. Of course, a real necessity about consciousness itself would be such that this necessity is true on the basis of some feature of consciousness; it will not be an intentional necessity since it does not *as a necessity* have this relation to consciousness, but only as something about consciousness.

The contrast between the real and the intentional does not require that there be entities that are not real. For to say that a modal proposition has an intentional basis is not to say that there is an entity other than a real one that is involved in the conditions that make this proposition true. Rather, it is to say, first, that the truth conditions for the modal proposition—necessarily *A*—involve not just the entities *A* is about but also the non-modal proposition *A*. Second, it is to say that the non-modal proposition—*A*—is by its role in human thought or expression (which makes it *about* other entities) involved in the truth conditions for the modal proposition—necessarily *A*. This conception of an intentional basis does not require us to say that either propositions, human thoughts, or expressions, are not real. (If, independently, propositions are shown to be unreal, a parallel characterization of an intentional basis might be given using, instead, the notion of a sentence.) In so far as propositions, sentences, concepts, and words are about entities, they are themselves intentional entities. But it cannot be inferred from their intentionality that they are not real.

It is important to see why the necessity of the physical necessities called for by the fact that experiences support or confirm propositions has to be a real necessity. When the necessity is real, certain physical features belong to entities on the basis of factors in these entities. The argument—point (I) of which is worked out in Chapter IV—is as follows.

(I) One cannot contend that past experience is the guide to the future and at the same time hold that there are no necessities. Ultimately, such guidance goes back to the simple inductive projection of features of observed individuals onto unobserved individuals. Such a projection—of, for example, the conditional feature of being *G* if *F*—is warranted only if there is a chance that, if observed individuals have the feature of being *G* if they are *F*, then any arbitrary unobserved individual is *G* if it is *F*. There would be no chance of this connection between the observed and the unobserved individuals if all the features of the former were contingent. It would then be only owing to the peculiarities of the circumstances that the observed individuals had the features they did. There would be no basis for claiming that an arbitrary unobserved individual would have any of those features.

(II) But is the necessity required real or intentional? Suppose it is intentional. Thus, if an observed individual were of necessity to have the feature of being *G* if it is *F*, the proposition that it has this feature belongs to a coherent deductive system, or it is propounded by an authority, or it cannot be denied without violation of certain linguistic conventions. Now the point of introducing necessities would be defeated if it were highly improbable that if one individual had a projectible feature of necessity, then any other individual, whatever its circumstances, would also have it. If it were highly improbable, then the necessity of the projectible feature would provide no basis for attributing that feature to other individuals. Yet it would be highly improbable if the necessity were merely intentional. No restriction put on the proposition that an individual is *G* if it is *F* in order to make this proposition intentionally necessary would tend to influence physical reality in such a way that we could expect another individual to be *G* if it is *F*. The feature of being *G* if *F* is a genuine part of reality, and how we happen to conceive of it will not, by itself, influence its distribution among individuals. Thus intentional necessity fails to satisfy the requirement that, for properties that we project by induction, the necessity of any such property in one individual provides a chance, however small, that it is realized in any other individual.

(III) One must conclude that only the real necessity of a feature's belonging to an observed individual can make it at all likely that an unobserved individual will have a similar feature. Observe that the projected features are those that individuals could have by law. Hence we could have said in (I) that some features of individuals must be had by law. The argument of (II) would then have reached the conclusion that lawfulness, like necessity, cannot be merely an intentional characterization of a truth. Necessity, and hence lawfulness, of the sort needed for induction, are real rather than intentional.

Yet it has become a dogma that the basis for lawfulness is intentional. It is thought, for example, that *A*'s holding by law is to be analyzed exhaustively in term.of *A*'s truth and with reference either to *A*'s place among other propositions of a deductive system[3] or to the place of expressions for *A* in the hierarchy of linguistic expressions arranged by familiarity.[4] Efforts based on this dogma may well prove fruitful as a means of identifying laws, but the dogma acts as a blinker that cuts off from view the ontological base of lawfulness. Since *a*'s being *F* by law implies *a*'s being *F* by necessity, when *a* is *F* by law, *a* has the property *F* on the basis of some factor about *a* other than *F*. Lawfulness is, then, real rather than intentional.

If the belief that lawfulness is intentional persists as a dogma, then there must be some reason favoring the intentional view of lawfulness. The remarkable thing is that a variation on Hume's argument against necessary connections is still used in this regard, with no effort to firm up its ontological foundation. If there were real lawfulness, then there would be real necessity. But, it is asked, do we ever encounter the necessity of a real necessity? We encounter temporal conjunctions, but nothing like the necessity of a necessary connection. Perhaps we have not looked hard enough. No; the necessity of a necessary connection simply cannot be found. But do I not observe that the door must shut when I push it or that the paper must flame up when I hold a lighted match to it? Against this appeal to perception, the Humean is forced to bolster his epistemological argument with an ontological one. We are to believe that there are no observations of necessity since things in the knowable world are merely collections of their conditions, and as to conditions it is obvious that what is distinct is separable. Accordingly, if there are no entities in the knowable world that can be necessarily connected, there is no necessity to be detected. But the only reason suggested for believing that things are reducible to conditions is that if they were not, necessary connections and hence real necessity would return to plague us. These are hardly impressive credentials for treating necessity and hence lawfulness as intentional.

Granting that lawfulness is real rather than intentional, what precisely is its real base? In answering this question, we also answer the same question for necessity. Let us consider several possibilities.

(A) Suppose *F*'s are *G* by law. Could the real basis for its being a law be an entity called a "necessary connection" that stands, somehow, between anything's condition of being *F* and its condition of being *G*? But then lawfulness, and hence necessity, would be based on the merely *contingent* presence of a special entity. This is absurd, however, for, if the special entity—the necessary connection—could be absent, then it is not a law or a necessity that *F*'s are *G*. So this entity *must* be present between anything's being *F* and its being *G*. Yet why should it be present between being *F* and being *G* rather than between being *F* and, say, being *H*, where, we suppose, being *H* does not always accompany being *F*. Our search in this direction for a real basis has come to a dead end.

To avoid confusion, it is well to digress now to note that even though it may be a law that if anything is an *F* it is *G*, the proposition that if anything is an *F* it is *G* is not, in general, a modal conditional. For, if it were, then the proposition that it is necessary that if anything is an *F* it is a *G* would be doubly modal. Thus in looking for a model best suited to conditionals that are laws, we must try to find a non-modal conditional. This requirement is satisfied by Anderson and Belnap's "relevant" implication[5] rather than by Lewis' "strict" implication,[6] which is modal.

Throughout this book I shall make frequent use of the concept of relevant implication, symbolizing it by the $\rightarrow$. It will be especially important in showing how necessities are based on natures, how relational properties are based on their foundations, and how capacities are reduced to actualities. Lewis' strict implication, symbolized by the $\prec$, is such that for any propositions A and B, $(A \prec B)$ implies $\Box \sim (A \cdot \sim B)$, that is, that it is necessarily not the case that both A and not-B. But, since a relevant conditional is non-modal, $(A \rightarrow B)$ does not imply $\Box \sim (A \cdot \sim B)$. Moreover, the paradox-free character of relevant implication makes it more desirable than "material" implication–to be symbolized by the $\supset$ –for the discussion of all the matters mentioned. That is, though $(A \supset (B \supset A))$ is valid, as is $((\Box A) \prec (B \prec A))$, neither $(A \rightarrow (B \rightarrow A))$ nor $((\Box A) \rightarrow (B \rightarrow A))$ can be a theorem of relevance logic. This agrees with the common-sense observation that, since A may be totally *irrelevant* to B, A will not in general imply that B implies A.

(B) Perhaps the real basis of lawfulness is to be found in a "middle term." If F's are H by law and H's are G by law, then H is the real basis for F's being G by law. H might be a feature of the micro-structure of entities that are F. Whatever the supposed middle term may be, however, this procedure leads to a regress. We now have two additional laws, those relating the middle term to the extremes. On the one hand, there is nothing to justify the assumption that however far the regress takes us, there will still be a middle term. On the other hand, even if the regress is infinite, lawfulness remains ungrounded, since each middle term appealed to at each stage must be appealed to as one that is related by law to the extremes. The regress is then vicious, as I shall establish in more detail in Chapter X, §5.

(C) What is needed, in view of (B), is not a third term that itself stands in connections that are lawful, but rather a third term whose role is merely to back up laws. This will have to be a very special entity indeed. For if we think of properties, dispositions, stuffs, and particles as the normal sorts of components, then components seem always able to enter into lawful connections with one another. But a nature is exactly the kind of component of an entity that is limited to the role of backing up laws without entering into them.

It is important to distinguish between a nature itself and what takes place by virtue of that nature. Even if it is the nature of salt to dissolve, the dissolving itself is not the component of the salt that is its nature. Rather this process takes place by the nature of salt. Digging behind appearances to the ionic structure of the salt crystal, we do not find the nature itself of the salt, but at best something it has by nature.

In view of (A), it is not enough to say that natures do not have lawful connections, but merely stand behind such connections. They must also inhere in individuals or things* as their "being" or "substance." For the being of or the substance of an individual will be selective in its support of connections between that individual's conditions. By contrast, the entity introduced in (A) was merely a relation between conditions. There was no basis for saying that it had to be a connection between certain conditions, but not others. It was external to individuals since it stood only between their conditions. Natures must, however, be internal to individuals in such a way that we can say that they are their being or substance.

When Aristotle asked what the being (*ousia*) of an individual is, he was aware that he was asking a question about a principle at the root of what the individual is, that is, about its nature. So he says "the nature of a thing is clearly its primary being (*ousia*)."[7] But his answer to this question involved a fatal compromise with epistemology. According to him, the being, substance, or nature of an individual is expressible by a definition of it.[8] Thus the properties or parts an individual has *by* its very being or nature become its very being or nature. Otherwise, he thought, the being or nature of an individual would not be "intelligible."[9] So the being or nature of an individual is identified with what properties or parts it has of itself.

Now, on the one hand, it does not appear to me necessary to turn the nature of an individual into what the individual is by its nature in order to make natures intelligible. Natures are intelligible in terms of the role that they play as the basis for certain properties and parts. On the other hand, making natures into properties and

*Things and individuals are to be distinguished from properties and conditions, but things are distinguished from other individuals as ones with capacities to act (Chapter XI, §1). Nothing here rests on the latter distinction.

parts leaves no basis for the necessity of these properties and parts to the individuals having them.

It is difficult to hold the idea of a nature as something behind essential properties and parts alike in face of the universal acceptance of Locke's belief that "If anyone will say that the real essence and internal constitution on which these properties depend, is not the figure, size, and arrangement or connexion of its solid parts, but something else, called its particular *form,* I am further from having any idea of its real essence than I was before."[10] Locke's idea of a nature as a constitution of parts is more restrictive than the Aristotelian idea that allowed for natures composed of properties. But both are united in denying the intelligibility of the idea of a nature as something behind essential properties and parts alike.

If the only components one can have ideas of are properties, particles, stuffs, and dispositions, then Locke is right that one cannot have an idea of what I have called a nature of an individual. But even an empiricist theory of ideas might allow that there can be an idea of a nature as a component distinct from all of these. Of course, one might have the idea of a nature merely by knowing that it played the role of a ground of necessity. But such an idea would lack solid empiricist credentials. There is, however, no need to settle for less than an idea of a nature that is tied to the experience of individuals' having natures. When I experience an individual's having a property that I am right in judging essential to it, it is entirely plausible to suggest that I then experience that individual's condition of having the nature that gives rise to this property. I then experience the individual as having its being or substance, thereby settling negatively the question of whether I am encountering a collection of distinct entities rather than a unitary individual. According to the view of Chapter VI, if natures, microparticles, and other components could not be experienced as had by individuals, then expressions for them would lack significance.

§3. *Possible Worlds Controlled by Population.* Can one get at the roots of necessity through the idea that necessity is truth in all possible worlds? One can say at least that if a possible world is simply a world in which laws hold or a world in which entities behave in accord with their natures, then the notion of a possible world is derivative from the notions we have already explored. Is there, perhaps, some conception of a possible world that gets behind the notions of law and nature and still reaches the roots of necessity? My conviction is that there is not and hence that the use of the notion of a possible world as a quasi-explanatory category in physical ontology leads away from rather than to the roots of necessity.

Once the restrictions imposed by laws and natures are passed by, there appears to be a great deal of arbitrariness in settling on any other single standard for possible worlds. So one is very understandably led to the point where any set of entities together with a distribution of properties over them can, if one chooses, be considered a possible world. The set of possible worlds is simply a set of sets of entities with specified properties.

This leads to the result that necessity is not univocal, for it changes its meaning each time the set of possible worlds is changed to a different set of sets of entities with specified properties. But to bring this view of necessity into line with our univocalist conception, it suffices merely to relativize the notion of necessity. Let '*L*' and '*P*' be constants designating different sets of sets of entities with specified properties. These designations are to be defined without reliance on laws and natures. They are defined by stating which entities with what properties are in the worlds included in the sets. Thus I shall say that they are designations for sets of possible worlds "specified by population."

An *L*-necessity will hold in all of the worlds designated by '*L*'. One can think of *L*-necessity and of *P*-necessity as being relative necessities. Both are then instances of the univocal concept of necessity relative to some set of possible worlds specified by population. The expression '*X*-necessity' will signify this univocal concept. Roughly, the relativizing of necessity to various sets of sets corresponds, in the semantics of modal logic, to interpreting formal modal languages containing non-relativized modal operators by means of models on various "model structures."[11]

Let us then grant that there is such a univocal concept of relative necessity, that is, the concept of *X*-necessity. However, it is so constructed as to be unilluminating about the basis of the necessity of whatever kind of necessary truth one considers. This can be seen in two ways.

First, suppose that the set *L* is *in fact* the set of logically possible worlds and that the set *P* is *in fact* the set of physically possible worlds. But *qua* *L*-possible and *P*-possible sets, they have not been specified, respectively, as sets of worlds in which logical and physical laws hold. *L* and *P* are, rather, sets whose worlds are specified by population. It will not then follow from the fact that a certain proposition is *L*- or *P*-necessary that the proposition is logically or physically necessary. In each case we get only an extensional equivalence. It would thus be absurd to claim that we are getting at the roots of logical and physical necessity through instances of the notion of *X*-necessity.

Now in applying the concept of *X*-necessity it will have been, in general, already assumed that the specific set of sets chosen conforms to logical laws. So any *X*-possible world is logically possible in a sense that relies on an appeal to logical laws. The different species of *X*-necessity are, then, determined by various "cut-downs" on the set of logically possible worlds. If, on the one hand, the cut-down to physically possible worlds is also made by an appeal to laws and hence to natures, then the whole project of getting at the roots of necessity through possible worlds in a way that by-passes laws and natures is abandoned. If, on the other hand, the cut-down to physically possible worlds is made by means of a specification by population, then not only is the treatment of physical necessity incoherent with that of logical necessity but also the specification by population can at most generate an extensional equivalent for the notion of physical necessity.

Second, let *Q* be the set of two worlds such that a single piece of paper is contained by both worlds and that neither contains anything else. In one of the worlds it is red, and in the other it is green. But in each world it is circular. It is then *Q*-necessary that the paper is circular. Yet if *R* is the set containing only the single world in which the same paper is red, then it is *R*-necessary that the paper is red. All that can be claimed for *Q*- and *R*-necessity is that they are only certain similarities between sets.[12] The sets of *Q* are similar in that they have the same piece of circular paper.

This is what it means to say it is *Q*-necessary that the paper is circular. When it is driven home by considering these simple examples that this is what any instance of *X*-necessity amounts to, one recognizes the vast conceptual chasm between *X*-necessity and the necessity involved in physics and logic. The former is related to the latter in name only.

The source of the trouble is the attempt to make philosophical use of the metalogically useful notion of a cut-down on logically possible worlds. The motivation for interpreting modal languages in a way that gives importance to the notion of a sub-set of the set of logically possible worlds was the desire to show the completeness of certain formal modal languages. To get completeness in these cases it will not do to define validity as truth in all logically possible worlds. It must be defined more demandingly as truth in all worlds in any sub-set of the set of logically possible worlds.[13] The idea is that, for any atomic proposition *A,* the proposition possibly-not-*A* is not a theorem in Lewis' system S5, but this proposition holds in every logically possible world. For, any atomic proposition fails in some logically possible world. A way of defining validity is then devised so that S5's failure to contain this logical truth is not a mark against this system. For *A,* take the proposition that *this* is red, where *this* is the piece of red paper in the sole world of *R.* With *R* as the reference set for deciding modal truths, possibly-not-*A* is false in the sole world of *R* since there is no other world in *R* and *a fortiori* no other world in *R* in which *A* is false. Hence, possibly-not-*A* is not valid in the demanding sense of being true in all worlds in any sub-set of logically possible worlds. The brilliance of this device for achieving completeness for S5 is not in question. But one should not be so dazzled by it that one confuses the heuristic value of deciding modal truths by reference to different sub-sets of logically possible worlds with a sign of philosophical fruitfulness.

Even if the above difficulties of getting at the roots of necessity *via* possible worlds are overlooked, the limited usefulness of the notion of possible world turns up in another way. On the assumption that natures are the real basis called for by necessity, one cannot ask what natures are possible. It may be impossible for an entity to behave in a certain way in view of its nature. But how could it be impossible for an entity to have a certain nature, say a nature to be contradictory? Perhaps there would be a conflict with a more basic aspect of the natures of entities; thus it would be the nature of any entity to be non-contradictory. But this can indicate only that 'entity' is not yet the broadest designation, as we intend it to be. In the intended broad sense, it is possible for an entity to have any nature. Thus the idea of all possible worlds is too broad to make any useful discriminations. Only after we have limited the worlds to those containing entities on the natures of which logical necessities or logical and physical necessities are grounded do we have a useful set of possible worlds.

§4. *Natural Necessity.* The kind of necessity required by the fact that at least some propositions are supported by prior experience is a real rather than an intentional necessity. Moreover, since natures are the real factors at the base of this necessity, it is appropriately called a natural necessity. In view of the identity between the necessity of physical and logical necessities, it must be recognized that logical necessity is a real necessity of the natural sort. The equivalence:

(1) Necessarily *A* if and only if *A* by nature

holds for both physical and logical necessity. (It is intended to hold only for so-called *de re* necessity, but it will soon be shown that natures also play an important role in regard to so-called *de dicto* necessity.)

There are several ways one might interpret 'by nature' in (1). It might be interpreted as an entity's manner of being something, where its manner is taken to be based on nothing else. Then the manner of Jones's being human—his being human naturally—would not point back to a further entity, a nature. The manner of being would itself be ontologically ultimate. This has two drawbacks. In the first place, 'necessarily' is already an expression of manner, and the search for a basis for necessity was a search for a basis for a manner of being. Simply saying that this manner of being can be equally well expressed by the phrase 'by nature' is to abandon the search for the basis of the manner of being. In the second place, unless a manner is based on objective factors, there seems no alternative but to treat the manner as having an intentional basis. That is, the notion of a manner of being that is ontologically ultimate is just not acceptable (cf. Chapter VIII, §4). Going in one direction—that which one takes with 'obviously', which is applicable on the basis of some relation between given data and the proposition in question—leads to an intentional interpretation of modality, which has already been rejected. Going in the other direction—that which one takes with 'swiftly', which is applicable on the basis of the kind of action performed and the rate of its being done—takes us beyond mere manners of being to the natures that are the real factors at the basis of necessity.

How then are we to express an interpretation of 'by nature' in terms of entities rather than of manners of being? As a first step, consider an interpretation of 'a is ϕ by nature' as 'The nature of a is such that a is ϕ'. But this does not unequivocally commit us to natures as entities. For, if we treat 'the nature of a is such that' as an operator on a par with 'some x is such that', then everything but 'a' in the operator might be relegated to the syncategorematic. I am then led to propose that 'a is ϕ by nature' be interpreted as 'There is a nature such that a has it and if a has it then a is ϕ'. Thus where 'n' is a variable for natures:

(2) ϕa by nature if and only if $(\exists n)$(a has the nature $n \cdot$ (a has the nature $n \rightarrow \phi a$)).

Or in general:

(3) A by the nature of certain entities if and only if there are natures that those entities have and A is implied by the fact that they have those natures.

The use of 'by the nature of certain entities' in (3) in place of 'by nature' in (1) gives recognition to the fact that (1) has been simplified on both the left and the right hand sides. In asserting a necessity, one must be clear as to which entities the necessity is of. Correspondingly, when something is asserted to hold by nature, it should be clear of which entities it is by nature. It will be taken for granted here that the *certain entities* whose natures support A are entities that A is about.

How does this treatment of necessity avoid an infinite regress?

Suppose ϕa is indeed necessary. If in addition (2) is true, then one must be prepared to admit still further necessities. For, first, *a* must have some nature, and it turns out that whatever nature it has it has necessarily. Otherwise, (2) would conflict with the modal laws of Lewis' S5. This can be seen as follows.

What would happen if *a* could have the nature *M* that is different from its actual nature *N*? Because of their difference, these natures will "support" different properties. That is, either (i) having *M* implies having some property ψ though having *N* does not imply having ψ, or (ii) having *N* implies having some property θ though having *M* does not imply having θ, or both. If (i) were the case, then by (2) *a could* have ψ by nature, and hence necessarily, even though by (2) *a actually* does not have ψ by nature, and hence has it only contingently. But this conflicts with the modal law of Lewis' S5 that the possibly necessary is actually necessary. If (ii) were the case, then by (2) *a might* have θ only contingently, even though by (2) *a actually* has θ necessarily. But this conflicts with the modal law of Lewis' S4, which system is contained in S5, that the actually necessary is not possibly not necessary. So if (2) and S5 are accepted, true instances of the formula that (*a* has the nature *n*) are necessary.

Faced with the additional modal claim that *a* has the nature *N* necessarily, one must ask how a regress is to be avoided. If this necessity required still a further nature, then a regress would be unavoidable. But our position does not require appeal to a further nature. Our position is that whatever *a* has necessarily it has because of its nature. So if *a* has *N* necessarily, this is simply because of *N* itself, and the regress to other entities is stopped.

Second, true instances of the conditional formula that (*a* has the nature $n \rightarrow \phi a$) will have to be necessary if (2) is to be satisfactory. Otherwise, even though the antecedent is necessary, the consequent might be false. But if ϕa might be false, the left side of (2) would be false. To accommodate this need for a necessary conditional, there is no need to retreat to a further nature. The nature, *N*, of *a* makes it true of *a* that it have the relevant conditional property. It supports the conditional property that any entity *x* has when it is true that (*x* has the nature $N \rightarrow \phi x$).

But are all the modal laws of S5 with relevant implication, and hence of the weaker systems S1-S4 with relevant implication, true here? That is, once (1) and (2) are used to interpret the modalities in these laws, are the modal laws of S5 and hence of S1-S4 demonstrable? The answer is that they are. The demonstrations are straightforward enough to need no presentation here. For example, in the case of the law of S4 used above, that the necessary is necessarily necessary, it is to be shown that, where 'P' is 'is the nature of', from $(\exists n)(nPx \cdot (nPx \rightarrow Fx))$, it follows by simple logical steps that $(\exists n)(nPx \cdot (nPx \rightarrow (\exists m)(mPx \cdot (mPx \rightarrow Fx))))$. For the law of S5, that the possibly necessary is actually necessary, one needs to add the assumption that any individual has a nature. These and the other laws of Lewis' modal systems are then seen to express truths about natures.

To apply the general idea expressed in (3) to cases beyond the atomic one that is considered in (2), a recursive schema would be desirable. In lieu of developing such a schema, I note only that (3) is intended to have these applications:

(4) $(x)\phi x$ by the nature of x if and only if (x) $(\exists n)$ (x has the nature n $\cdot$ (x has the nature $n \rightarrow \phi x$)),

(5) $\phi a \rightarrow \psi b$ by the natures of a and b if and only if $(\exists n,m)$ (a has the nature n $\cdot$ b has the nature m $\cdot$ ((a has the nature n $\cdot$ b has the nature m) $\rightarrow$ ($\phi a \rightarrow \psi b$))).

The right-hand sides of (2), (4), and (5) indicate in exactly what sense natures are real bases, grounds, or foundations of necessity. Necessity and lawfulness are not themselves entities. But if there is a true proposition asserting the necessity or lawfulness, for certain entities, of a certain fact, then the condition for its truth is that there be natures that those entities have and that their having them implies that fact. So natures ground necessity and lawfulness in that the existence of natures and of their implications are conditions for the truth of claims of necessity and lawfulness.

§5. *Natures and de Dicto Necessity.* The necessity claims thus far considered were called *de re* necessity claims. In making such claims, certain entities are said to be certain ways necessarily. Now these are the entities that the corresponding non-modal claims are about. Since the proposition that Jones is two-footed is about Jones and no one else, the corresponding *de re* necessity claim asserts of Jones and of no one else a necessity to be two-footed. But what I termed a *de dicto* necessity claim is not limited in this way. The entities whose natures are relevant to the truth of this claim need not be entities limited to the ones that the corresponding non-modal claim is about. This does not mean that intentional entities enter the truth conditions of *de dicto* claims. It means only that the natures of entities beyond those referred to are often involved.

Suppose there is a cage that contains only cats. Cats, we assume, purr by nature. But the nature of the cage is not such as to make animals in it purr. Now interpret the proposition that all animals in the cage purr as being about any animal in the cage, rather than about any entity whatsoever. It might then be expressed as '$(x \in \{C\})Px$'. Here '$x\in\{C\}$' is a restricted variable of quantification. And so the sentence reads 'Any animal-in-the-cage, *x*, is such that *x* purrs'. Under the suggested interpretation, the proposition would not be expressed with the unrestricted variable as '$(x)(Cx \rightarrow Px)$'. For this is about any entity whatsoever, and not just about animals in the cage. When the cage is empty, '$(x)(Cx \rightarrow Px)$' but not '$(x \in\{C\})Px$' would still be about entities. Now the modal claim that all animals in the cage necessarily purr —that is, that any animal-in-the-cage, *x*, is such that *x* necessarily purrs—is a true, *de re* claim. For the natures of the entities that the corresponding non-modal claim is about suffice for the truth of the modal claim. (Where it is feasible, a *de re* claim will be distinguished from a *de dicto* claim by the convention of placing the modal adverb adjacent to the main verb.)

Universal modal propositions such as:

(1) All animals in the cage necessarily purr

that depend for their truth on the natures of just the entities of a restricted class are familiar enough. It is clearly a mistake to try to analyze them by using the universal conditional with an unrestricted variable. For (1) says what the entities in the cage necessarily do. It does not say that any entity is necessarily such that, if it were an animal in the cage, it would purr. This would make the truth of (1) depend on the natures of all entities, whereas it depends only on the natures of those in the cage. Moreover, it does not say that any entity is such that, if it were in the cage, it would necessarily purr, thereby limiting the modality to the consequent. The proposition (1) does not say this since it speaks categorically, not hypothetically, about the animals in the cage.

On the other hand, suppose one wants to say not just that all the animals that happen to be in the cage have a nature to purr but also that any entity is by nature such that if it is an animal in the cage it purrs. Here one considers not just the entities in the cage but all others as well. Thus, not only must it be true that $(x \in \{C\})Px$ by the nature of $x \in \{C\}$, but it must also be true that $(x)(Cx \rightarrow Px)$ by the nature of x. The proposition that is true under these stronger conditions will be the *de dicto* counterpart of the *de re* proposition (1). (The *de dicto* claim will be expressed with the modal adverb as prefix, rather than as adjacent to the verb.) So the *de dicto* proposition:

(2) Necessarily all animals in the cage purr

is true precisely when the animals in the cage purr by nature and it is by the nature of any entity to purr if it is an animal in the cage. Since one could put a dog in the cage, (2) is false even though (1) is true on the supposition that only cats happen to be in the cage.

Though it goes beyond the corresponding *de re* claim, a universal *de dicto* claim in no wise introduces a necessity based on intentions. The *dictum* is the scope of the necessity operator and not the basis of the necessity. In fact, the *de dicto* necessity is grounded in natures and is thus a real necessity. The reason it is not *de re* is that it goes beyond the *res* of the corresponding non-modal claim. In going beyond what the corresponding non-modal claim is about, it still has its ground in the real rather than the intentional.

This view of universal *de dicto* claims is summed up by the following schema, where '$(x \in \{F\})Gx$' means 'Any F, say x, is such that Gx' which means 'All F are G':

(3) Necessarily $(x \in \{F\})Gx$ if and only if (i) $(x \in \{F\})Gx$ by the nature of $x \in \{F\}$, and (ii) $(x)(Fx \rightarrow Gx)$ by the nature of x.

It follows from (3) that when $\{F\}$ is the class of all entities—when the variable of quantification in '$(x \in \{F\})Gx$' is unrestricted—the universal *de re* and *de dicto* claims are equivalent. So it follows from (3) that the two Barcan laws hold—that all entities are necessarily *G* implies that necessarily all entities are *G*, and conversely that necessarily all entities are *G* implies that all entities are necessarily *G*. The reason for this result is that '*x*' has been assumed to range only over actual entities. Had this not been assumed, had non-actual entities been introduced into the range of '*x*', then even when $\{F\}$ is the class of actual entities, it would impose a significant restriction on the range of '*x*', and the equivalence would fail. The reason for this assumption is that non-actual entities are no part of the ontology required by the practice of action based on prior experience. The required ontology is then uncompromisingly actualist. "No new entity is spawned in a possible world."[14] Apparent non-actual entities admit of reduction *via* an analysis of the acts of which they are the intentional contents.

So far there is no reason to regard Quine's claim that necessity "resides in the way in which we say things, and not in the things we talk about"[15] as even partially true. But we have yet to consider the most troublesome case, that of singular *de dicto* claims. The invalidity of existentially quantifying into such claims seems to warn us that here we are dealing with how things are conceived rather than with the natures of things. I contend, however, that the necessity of a singular *de dicto* claim need not be an intentional necessity.

Assume that the first human born at sea was the first animal born at sea. Now the singular *de dicto* claim that necessarily the first human born at sea was risible is true since two important conditions are satisfied. First, the corresponding *de re* claim is true. That is, the first human born at sea was necessarily risible just because it was an individual whose nature was to be risible. Second, anything is necessarily such that if it is the first human born at sea then it has the property humanness; and, if it is human, then necessarily it is risible. So the conditions involve both a singular and a general *de re* claim. By contrast, the singular *de dicto* claim that necessarily the first *animal* born at sea was risible is false. For, the second condition fails. There is no property necessarily implied by being identical with the first animal born at sea that in turn implies being risible.

The schema for singular *de dicto* claims is then:

(4) Necessarily Fa if and only if (i) Fa by the nature of a, and (ii) $(x)(\exists \phi)((x = a \rightarrow \phi x) \cdot (\phi x \rightarrow Fx))$ by the nature of x.

It is clear from this why there is a difficulty about quantifying-in. If $(\exists y)$ (necessarily Fy) is true, then it will be true that $(\exists y)(x)(\exists \phi)((x = y \rightarrow \phi x) \cdot (\phi x \rightarrow Fx))$ by the nature of x. But plainly the latter is not true, except where F is merely a property implied by the properties of identity. For there is no individual mere identity with which as an individual will imply having a property such as humanness. The device of quantification abstracts from any content that supports such an implication. Though, for any x, it is true that ($x =$ the first human born at sea $\rightarrow x$ is human), it is not true that $(\exists y)(x = y \rightarrow x$ is human).

If this is why existential quantification is not valid, the nonintentional character of the necessity is left intact. One cannot quantify-in because the mechanism of denoting individuals has been made crucial use of also to signify properties of those individuals. Quantifying wipes out the signifying role of the mechanism of denotation. But even though that role has been relied on, it is decidedly not the case that the truth of the proposition expressed by mobilizing that role depends on anything other than nonintentional factors. Thus its being true that anything identical with the first human born at sea is a human is based simply on the nature of any entity that one may care to consider. Still one cannot quantify into this proposition since the denotational expression 'the first human born at sea' is also relied on to signify the humanity of the denoted individual.

A case has already been considered in which clause (ii) of (4) failed. Failures of clause (i) present an interesting variety. It is not true that necessarily the first human born at sea was born at sea. For though the nature of the first human born at sea is to be human, it is not of the nature of this individual to be born at sea. To accommodate this and like cases, one can define a special sense of *de dicto* necessity by clause (ii) alone. This kind of necessity could be called "incidental." For it is grounded not on the nature of the individual but on some feature incidental to it. It is incidentally necessary that this human, who is a ϕ, is ψ, where a human is not by nature a ϕ but where a ϕ is necessarily a ψ. (For Aristotle, a man born at sea is an "incidental being" since he is not of himself born at sea, but any man is a "*per se* being" since he is of himself a man.[16])

Moreover, it is also false, in view of (i) of (4), that necessarily the president is a citizen, assuming no one is a citizen by nature. But here even (ii) fails, since being president implies being a citizen not by nature but by the Constitution. This can then be defined as an intentional necessity. It will be intentional not because of failure of quantifying-in, but because the necessity is based on an intentional entity, the Constitution.

Having reduced real *de dicto* necessity to real *de re* necessity, it is well to consider the alternative of making the reduction go the other way. The motivation for this converse reduction might well be a prejudice against natures. But since the *de re* necessities I am concerned with must be real, this reduction cannot lead to *de dicto* necessities based on intentions. Suppose somehow the reduction to *de dicto* necessity could be effected, what account could then be given of *de dicto* necessity itself? Aristotle's concept of nature seems suited to the job in view of the peculiarity that his is a kind-relative concept of nature. It differs in this respect from the concept of nature I am using. For him, a given entity has a nature as, say, a yew, but not as a topiary, even though the given entity is a topiary and this topiary is just a yew fashioned by the gardener's art as a bird. On the other hand, the view taken here is that an entity has a nature by itself, irrespective of kind. Yet Aristotle's concept gives a direct basis for *de dicto* necessity, without detour through *de re* necessity. The *de dicto* claim that necessarily every cat, or even this cat, purrs amounts to the claim that, in view of its kind-relative nature, a cat, or this cat, purrs. The non-relative natures of the cats would, as we have seen, be powerless to support these *de dicto* claims. What then are the kind-relative natures? The nature of an *F*, or of this *F*, is an explanatory principle of change in an *F*, or in this *F*, *qua F*.[17] In other words, a topiary, being a product of art, has no nature as topiary since any principle of its growth is in it not *qua* topiary but *qua* yew. Either the reduction of the *de re* to the *de dicto* is bought at the expense of adding the primitive concept of *qua*ness, or this concept is itself reducible. But when we go to reduce it, we are led straight back to *de dicto* necessity, for which we were presumably getting a real basis. An *F*, or this *F*, *qua F* is *G* if and only if necessarily an *F*, or this *F*, is *G*. On the Aristotelian kind-relative view of natures there is either no grounding of *de dicto* necessity or there is the addition of *qua*ness.

CHAPTER III

Nature and Sameness

§1. *The One and the Many.* Since natures are to be part of the required ontology, there are some questions about them that call for an immediate answer. Chief among these is the question of the relation of entities to their natures. If the nature of an entity is numerically distinct from that entity, then how can it be the basis for what the entity must be? Moreover, since terms for natural kinds appear in universal necessity claims, it is important to understand the relation of natures to natural kinds. Do all individuals in a natural kind have similar natures, and if natures are not properties, what can it mean to say two entities have similar natures?

The question about the distinctness of entities from their natures is best approached with some general machinery in hand. As far as sameness is concerned, ontologies divide into two basic kinds. According to those of the one, individuals are simples. According to those of the other, individuals have components. For an "ontology of simples" a potentially divided individual cannot be a genuine individual. It is a complex of many individuals. If it were one, it would, in contradiction to an ontology of simples, have many components. For the parts which could be separated from it are components of it. In effect, potential dividedness, for an ontology of simples, is always only an appearance overlaid on actual dividedness.[1] Moreover, for an ontology of simples, a property of an individual cannot be a component of it, for then the individual would not be simple. In the ontology of simples there are only two possibilities for a property.

First, the property might be something that is not different from the individual having it. Thus, Hume held that a cube of marble is "neither distinguishable nor different nor separable" from the shape of the cube.[2] For such an extreme nominalism, the basic individuals, whether they are things, impressions, or events, are alone in the world. There are no entities that are their properties or parts.

Second, the property might be a totally distinct entity from the individual having it. Thus, for example, the quality in one of Russell's monadic atomic facts is distinct from the simple that is the particular in that fact.[3] For such a Platonizing ontology of simples, the distinctness of particulars is precisely like that between particulars and universals.

In short, an ontology of simples rejects sameness without identity. By "identity" I mean not being discernibly different. Identical entities are such that if one has a property the other has it, too. But by "sameness" I mean not being numerically distinct. For an ontology of simples, no distinction is drawn between these two notions; for such an ontology, if a property and an individual are the same particular, they are identical. If the property were different from the individual while remaining the same particular —*idem subjecto*—then the individual would have an entity as a component, and would thus not be simple.

When a property is the same particular as an individual, one of them depends for its existence on the other. The very idea of a complex entity brings in the idea of existential dependence, which will be discussed in Chapter XI, §4. As will be pointed out there, existential dependence is only a necessary condition for sameness; some entities are existentially dependent on individuals while distinct from them. Here it is to be pointed out only that existential dependence is not dependence in the usual causal sense. Jones may bring it about that a book comes into being, but though he is the cause of its coming into existence, he is not the cause of the existence that it has. Similarly, Jones may bring a circular cookie into being, but he does not thereby cause the property circularity itself. If individuals are not dependent as regards their existence and if properties are the same particulars as their respective individuals, properties will exist only in the sense that individuals exist with them and hence will be existentially dependent on individuals. The conflation of sameness with identity by the ontologist of simples is a first step toward denying that properties are existentially dependent on individuals. For this conflation leads us to say that properties are distinct from individuals since they are different from individuals. And only distinct entities can be existentially independent. In this chapter and in Chapter VII, I shall state my misgivings about the thesis that properties, natures, and relations are not the same particulars as individuals with them.

An "ontology of components" neither collapses the difference between physical individuals and their properties—as extreme nominalism does—nor represents them as numerically distinct entities—as the Platonizing ontologist of simples does. Collapsing the difference puts grave problems in the way of understanding how there can be real dissimilarities between individuals. How are a red and a green patch dissimilar if there are patches but no colors, or no bases for what one takes to be colors? To say that their dissimilarity is merely their distinctness will not do, since two red patches are distinct without being dissimilar.

Suppose then we take the view that properties are distinct from particulars as the most promising form of the ontology of simples. The undeniable unity of a pale man then becomes the unity of a fact, not of an individual. For an encompassing fact is needed to unite the man and his paleness. On this view, such a fact is not made up of concepts since the individual and the property are parts of the fact. Moreover, such a fact is not an intentional entity, and hence is not *about* the pale man. For the unity of the fact is to be the unity of the pale man, and not the unity of some entity about him. So the unifying fact is not the fact *that* the man is pale, for facts-that are intentional. Rather the unifying fact will be the fact *of* the man's being pale, since facts-of are not intentional.

But how can unity be generated from distinct entities? On the one hand, suppose the property is held to be just the sort of entity that does join an individual together wiıh it into the unitary entity I have called a fact without the assistance of a third entity. So the property joins together, it unifies, entities. This uniting is either an entity distinct from both the individual and the property, or an entity that is a component of the property that does the joining together, or finally an entity that is not different from the property itself. If the unifying is a distinct entity, then our supposition that the property acts to unify without the assistance of a third entity would be violated. If the unifying is a component, then we violate the conclusion that all basic entities are simples—a conclusion which follows from the premiss that for such entities sameness implies identity. If the unifying is not different from the property, then the fact is only the unification of an individual, but since individuals are simples, there is nothing in them to be unified.

So we are led to suppose, on the other hand, that the unity of a fact requires a third entity. Call it the copulation, the *being* in the fact of the man's *being* pale. As a third entity, distinct from the property and the individual, it will not be a component of either of them. One can say that its function is simply to unite,[4] but how can it perform this function within an ontology of simples? If the uniting is distinct from the copulation, a fourth entity is introduced and a regress has been started. If the uniting is a component of the copulation, we no longer have an ontology of simples.

One is left with the alternative that the uniting is not different from the copulation itself. But this uniting is then included in the fact since the copulation is. The copulation must account not only for the uniting of the property and the individual in the fact but also for a uniting of them together with itself in the fact. This is just our original problem, but now with three rather than two entities to be united. A further entity is needed to unite the uniting to the other entities in the fact, and so on endlessly. In short neither a property and an individual nor a property, a copulation, and an individual account for the unity of a fact on the ontology of simples.

In order to skirt this difficulty one might demote individuals and properties to dependent entities that are mere components of facts. But this carries us over to an ontology of components in which individuals and properties are not *distinct* from one another or from facts, but are merely *different* from one another and from an encompassing fact. The advantage of this is that individual and property as non-distinct require no unification, and thus the copulation need not be a distinct entity. According to one version of this view, the copulation in a fact-of is a "tie" but this tie is not identical with any entity allowed in the ontology.[5] It becomes possible to treat the copulation in this way when components are substituted for the distinct entities of the ontology of simples. Such an anomalous tie, like any non-entity, suffices when there is no work to do, and there is no uniting to be done when, as in this case, there are no distinct entities. Likewise, the view that since properties are "unsaturated" they can be united with particulars in facts without a third entity is an awkward version of the ontology of components.[6] For, on this view, to say that the paleness is distinct from the man would be to treat the paleness as a particular and no longer as a property with its characteristic unsaturatedness. The awkwardness comes from not being able to say they are the same either.

So for an ontology of components there is no question as to how a particular and a property are united, since they are not distinct. The only question that could be raised is how, being one particular, they are different. An unacceptable way of answering this question is to say that difference is rooted in conceptual distinctness. But then difference is not real but only intentional, and this position reduces to Hume's form of the ontology of simples. Other means of accounting for differences also invert important ontological priorities. It is best then to ask, not how components are different, but how difference shows up. Though facts-of were unsuccessful in the role of unifying distinct entities, they can be employed as a criterion for differentiation. Thus entities that are the same but are associated with distinct facts-of are different. Consider Jones and his paleness. Jones is different from his paleness, even though he is not distinct from his paleness. This difference shows up as the distinctness of the fact of or, to revert now to our earlier expression, the distinctness of the condition of being Jones from the condition of being pale. For the property paleness the associated condition is the condition of being pale. As I shall argue in Chapter VIII, §4, conditions, unlike components, are distinct from the particulars with them. Only because of this distinctness of conditions from particulars having them can the difference between components show up as the distinctness of the conditions of having those components. Note also that by the above criterion, a property is different from a similar one that recurs in the same particular. Jones's hunger today is different from his hunger tomorrow, assuming he ate an ample meal in between. For his condition of being hungry tomorrow will be a new condition. None of this commits one to the view that components of individuals or individuals themselves are ontologically dependent on conditions. I shall argue the converse in Chapter XI, §4. Here I am saying only that difference is shown in distinctness of conditions.

A necessary equivalence between facts-that is neither a sufficient nor a necessary condition for the sameness of the corresponding facts-of. Where *a* is a plane figure, the fact that *a* is a tri-lateral necessarily implies and is implied by the fact that *a* is a tri-angle. But being a tri-lateral and being a tri-angle are distinct facts-of or conditions of *a*. This distinctness results from the obvious difference between the components tri-laterality and tri-angularity.

Further, the fact that *a* is a figure does not necessarily imply that *a* is a tri-lateral. But *a*'s being a figure and *a*'s being a tri-lateral are not distinct conditions. Of course, the terms 'figure' and 'tri-lateral' have different significations. However, they signify not just properties of *a* but of other entities as well. When one comes to consider what it is in *a* that makes these terms truly applicable, one is no longer concerned with the properties of other entities, which properties happen to be in the significations of the terms 'figure' and 'tri-lateral'. There is no special component in *a* that makes it a figure beyond the component of tri-laterality. There is, that is to say, no "figureness" in *a*. Of course, *a* may have the property that is the disjunction of all the properties in the signification of 'figure'. But that is clearly not the property one wants. For the property that makes *a* a figure is the same even when there are some variations in what properties are included in the signification of 'figure'. In short, it is futile to go beyond facts-of to facts-that in order to get a grounding for difference.

It follows from the picture I have drawn of the contrast between an ontology of components and an ontology of simples that most fundamental issues will be handled differently by the two schools. In particular, they diverge on predication and on sameness.

In the ontology of components, a predication is true when, among the components of entities signified by the predicate, there is a component of the individual referred to by the subject. Since components are not distinct from their individuals, the truth of a monadic predication requires the sameness of the individual with its component. In the ontology of simples, however, a predication is true when the predicate signifies an entity that is exemplified by the individual referred to by the subject. Since the individual referred to is simple, it cannot exemplify a component of itself. So exemplification stands between it and a distinct entity.[7]

A true monadic proposition requires, for the ontology of components, only a single entity as its objective counterpart. Nonetheless, that entity has components that are different from it but not distinct from it. This difference in sameness is reflected by the propositional copula. But the ontology of simples requires a structure of distinct entities, if there is to be a true monadic proposition. Even exemplification itself must be a distinct entity in such a structure. If it were a non-entity, there would be no structure. If it were a component of the individual or of the property, they would no longer be simples. And, finally, if facts-of were the basic entities of which individuals, properties, and exemplifications were the non-distinct components, there would be no simples among the basic entities.

Identity is characterized by lack of a discernible difference. But is there for sameness an analogue of the Principle of the Indiscernibility of Identicals? It will not in general be the case that entities counting as the same particular lack a discernible difference. That is, it will not in general be true that the Principle of the Indiscernibility of Sameness holds. Indeed this principle holds only within the ontology of simples. Within the ontology of components entities that are the same need not have all their properties in common. From the standpoint of his own ontology of components, Aristotle noted that entities may be the same that do not have all their properties in common.[8] The implicational form (x is the same particular as y) $\rightarrow (\phi)(\phi x \leftrightarrow \phi y)$ does not have all true instances in the ontology of components. For, though Jones and his paleness will be the same particular, Jones will be carnivorous, even though his paleness is not. (My primary reason for saying that the relation of an individual to one of its properties is that of sameness, rather than identity, is that if it were the relation of identity, the widely held indiscernibility of identicals would fail.)

The above implication (that the same particulars have all their properties in common) holds even in the ontology of components if the ranges of the variables *x* and *y* are restricted to individuals and exclude their components. But, without this restriction, if individuals are not simples, there are propositions claiming that one entity is the same particular as another for which the implication does not hold. Individuals are the same particulars as their properties; they are distinct from other individuals and distinct from the properties of other individuals.[9] The properties of a single individual are the same between or among themselves[10] and are distinct from those of another individual. These cross-categorial samenesses between individuals and properties do not hold for the ontology of simples. This has the consequence that an entity in one of these categories cannot be regarded as more than an external factor in accounting for the behavior of an entity in another category. Since simples have no make-up, they make no contribution to their own behavior. The chief factor in the behavior of simples is not the simples themselves but the entities they exemplify.

It is far from clear that the authority of Leibniz can be appealed to in favor of the Principle of the Indiscernibility of Sameness. It might be thought to follow from his principle of interchangeability *salva veritate* construed as a principle governing concepts. For, as applied to the same concepts of individual substances, it seems to imply that the corresponding same individual substances have the same properties.[11] Nonetheless, Leibniz stated explicitly that distinct subjects could not have the same property, "it being impossible that the same individual accident should be in two subjects or pass from one subject to another."[12] This impossibility can stem only from the fact that, by being "in subjects," accidents are the same particulars as their subjects. Thus Leibniz would be forced to reject the indiscernibility of particulars that are the same. I shall then speak of the Principle of the Indiscernibility of Sameness as the pseudo-Leibnizian Principle.

It seems clear only that Leibniz did assert the converse principle, the Principle of the Sameness of Indiscernibles. Thus he held that $(\phi)(\phi x \leftrightarrow \phi y) \rightarrow$ (x is the same particular as y) since it seems clear that if x and y are identical they are the same. This principle is logically true when the range of the property variable, ϕ, is extended to include the relational property of being the same as some specific individual. But when ϕ is restricted to physical properties, there are objections to this principle. Since electrons are described by antisymmetric state functions, two electrons cannot be distinguished by physical properties, even though their distinctness—their being two—leads to different observations from those that would be met with when there were only one electron.[13]

But is it not downright absurd to reject the Principle of the Indiscernibility of Sameness and thus to hold that Jones is the same particular as his paleness even though he is carnivorous and his paleness is not? Indeed it is absurd if Jones and his paleness are related as a simple to one of its properties. The absurdity disappears if Jones has components. Even so, one might try to avoid rejecting the pseudo-Leibnizian Principle. For one might say that the relation between Jones and his paleness is not *true* sameness but a sameness *of composition*. This sameness of composition is expressed with an 'is' of composition.[14] On the one hand, this splitting of senses of sameness is, in the context, a merely *ad hoc* way of salvaging the pseudo-Leibnizian Principle. On the other hand, it is a failure to come to grips with the basic fact that the component of any real entity—which must be a unity—cannot be a distinct entity. So in the end, the rejection of the pseudo-Leibnizian Principle is unsatisfactory only if one is committed to an ontology of simples. It may be said that the pseudo-Leibnizian Sameness is the only clear kind of sameness and that for this reason one should in no event give up the ontology of simples; but Aristotle's classical theory of sameness is surely clear if one grants the use of the notion of components. And if one refuses, then it is fair for the component ontologist to counter that pseudo-Leibnizian sameness is not clear since the notion of exemplification is not clear. For the pseudo-Leibnizian view of sameness requires that properties, as entities that are necessarily distinct from individuals, be relevant to individuals only by exemplification. If there is no advantage to be gained by polemics of this sort, is there anything in the offing that would genuinely support either side?

§2. *Natures the Same as Things.* The ontology of components receives rather strong confirmation from the fact that natures are part of the required ontology. We have seen that natures come to be part of the required ontology as bases for necessity. That is, if it is a necessity of *a* that it is ϕ, then there is an entity that is the nature of *a* and *a*'s having this entity implies that *a* will be ϕ. But could natures be bases for necessity if they were distinct from the entities whose natures they were?[15] If not, then physical individuals can no longer be regarded as simples, since they have natures as components. Once their simplicity has been compromised by natures, we are led, for the sake of coherence, to consider properties and parts also as components.

If natures are distinct entities, then one has to ask what the conditions of their association with individuals are. There is no comparable question for the component ontologist. For if a nature is a component and thus the same particular as the individual having it, there are not two entities whose association can be in question. Now if *N* is a nature distinct from Jones, then *N* is "associated" with Jones provided it is a necessity of *N* that if *N* supports (say) mobility, then Jones is mobile. If this condition were not satisfied, how could we say that *N* is the nature of Jones? Jones has whatever property flows from or is supported by the nature of Jones. Furthermore, this is not just a contingent fact; for otherwise Jones could fail to be mobile even though his nature supports mobility. Now this necessity required for association is a necessity of *N*, not a necessity of Jones. For, a necessity of Jones would be grounded on a nature associated with Jones. Our condition of association would then presuppose, rather than itself fix, the associated nature.

Since the necessity is of the nature *N*, it must be grounded on a further nature, *M*. This supposes, of course, that *M* is associated with *N* so as to be the nature of the nature *N*. And the condition of association is a necessity of *M*. There will be a necessity of *M* only if there is a further nature associated with *M*, and so on without stop. So for the distinct entity N to be the nature of Jones, N must be the beginning of an unceasing chain of natures of natures.

Before asking whether this regress is objectionable, let us see whether our argument for it is sound, by facing it with two questions. (I) The regress develops supposedly because at each stage the association of a nature with the entity that it is the nature of depends on the nature of the nature. But is there really such a dependency?

Consider the difference between the following propositions:

(1) $\Box\, a(\phi a \rightarrow \psi b)$,
(2) $\Box\, b(\phi a \rightarrow \psi b)$,

where '$\Box\, a$' means 'it is a necessity of a that'. So the difference is that (1) expresses a necessity of a and (2) a necessity of b. Suppose that a—being a piece of fresh litmus paper just dipped in a solution b—is of such a nature that if it is blue then b is alkaline. This amounts to supposing that:

(3) $\Box\, a(a \text{ is blue} \rightarrow b \text{ is alkaline})$.

But from this it does not follow that:

(4) $\Box\, b(a \text{ is blue} \rightarrow b \text{ is alkaline})$,

for since we are concerned in (4) only with a's blueness and not with a's nature, *a could be* a shard of blue pottery rather than a piece of litmus paper. Even when (3) is true, it is surely not in the nature of the solution b that the blueness of whatever might be a—including the shard—implies the alkalinity of b. Conversely, though it may be true that:

(5) $\Box\, a(b \text{ is alkaline} \rightarrow a \text{ is blue})$,

it may still not be true that:

(6) $\Box\, b(b \text{ is alkaline} \rightarrow a \text{ is blue})$.

For, again, it is not the nature of a but a's blueness that is the concern of (6). So *a may be* any object dipped in b.

Applying this to the case of the association of natures with individuals, one sees that neither of the following implies the other:

(7) $\Box N$(the nature N supports mobility $\rightarrow j$ is mobile),
(8) $\Box j$(the nature N supports mobility $\rightarrow j$ is mobile).

This is relevant since there would be no regress set off by appealing to (7) if it were the case that (7) co-implied (8). For then one could say that (7) is grounded on the nature of Jones, which is simply *N*, rather than on the nature of the nature *N*. But since there is no implication between (7) and (8), the appeal to (7) sets off a regress.

(II) This leads directly to our second question. Why appeal to (7) in the first place? Would not an appeal to (8) suffice to establish an association of nature with individual? The problem was to give some sense to the notion of a nature's being the nature of an individual when the nature is distinct from the individual. But when one uses '$\Box j$' in (8), one presupposes that one has in hand a sense for the notion of a nature's being the nature of Jones. Using (2) of Chapter II, §4, (8) above becomes:

(9) $(\exists m)$(j has the nature m · (j has the nature $m \rightarrow$ (the nature N supports mobility $\rightarrow j$ is mobile))).

The trouble is that '*j* has the nature *m*' in (9) is not supposed to be intelligible until we have explained the association of *j* with its nature. But (9) is one of the conditions for association, that is, for a nature's being the nature of Jones. Of course, our expansion of (7) will contain '*N* has the nature *k*'. But if this is susceptible of independent explanation, it can be used in explaining '*j* has the nature *m*'.

Thus when entities are distinct from their natures, one must go in either of two directions. Either entities are associated with natures through natures of these natures (in which case association is obtained at the price of an endless sequence of natures of natures); or entities fail to have an association with natures because an appeal to natures of natures is found objectionable (in which case entities are contingently connected with their natures, and thus any real necessities for these entities are precluded). The price for an ontology of simples with real necessities seems to be merely a regress of natures of natures. Is there any objection to such a regress?

An observation about the logic of *de re* modalities of the kind being used here is relevant now. Given (1) or (2), it does not matter which, and the additional premiss that $\Box\, a(\phi a)$, it follows directly that $\Box\, a(\psi b)$, but not that $\Box\, b(\psi b)$. For example, suppose God's nature is such that if He exists, then the World exists. So, if He exists by His nature, then it follows not that the World exists by its nature, but that it exists by His nature. Thus:

(10) $\Box$ God (God exists → the World exists) → ($\Box$ God (God exists) → $\Box$ God (the World exists)).

Even if the existence of the World is not the result of a free choice made by God—as Leibniz thought it was—but is determined, it does not follow that the World necessarily exists of itself—as Spinoza seems to have thought.[16]

This calls for a qualification on the view of *de re* necessity expressed in Chapter II, §5. *De re* necessities cannot be limited, as they were there, to those that were necessities *of* the entities that their non-modal components were *about*. For the proposition that $\Box$ God (the World exists) is a necessity of God about the World. We may, however, call such a necessity a "derivative" *de re* necessity. For $\Box\, a(\psi b)$ will follow from its being the case that $\Box a(\phi a)$, for some ϕ.

How does this conclusion apply to the regress problem? If natures are distinct entities, it will not be a necessity of Jones but at best of his nature that he is mobile. For it is *false* that:

(11) $\Box\, N$(the nature N supports mobility → j is mobile) → ($\Box\, N$ (the nature N supports mobility) → $\Box\, j$(j is mobile)).

(Clearly, (11) does not cease to be false when only the left-most '$\Box\, N$' is changed to '$\Box j$'.) Perhaps then one should simply settle for necessities *about* individuals in the world that are not necessities *of* those individuals, but *of* entities distinct from them. Such necessities would still be real. The difficulty is that such necessities are derivative and must then be derived from non-derivative necessities. But it turns out there are, on the ontology of simples, no non-derivative necessities. At first this might not seem to be the case. It seems as though $\Box\, N$(j is mobile) derives from the non-derivative $\Box\, N$(the nature N supports mobility) *via* the antecedent of (11). Yet there is no such non-derivative necessity. For, by all the above reasoning, the necessity that N support mobility is a necessity of the nature M of N, not a necessity of N, despite the way we have written it. After all, N must be associated with M, and only on the basis of that association are there any necessities about N. But then such a necessity about N will be a necessity of M. However far back one goes, one never reaches a non-derivative necessity.

The need for non-derivative necessities to back up derivative necessities runs deeper than the mere fact that I have defined derivative necessities in terms of non-derivative ones. To reject the definition is to say that the way one individual affects another in no way depends on the components of the former. But it seems clear that a's being ϕ will be a necessity for the distinct individual b only because of what b is itself by its nature. Otherwise, it would be possible for b and a third individual c to have natures that are exactly alike in regard to what they imply for themselves, but are dissimilar only in that they imply different properties for a. The most detailed probing of b and c would show no dissimilarities in them. Yet they would necessitate dissimiliar properties for a. On this basis, I judge the regress of natures of natures to be objectionable. Neither non-derivative nor derivative *de re* necessities for individuals are allowable on the view that entities are distinct from their natures.

The Platonic view that forms and physical individuals are distinct leads to just this view. There may well be necessary connections among the forms. But for an individual to be something necessarily it is not sufficient that there be a corresponding form. The form must be such that it is necessarily exemplified by the individual, and this is a necessity either of the form or of the individual. We have just seen, however, that neither of these conditions is true. It can then be no more than likely that the individual will exemplify the form. Only if the forms were indwelling natures, rather than distinct entities, would the world of becoming be a domain of necessity rather than one of the merely likely (*eikos*) and hence as well a domain of the real rather than of the mere image (*eikon*).[17]

Once natures are recognized to be components, reservations based on the pseudo-Leibnizian Principle can no longer stand in the way of recognizing properties and parts as components. For if natures are components, then Jones and his nature are the same even though Jones is pale and his nature is neither pale nor dark.

The consequences of avoiding the problem of association by taking natures to be components are theoretically quite satisfying. Consider, for example, how Jones does not fall short of what his nature requires. For the ontology of simples, Jones could be kept from falling short of his nature only by the nature of his nature, and the regress thus generated was found to be objectionable. But with natures as components there is no circularity to the claim that Jones's nature grounds the necessity of his being mobile if it is his nature to be mobile. There is no circularity since this claim is not needed to say what nature it is that is associated with Jones. There is no need to pick a nature out of heaven and tie it to Jones, for he is the same as his nature. This sameness with his nature is, of course, a necessity of Jones. As a necessity, it is grounded by Jones' nature. But also it is a necessity of Jones' nature that it is the same as no other entity than the one it is actually of, that is, Jones. Jones cannot switch natures, and his nature cannot switch subjects. It might seem that the necessity of the nature could be grounded only in the nature of the nature. But since the original nature is the same as Jones, one is free to say that the necessity of the nature to be the same as its subject is just a necessity of the subject for its nature to be the same as its subject. Thus where j is the same as N, '$\Box j$' can replace '$\Box N$', when the necessity is real. So with natures as components, an appeal to natures of natures is superfluous.

Despite this necessary sameness, natures are different from the entities that have them. The difference between individual and nature is not, as Aristotle thought, a difference between the indefinable and the definable.[18] What is definable is not the nature but certain components that the individual has by nature. The difference between an individual and its nature is that between what has but is not a component and what is a component that cannot be expressed by a definition.

The view that natures are not different from properties had by nature comes to grief over the matter of necessity. A property had by nature is a property that something necessarily has. But if F is both a nature and by nature, what grounds the necessity with which an individual has F? Since natures ground necessities, F will ground the necessity with which the individual has F. Clearly this cannot mean, as our nature model for $\Box\, a(Fa)$ might suggest, that there is a nature, namely F, that a has and, if a has it, then Fa. For then natures fail to perform a function that other properties cannot perform, since any property implies itself. What it must mean is that F has a special power over individuals whereby each of them will have a property exactly similar to F. But it is simply false that the properties signified by a real definition of an entity are universally distributed. Otherwise, every individual would simultaneously be a man, a tree, and everything else.

Logical properties are alleged to apply universally. But this can hardly be evidence that these properties ground the necessity of things for having them. That is, it is no indication that the properties themselves have a special power over individuals whereby the individuals submit to being their instances. If this were the case for the property of being non-contradictory, why should it not be the case for the non-logical property, characteristic of men, of being capable of consciousness. The mere fact of wider applicability is not going to make the difference. It is not a property that grounds the necessity of an individual to have it. Rather it is the nature of an individual that determines whether a property, however widely or narrowly distributed, is had necessarily.

§3. *Natural Kinds and the Primacy of Individuals.* Natural kinds are in some way related to natures. If two individuals belong to the same natural kind, they are not just individuals that share some properties (or some components other than properties such as actions or parts). They are alike in sharing properties that they have by nature. Normally an even stronger interpretation is put on the concept of natural kind. Thus two individuals belong to the same natural kind not just when they share some properties that each has by nature but when the properties which one has by nature are just those that the other has by nature. A simpler way of putting this would be to say that two individuals belong to the same natural kind if they have exactly similar natures. Now since natures are the same as the individuals having them, two individuals cannot have precisely the same nature. They can nonetheless have exactly similar natures in the sense that those and only those properties that are by the nature of the one are by the nature of the other. Of course, this only pushes the problem back to properties. For, properties, too, are the same as the individuals having them. So the properties that one individual has by nature are exactly similar to but not the same as those that another has by nature. To say what natural kinds are I must, then, first say what similarity is.

There are some component ontologies that yield a ready answer to the question of the nature of (exact) similarity. Thus, suppose one admits, in addition to properties-in-individuals, universal properties as well, that is, those that are both distinct from individuals and capable of being exemplified by several individuals. Then one can say that property A in individual a is similar to B in b if there is a universal property ϕ such that A is an exemplification of ϕ in a and such that B is an exemplification of ϕ in b.[19] If, however, there is an alternative explanation of similarity that dispenses with universal properties, there is no reason to add universal properties to the required ontology.

I think there is such an alternative. Parts, as well as properties, are components. Possibly then some interesting truths about parts can be deployed in respect to properties. One fact about parts is that they can often times be transferred from one individual to another. But can properties be transferred? The blackness of this newstype comes off onto my hand; the stickiness of this candy gets onto my fingers; the heat of this tea is transferred to my mouth. Protoza, which are single cells, divide to form new cells. The parent cell transfers, not just parts, but also properties to the daughter cells. There is then some basis for extending the notion of transferral from parts to properties. Now a part that is taken from one individual and inserted in another does not remain the same as the former individual since, successively, it is a component of two individuals. The familiar notion of transferral is, I am assuming, broad enough to allow for such a double sameness. The part that is transferred is similar to but not the same as itself at the end of the transfer. Likewise, blackness, stickiness, or heat is transferred despite the change of sameness that occurs as the property finds a new seat. Taking this notion of transferral as basic, one can account for similarity by means of it.

Thus, property *A* in individual *a* is (exactly) "similar" to *B* in *b*, when, if the result of transferring *A* of *a* to *b* is some component *C* of *b*, then *C* and *B* are not different. It will be recalled that *C* and *B* are not different only if *b*'s condition of being *C* is the same as its condition of being *B*. Of course, for this account of similarity to be adequate there need not be a way of transferring every property. Color is transferred from a worm to each of the two smaller worms resulting from splitting it. But communicating ideas is not a transferral, since there is an intermediate causal link here in which the ideas are not present. All that is required is that the general notion of property transfer be meaningful. This account of similarity does imply a regress, but, *pace* Russell, a harmless one.[20] If *A* and *B* have the similarity property, then *D* and *E* could have a similar similarity property. But one can treat this similarity of similarities in a similar way, and so on. One can let the regress run on for, since it is harmless, there is no need to introduce universals to stop it.

In the strong sense of natural kind, two individuals belong to the same natural kind if they have natures supporting similar properties, that is, properties that would not differ if all of them in the one individual were transferred to the other. But, as far as the practice of action on prior experience goes, that is, as far as the required ontology goes, it will be unnecessary to give this stronger interpretation to the concept of natural kind. It will, that is, be unnecessary to think of individuals of a natural kind as having (exactly) similar natures. So it may be that no two individuals in the universe are such that every necessary property of one is matched by a similar necessary property of the other.

Moderate empiricism requires *at most* that there be classes of individuals that are similar in respect only to certain of their necessary properties. The requirement that the universe be segregated into a manageable number of classes of individuals with similar natures is seen to be excessive. This point will be developed in Chapter V, §2. For the present we shall say that in the weak sense of natural kind to be developed there, a natural kind is natural only in that the properties determining the kind exist in the individuals of that kind by virtue of their natures. Individual variations in a natural kind in the strong sense can be regarded only as accidents. But it is well to have the option, provided by the weak sense of natural kind, of thinking of important differences between men, say, in different cultures, not as mere accidents of culture, but as differences in the necessary properties of individual men.

Associated with a natural kind, such as the class of men, there may be a natural-kind noun, such as 'man'. Like many other terms it both refers and signifies. This noun refers, distributively, to the members of the associated kind. It does not signify a universal, but like other terms, it signifies components of entities. 'Red' signifies the rednesses of red entities, and 'frictionless surface', though meaningful on the basis of its construction from terms with significations, signifies no entity. So the sentence '*a* is red' is true when *a* is the same as one of the rednesses signified by 'red'. The rednesses signified by 'red' are, of course, similar in the above sense.

Now if *K* is a natural kind, the following three conditions are to be satisfied by a natural-kind noun, '*N*', for members of *K*. (1) '*N*' must signify components. These components will be similar among themselves, and each will belong to a distinct member of *K*. Since natural kinds are to be non-empty, '*N*' will never fail this requirement because of *K*'s being empty. (2) As a natural-kind noun, '*N*' will signify these components as ones that belong to members of *K* by the natures of these members. Thus when '*a* is an *N*' is true and '*N*' signifies the component ϕ of *a, a* has ϕ by its nature. If a term signifies components as had by nature when in fact these components are contingent to some of the individuals referred to, it is at best a "purported" natural-kind noun. Likewise, when *K* is empty, '*N*' is at best a purported natural-kind term. (3) The components signified by '*N*' must be "representative" of other components that are similar among members of *K* and had by the natures of its members. That is, though the component that '*N*' signifies for any member of *K* need not be the only component that member needs to belong to *K,* still no entity outside *K* will have, by nature, a component similar to the one signified by '*N*'.

The component of a member of *K* signified by '*N*' I shall call "the kind component" of that member in respect to '*N*' and *K*.

So if *'N'* signifies ϕ for *a,* then, assuming *'N'* is a genuine natural-kind noun, ϕ is the kind component of *a* in respect to *'N'* and *K*.

Suppose the kind component, ϕ, of *a* in respect to *'N'* and *K* is in fact a property. Then ϕ can be in the signification not only of the natural-kind noun *'N'* but also of the property predicate, say, *'F'*. Thus the kind component humanness is signified both by the natural-kind noun 'man' and the property predicate 'human'. The two terms do not differ in what is signified. In particular, 'man' does not differ from 'human' by signifying a putative entity called a species. The difference is only that 'man' does, though 'human' does not, signify humanness as had by nature and as representative of other components that are both similar among and had by the natures of members of mankind. If the semantics of natural-kind nouns does not require species and genera as special components of individuals over and above their properties, parts, and actions, it is unlikely that there is any reason why such special components should be countenanced.

Aristotle made this point by saying that the last differentia reached in defining a species is the being of or the nature of any entity of that species.[21] The generic term in the definition adds no new entity; the property it signifies is already implied by the property signified by the differentia term. And the species term introduces no new entity; it signifies exactly what the differentia term signifies, though only the former signifies the property as one had by nature. The term expressing *what an entity is* (*ti estin*)—the species or natural-kind term—does not signify a new entity—a species. This term signifies, rather, *what makes the entity be of its kind* (*to ti ēn einai*), and this is what the differentia term signifies, though in a different way.

The old dispute as to whether natural kinds are real or conventional has the following resolution here. Natural kinds are, at least in our weak sense, not real if by being real one means that within each of them all members have exactly similar natures.[22] The members of a natural kind need be similar only in respect to some, not all, of the necessary properties of their members. This leaves room for an element of conventionality. For a natural kind in this weak sense will be overlapped by numerous closely related natural kinds. But one cannot think in terms of all these natural kinds. A selection is made from competing kinds, and this fact is recorded linguistically in the use of certain natural-kind nouns. Despite the fact that this selection is not imposed by natural divisions, and is to that extent conventional, natural kinds are real in the limited sense that an individual is bound by a real necessity to its kind component. So what a genuine natural-kind noun signifies for an individual is a component the individual has necessarily. Contrary to Locke, this necessity does not derive from the fact that the individual is brought under that noun.[23]

Even though a natural kind is not based on exactly similar natures or upon special components called species and genera, the concept of natural kind is still a useful one, as I shall try to illustrate. We know that when charges are accelerated through radio-transmitter towers, electromagnetic waves are radiated. We are convinced it is the nature of such things to emit radiation when charges are accelerated through them. But on this basis we are unwilling to say of an arbitrary individual that it emits radiation by its nature when a charge is accelerated through it. One feels safe in making an inductive generalization only to things within some restricted natural kind. I shall indicate the reason for this in Chapter V. But even here it is easy to recognize the pitfalls of ignoring the restriction to natural kinds. For according to early quantum theory at least, electrons revolve in atoms for extended periods without emitting radiation. They do not emit continuously and in their ground states there is no emission. It is only of systems of a certain kind that it can be said they emit energy when charges are accelerated through them. Of course, when an induction is made for a natural kind, the kind may not be restrictive enough, but without some restriction by kind, the field is so wide open that no induction is warranted.

In other words, even if it is true that:

(1) $\Box\, a(Fa)$,

where a is a metal bar and F is the property an object has of being an emitter of electromagnetic energy when a charge is sent back and forth through the object, this statement hardly constitutes support for the unrestricted claim that:

(2) $(x)\, \Box\, x(Fx)$.

Where 'N' is the natural-kind term for metal bars, one can seriously raise the question whether, on the basis of (1), there is a chance that:

$$(3) \qquad (x)(Nx \rightarrow \Box x(Fx))$$

is true. The restriction imposed by 'N' makes the difference. The idea is that if one is convinced that a is F by nature, then one is warranted in believing that other individuals are F by their natures only if one assumes that those other individuals are somewhat close to a in nature. How close will be specified in Chapter V.

I noted earlier (Chapter II, §2) that a necessary condition for induction is that the property to be projected have a chance of being possessed necessarily by the observed individuals. What I am saying here, in denying that the induction to (2) from (1) could be warranted, is that the chance of the observed individuals' necessarily having the projectible property is not a sufficient condition for warranted induction. A further requirement is being sketched here, and it introduces the notion of natural kind. This additional requirement will ultimately be that the projected property be a conditional property in respect to which there is a chance that the antecedent will specify a natural kind.

Now (3) says that entities of a certain natural kind have a certain property by their natures. On its surface at least, this is not the same as saying that any entity is such by nature that if it is of a certain natural kind it has a certain property. That is, it seems different from:

$$(4) \qquad (x) \Box x(Nx \rightarrow Fx).$$

If we call (3) a "kind-specific" necessity, then inductively generalizing claims like (1) involves moving to a kind-specific necessity. But to generalize only in this way, and not to (2), does not mean we have lost faith in the original singular claim, (1), and wish to replace it with the more qualified claim that:

$$(5) \qquad Na \rightarrow \Box a(Fa).$$

For, an individual's necessary properties are not conditioned by its assignment to a kind; rather, its kind is conditioned by the necessary properties it has.

Though (3) seems to say something quite different from (4), the two are in fact interderivable *via* a principle for natural kinds that follows from the way we have described natural kinds. This is the Principle of Essentialism, which says that whatever may be of a given natural kind must be of that kind; that is:

(6) $(x)\,(\Diamond x(Nx) \rightarrow \Box x(Nx))$.

The principle is clearly equivalent to the conjunction of:

(7) $(x)\,(\Diamond x(Nx) \rightarrow Nx)$,
(8) $(x)\,(Nx \rightarrow \Box x(Nx))$.

In discussions of essentialism, emphasis is ordinarily placed on (8) to the neglect of (7).[24] From (3) with the aid of (7) one derives (4) by an indirect proof. The idea is that if an individual might be *N* but not *F*—that is, if (4) is false—then the individual will be *N* in view of (7) and thus by (3) it must be *F*. On the other hand, from (4) with the aid of (8) one derives (3) by distributing the modality in (4). So either (3) or (4) is an acceptable way of generalizing (1) inductively.

It remains to justify the Principle of Essentialism itself. I rely entirely on the notion of a natural kind, in the weak sense, and on the characteristic laws of S4 and S5, which are, as I noted in Chapter II, §4, true on the nature-interpretation of necessity. To prove (7), assume that an arbitrary individual *might* belong to a certain natural kind. Thus it is possible that this arbitrary individual has certain properties necessarily. Now that the possibly necessary implies the necessary is a direct result of the characteristic law of S5 that the possible is necessarily possible. So the individual necessarily has those properties and thus actually belongs to that natural kind. So (7) holds. To prove (8), assume an arbitrary individual belongs to a natural kind. It will then have certain properties necessarily. Now that the necessary is necessarily necessary is the characteristic law of S4. So the individual necessarily has those properties necessarily, and thereby necessarily belongs to that natural kind. So (8) holds.

§4. *Ontological and Methodological Essentialism.* Karl Popper has quite rightly objected to the view I shall call "methodological essentialism."[25] Among other things, the methodological essentialist holds that the scientist can ultimately acquire indubitable knowledge and that natures provide an end to the chain of scientific explanation. On the other hand, the view expounded here that natures are the grounds of the necessity of necessities and that every individual is subject to necessities and hence has a nature is a view I shall call "ontological essentialism." Now, must ontological lead to methodological essentialism? If it must, then in view of Popper's criticism, one should abandon real necessity altogether. One should settle for what philosophers have long been settling for—intentional necessity. The practice of action on prior experience would, however basic to human practice, have to be declared an illusion. What that practice would have us believe about the world, we simply should not believe.

As to the matter of indubitability, there is nothing in what has been said about a necessity to imply that it is indubitable. To assert that what entities are necessarily proceeds from their natures does not imply that the kind of evidence that one has for a necessity, or could have for it, puts any doubting of the necessity out of the question. Moreover, my position does not imply that a necessity is *a priori* in the technical sense of being supportable up to any degree without recourse to sense experience. Quite the contrary, it seems clear, in general, that, whether an entity has a character contingently or by nature, justifying the claim that the entity has the character can be accomplished by an empirical procedure.

It is also well to point out that the Principle of Essentialism—that what could belong to a natural kind must belong to it—implies no objectionable apriorism. It might be alleged that the principle commits us to holding *a priori* that men cannot change into bats and that lead cannot change into gold. Indeed, it commits us to holding that *if* 'man' and 'bat' signify properties that are necessary but incompatible, *then* a man cannot change into a bat. (I revert here to Platonizing talk about a property that many individuals have as short for talk about many exactly similar properties.) But assuming their incompatibility, inductive considerations are involved in determining whether the two properties should be treated as necessary properties and thus, possibly, as kind properties. Our judging that a man cannot change into a bat is not then automatic. It waits upon the empirically motivated decision to treat the properties in question as necessary, or even as kind properties. Once it is decided they are necessary properties, or kind properties, we must judge either that Count Dracula was an impossible being or that he was not both truly a bat and truly a man, even though on different occasions he resembled each.

As to the second matter of natures being ultimate scientific explainers, nothing I have said about natures implies that they enter scientific explanation as explainers at all. In fact, it is consistent with ontological essentialism that there be no terminus to scientific explanation. There might, that is, be a level below any level that scientific explanation will ever reach. Natures are not, however, at the bottom level of any scheme of scientific levels; they are altogether outside any such scheme of levels. The necessity of the explanatory principles at each level and between the levels is grounded by natures; what the principles say entities are flows from the natures of these entities. Even though a principle is explained by parts or properties at a more basic level, it is nonetheless a principle that holds by nature. Those entities—whether properties or parts—explaining it are simply some of the manifestations of the natures by which the principle holds.

The reductionist may complain that this requires that we treat the existence of complex macro-individuals as irreducible. For it seems that the explaining parts and properties are always to be manifestations of the natures of individuals that contain them. But even this is not a consequence of ontological essentialism. When we speak of what a proposition says about individuals, we always mean what it says about unreduced individuals. These may not be the individuals that the proposition seems to be about. So it is the natures of unreduced individuals that ground the necessities at the infinity of possible levels.

Suppose, for illustration, that certain individuals, taken to belong to the natural kind, the class of volumes of gases, are found to obey certain relations, Q, between temperature, pressure, and volume. Assuming this behavior is by nature, and letting 'N' be the appropriate natural-kind noun, we have the truth that $(x)(Nx \rightarrow \Box_x(Qx))$. It may be wrong to take volumes of gases as unreduced to molecules, but we start with that assumption. Now we wish to inquire what, if anything, about the natures of gases makes them Q by their natures. Are there properties flowing from their natures from which Q is derived? Is there, that is, some E such that both $(x)(Nx \rightarrow \Box x(Ex))$ and $(x)(Nx \rightarrow \Box x(Ex \rightarrow Qx))$? In this case, E might be the molecular structure of gases.

Now suppose it is the case that there are no volumes of gases, but only the molecules said to compose them. The truth conditions for propositions apparently about gases will be the truth conditions for propositions actually about molecules. As a consequence of this and of the way we have described E, the proposition that $(x)(Nx \rightarrow \Box x(Ex))$ becomes a bare tautology, and the above step ceases to be an explanatory one in the inquiry. In order to start the inquiry again, a new natural-kind term is required that represents a kind of unreduced individuals. What matters here is not whether gases are unreduced or not. What matters is rather that, whatever the unreduced individuals, an explanatory step consists not in introducing a nature but in discovering behind the properties already deemed to be by the natures of the unreduced individuals properties that are "more fundamental" in respect to the same natures. The explainer of E's implying Q might be G, where, assuming gases are unreduced individuals, $(x)(Nx \rightarrow \Box x(Ex \rightarrow Gx))$ and $(x)(Nx \rightarrow \Box x(Ex \rightarrow (Gx \rightarrow Qx)))$. In this case, G would be a complex property combining a certain probability distribution for molecules of a gas with their mechanical behavior.

On the one hand, the grounding of necessity in natures requires no end term for an inquiry of this sort. On the other hand, it is not natures but properties or parts had by nature that are introduced at each step. Ontological essentialism is then incompatible with methodological essentialism, since the former can be joined quite naturally with an account of scientific explanation that requires no end point.

CHAPTER IV

Induction and the World

§1. *Reasonable Practice.* The inclusion of natures in the required ontology is based on the premiss that there are physical necessities. Having just elaborated on the notions of necessity and nature, we must now establish that premiss. This will be done by showing that ontologies excluding necessity come into conflict with the requirements of the practice of action based on prior sense experience.

I shall say of a practice whose requirements are satisfied by a given ontology that it is a "reasonable" practice relative to that ontology. Suppose a practice is not reasonable relative to two different ontologies. If one ontology can be extended so that the practice becomes reasonable relative to it, then it is merely insufficient relative to the practice. If the other ontology is incompatible with such an extension, then it and the practice, taken together, are "incoherent." But to avoid incoherence, does one adjust practice to ontology or ontology to practice? The practice of action based on prior experience is fundamental in that without such a practice there would be no human practice at all. And an ontology is a theory that, like other theories, has practice as its context. Thus whenever an ontology is incoherent with the practice of action based on prior experience, one must adjust the ontology to the practice. There can be no harmonization of theory with practice that requires abandoning the practice of action on prior experience. I shall try to show that, as a consequence, any harmonization of ontology with practice requires an ontology that does not exclude necessities, as an ontology of simples does. This can be shown by demonstrating that the practice of action on prior experience is reasonable only in respect to an ontology that supports necessities.

The argument for an ontology with natures will then be a "presuppositional" argument. That is, natures are introduced as presuppositions of the practice of action based on prior experience. To reject natures means that the criteria for warranted action on prior experience cannot be fulfilled. But presuppositional arguments are often notoriously unsatisfying. For example, why not respond to this one by criticizing the practice of action on prior experience? If it has such repugnant presuppositions, perhaps it is only a bad habit. So to have force this argument must be accompanied by a "vindication" of the practice itself. It was vindicated by showing that it is an indispensable means to a clearly desirable end.[1] For unless there is a practice of action on prior experience, people will not communicate, make judgments, order their behavior, or create works of art. In short, there would be no human practice. Without vindication of this practice, its ontological presuppositions would remain hypothetical; without the presuppositions, the vindication would carry no ontological message. The two must be combined. One can then assert categorically that any satisfactory ontology contains all that the existence of necessary connections requires.

But the combination is not a "justification" of the practice. That is, it in no way shows that this practice will continue to be a reliable guide to the future on the basis of general principles about the world that are themselves justified without reliance on induction. We do arrive, of course, at the general principle that there are necessities. By itself, though, this principle is not sufficient to guarantee continued success with the practice. If it were sufficient then a genuine justification would have been effected. For since the vindication makes the practice of action on prior experience essential to human practice generally, there is no way within a coherent whole of theory and practice to cast doubt on a principle about the world presupposed by this practice. Thus the familiar objection to justifications—that the general principles appealed to need justifying themselves—would be circumvented. Let us now consider that aspect of the practice of action on prior experience which leads in the direction of necessity.

Not every action based on prior experience is itself an act of judging some proposition true. Even if—as seems unlikely—every such action involved a judgment as an analytical component, it would not itself have to be a judgment. Let us agree to the following rather limited sense of induction. The conclusions of inductions are to be judgments made on the basis of prior sense experience. In this sense, not all actions made on the basis of prior sense experience are arrived at inductively. Nonetheless, I shall treat of inductive judgments in order to draw certain conclusions about the practice of action on prior experience as a whole. This procedure will be legitimate since to every action based on prior experience that is not a judgment one could correlate a judgment as to that action's success. For such an action to be warranted as a step to a given goal, there must be support for the corresponding possible judgment. So whatever is needed for support of inductive judgments is needed for giving a warrant to a corresponding action based on prior experience that is not a judgment.

In the methodology of science, one cannot neglect inferences to structures that are not similar to objects of prior experiences. For example, one cannot neglect an inference from constant ratios of the weights of combining chemicals to the atomic structure of matter. Yet these inferences that C. S. Peirce called "abductive" are not, in our sense, actions on prior experiences, for actions on prior experiences concern possible features of new situations that would be similar to experienced features of earlier situations. Nonetheless, abductive inferential practice, like all human practices, exists only in a context of action on prior experience. It would then be incoherent with an ontology that rejects the presuppositions of induction. The reason for this is that abductive inferences are made only when the ground has been prepared by the acceptance of regularities on the basis of prior experience.

The abductive inference to the atomic theory, from the experience of constant combining ratios in *some* cases, requires the belief, which we can assume has the same empirical basis, that, in general, chemicals can be expected to combine in constant ratios. Otherwise, the acceptance of the atomic structure of unobserved chemicals would here lack an empirical basis. The atomic structure of matter is hypothesized precisely because it accounts for constant combining ratios. To hypothesize it where there is no belief in such behavior is to reason in the absence of any posited analogy with observed cases. Thus the premiss of the abductive inference would be irrelevent to it, and it would not be a legitimate inference at all.

There are many possible inductive rules that might be used in judging propositions to be true on the basis of empirical data. Which of these rules is involved when one asks whether an ontology without a ground of necessity is coherent with inductive practice? One rule would tell us that if $\frac{m}{n}$ of the observed F are G, then if any hypothesis is to be accepted as true, the hypothesis that an F has an $\frac{m}{n}$ chance of being a G is to be accepted. But another rule, that appears counterintuitive, would favor, on the same observations, the hypothesis that an F has a $\left(1 - \frac{m}{n}\right)$ chance of being a G. To accept the favored hypothesis in either case would be to judge it true on the basis of prior experience. Suppose I construct an argument for necessity on the assumption that the first rule is the one used. Let me call it the "uniformity" rule, and the second one the "counterintuitive" rule. But when I showed that the practice of acting on prior experience was a fundamental practice, there was no reference to one inductive rule rather than another. So consequences that follow from limiting the practice to one involving the uniformity rule need not be consequences that are required for any human practice. In particular, the consequence that there are necessities would become a consequence of limited significance. To preserve its general significance, one would have to show that a practice involving any rule other than the uniformity rule would be incoherent. But no one has succeeded in showing this.[2]

This is not a problem that faces us. I am concerned with the general fact that, whatever the rules of induction may be, the conclusions of legitimate inductions are supported, to some degree, by their premisses. There are important common features of the notion of support, features not tied to specific rules for saying what supports what and to what degree. One of these common features is that if there is support for a proposition about the unobserved, then there must be real necessities.

Let us now return to the above idea of a reasonable practice. It will be interesting to contrast it with the ideas of reasonable practice inherent in pragmatic and conventionalist treatments of induction.

For the pragmatist, induction by a certain rule is reasonable on the following condition: successful predictions can be made by that rule, if they can be made at all by any rule.[3] Suppose they can be made by the counterintuitive rule. Then the uniformity rule can make at least one successful prediction. It can be used to predict—at a second level—that the counterintuitive rule makes correct predictions at the first level. But being reasonable in this pragmatic sense does not mean being reasonable relative to any ontology. Pragmatic reasonableness fails to carry over to ontological reasonableness. A pragmatically reasonable practice will, nonetheless, be incoherent with a Humean ontology, and hence not be reasonable relative to it. The practice requires necessities whereas the ontology rejects them.

Perhaps, though, pragmatic reasonableness is sufficient without bothering about reasonableness relative to an ontology. This would be true if one could infer from pragmatic reasonableness to genuine support. But in the context of an ontology that excludes necessities, there is no support, and thus the inference is blocked. By the pragmatic argument, inductions by a certain rule are reasonable when successful predictions can be made by that rule if by any rule. The pragmatist wants to be able to make the next step and say that pragmatically reasonable inductive conclusions are genuinely supported ones, without appeal to any ontological principles. But, as we shall show, support for hypotheses and an ontology that excludes necessities form an incoherent pair. Thus the step from pragmatic reasonableness to support fails. Pragmatic reasonableness is concerned exclusively with a connection among inductive rules. It implies nothing about the world, though support does. Thus, the inadequacy of a Humean ontology is only temporarily concealed from view by the statement that a certain inductive practice is pragmatically reasonable irrespective of what ontology one adopts. If one's ontology precludes necessities, one cannot coherently claim support for hypotheses, however pragmatically reasonable their induction may have been.

Goodman has given the most elegant statement of the conventionalist argument.[4] He feels that standard inductive practice is a sufficient basis, just by its being standard, for its reasonableness. In view of this, we can "stop plaguing ourselves with certain spurious questions about induction." But, once again, conventional reasonableness fails to carry over to ontological reasonableness. A conventionally reasonable practice that assigns support to hypotheses is still incoherent with a Humean ontology. This is not to say that the tribe whose conventions are the source of the conventional reasonableness must have ontological convictions. It is only to say that the philosopher, who will have ontological convictions, is not left free, despite the soothing association of convention and reasonableness, to choose a non-necessitarian ontology.

Moreover, for Goodman, a crucial factor in determining whether hypotheses are supportable by data in standard inductive practice is the "entrenchment" of their predicates in the language. In effect, hypotheses can be inductively supported if their predicates have occurred in hypotheses that people have in fact inductively inferred. This presumably takes the matter of support out of the hands of metaphysicians. But if one's ontology fails to contain a basis for necessities, then, it turns out, the connection needed between data and an hypothesis, if the former is to support the latter, is broken. Relative to such an ontology, the conventional reasonableness of assigning support in a given way is just a tribal illusion.

§2. *Inductive Support.* It is important to distinguish acceptance from support. If from a given set of data I infer inductively a given hypothesis, then I accept that hypothesis as true on the basis of those data. But the acceptance will not be warranted unless the hypothesis is supported by the data. The support of the hypothesis is not an act, though acceptance is. Moreover, the degree to which data may support an hypothesis may be too small to warrant its acceptance.

In this discussion, I am beginning with the practice of inductive acceptance of propositions and moving toward the notion of support. That is, I shall try to claim that warranted acceptance on the basis of certain data implies support from those data. I am not, conversely, starting from support and moving toward inductive practice. That is, I shall not try to claim that acceptance is automatically warranted when a certain high degree of support is reached.

Fortunately, there is no need to make this claim, for it has paradoxical results. In a large, fair lottery there is little support for the proposition about any given ticket that it will win. Conversely, there is a high degree of support for the proposition about any given ticket that it will not win. So, on the view that a high degree of support suffices for acceptance, one would accept the proposition about any given ticket that it will not win, assuming the lottery is large enough. One would likewise accept a similar proposition about every other ticket. So one ends up accepting the proposition that no ticket will win, which is absurd. A high degree of support then, is not a sufficient condition for acceptance.

I shall make the assumption, simply for purposes of exposition, that support can be treated as a numerical function. Having made this assumption, it is natural to assume further that it is a function with the formal features of a probability function. Here, $p(h/e \cdot f) = n$ shall mean that, relative to the data recorded by the proposition e and the background features recorded by f, the support for the hypothesis h has the degree n, where $0 \leqslant n \leqslant 1$. However, to say that, given f, h is supported by e to degree n or that, given f, e gives h the support n is to say that $p(h/e \cdot f) = n$ while implying that $p(h/e \cdot f) > p(h/f)$. In other words, though 'The support for h relative to $(e \cdot f)$ is n' does not imply e is "relevant" to h, 'Given f, h is supported by e to degree n' does imply the relevance of e to h. Our moderate empiricism commits us to the view that some hypotheses are acceptable only if they are given support by empirical data and are not just supported relative to such data (Chapter I, §3). We are then concerned with the consequences of the fact that hypotheses are given support by empirical data.

Whatever the full requirements of acceptability, they will include the minimal requirement of support. But here also there is room to distinguish *h*'s being acceptable given (*e* · *f*) from *e*'s making *h* acceptable given *f*. Thus *h* might be acceptable given (*e* · *f*) simply because it is acceptable given *f*. But if *e* makes *h* acceptable given *f*, then not only is *h* acceptable given (*e* · *f*), but also *h* is not acceptable given merely *f*. The requirement of support that is of interest here follows from the claim that some hypotheses are made acceptable by empirical data. When *e* makes *h* acceptable given *f*, then, as I shall show, it is required that *h* be supported by *e* given *f*, not just that *h* have support relative to (*e* · *f*). If this were not the case, then moderate empiricism would not require giving support, but only that some acceptable hypotheses be made acceptable by empirical data.

There have recently been various proposals for conditions for acceptability of *h* given (*e* · *f*) that avoid the lottery paradox. In general, these conditions include the requirement that there must be support for *h* relative to (*e* · *f*). For example, the proposal made by Levi involves a comparison of support for any hypothesis with the disutility assigned to its acceptance should it be false.[5] Here disutility is of an epistemic variety. Specifically, the disutility of accepting a false hypothesis that is rich in content is less than that of accepting a false hypothesis that is trivial, for hypotheses that are rich in content have a greater potential for relieving doubt. The proposal is that one is to reject *h* when the support for *h* relative to (*e* · *f*) is less than the disutility of accepting *h* given (*e* · *f*) if *h* is false.* It turns out, on this proposal, that for *h* actually to be accepted given (*e* · *f*) and its competitors to be rejected, *h* will have to have support relative to (*e* · *f*).

But now consider the case in which *e* makes *h* acceptable given *f*, rather than that in which *h* is merely acceptable given (*e* · *f*). Where *e* makes *h* acceptable given *f*, *h* is not acceptable given *f*. Thus relative to *f* alone, it either is rejected or, though not rejected, is a disjunct in an acceptable hypothesis. In either case, for *h* to be acceptable given (*e* · *f*), some competitor to *h* must be rejected because of *e*. This means that in respect to *e* the disutility of believing the competitor when it is false should be larger than the support for the competitor.

*One need not reject *h* when it has zero support, for there might be zero disutility in believing it when it is false.

On the one hand, this might occur by decreasing support for the competitor. But since the competitor will imply $\sim h$, support for h will increase as a result of e. On the other hand, this may occur by increasing the disutility of accepting the competitor should it be false. That is, e may decrease the content of the competitor, and hence of $\sim h$. This would mean an increase in content for h in view of e. For example, e might reduce the number of possible situations satisfying h from two to one by increasing the number of possible situations satisfying the competitor from eight to nine; h would then have more content since it would be satisfied in a smaller proportion of cases.

But when we speak of action on prior experience, it will be true that, since experience does not limit possibilities for unexamined cases of unrestricted hypotheses, it in no way alters the content of the hypothesis corresponding to the action. To observe that water boils at 100° C on many occasions does not reduce the content of the hypothesis that the next pan of water will boil at 100° C. So increasing the disutility of a competitor when it is false is not open to us as a means of rejecting competitors. One must accept the conclusion that if e makes h acceptable given f, then e gives support to h in respect to f. It seems likely that this would hold, not just for Levi's proposal, but for any proposal adequate for inductive acceptance.

In what follows, I shall have in mind three kinds of inductive claim: universal generalizations, statistical generalizations, and qualified instantial claims. I shall suppose the generalizations are cast in the form of relevant conditionals. Since the universal generalization 'Any x is such that if it is F then it is G' is represented as '$(x)(Fx \rightarrow Gx)$', the statistical generalization 'Any x is such that if it is F then it has an $\frac{m}{n}$ chance of being G' shall be represented as '$(x)\left(Fx \rightarrow \frac{m}{n} Gx\right)$'. I shall also suppose that 'All F are G' can be represented in the first way and that 'All F have an $\frac{m}{n}$ chance of being G' can be represented in the second way, even though in each case this involves the false assumption that one is talking about the x's rather than merely about the F's. Now it might be highly unlikely that there are no exceptions to a universal conditional. But still it might be likely that any new instance taken by itself that satisfies the antecedent of the conditional will satisfy the consequent. There is support, not for the universal claim, but for instances of it qualified as satisfying its antecedent. Thus though $p((x)(Fx \rightarrow Gx)/e)$ is negligible, for any x, $p(Gx/Fx \cdot e)$ is not negligible.

We want our conclusions to be valid for the practice of action on prior experience generally. Thus we want our conclusions to hold at least for induction generally. We cannot, then, limit ourselves to considering, say, only inductions to universal claims. Consequences derived from the fact that there is support given by evidence to inductively acceptable universal claims need not be part of the required ontology. For the practice of action based on prior experience is possible without the practice of inductions to universal claims. The same is true also of statistical claims and of qualified instantial claims. We must then look for consequences of support that do not depend on the kind of claim that is supported. We shall, then, be looking for consequences that are common to support for all three types of claim.

§3. *Conditional Support and Support for Conditionals.* How, then, does necessity become a requirement for support? Necessity is involved, it turns out, in several ways. But one among them is fundamental in that only by noticing it does one see how the others are required. The key idea in regard to this fundamental way is this. There is to be a chance that the individuals from which the data for an hypothesis are gathered have necessarily, or by their natures, the feature that the hypothesis projects onto other individuals. For if it is certain that the individuals in the data have the projected feature only contingently, their having it depends on their circumstances. Thus their having that feature would be irrelevant to the question of whether other entities, which may be in quite different circumstances, stand a chance of having it.

This requirement of necessity is not very useful by itself. It is useful only if unobserved individuals covered by an hypothesis have a chance of belonging to a natural kind to which the individuals in the data belong. Through natural kinds necessity enters in a second time, as will be discussed in the next chapter.

The first step in my argument involves a seemingly innocent transformation from one expression for support to another. It seems undeniable that an hypothesis can be supported by data only if there is some chance that if the data exist, then the hypothesis is true. If there were no chance that the data implied the hypothesis, then the data simply fail to support the hypothesis. My claim is for the case in which data increase support. When there is merely support relative to the data, there need be no chance that the data imply the hypothesis, since the data may have nothing to do with the hypothesis. So my claim is made only when e is positively relevant to h, that is, when $p(h/e \cdot f) > p(h/f)$.[6] The claim is then that:

(1) If not only $p(h/e \cdot f) > 0$ but also $p(h/e \cdot f) > p(h/f)$, then $p(e > h/f) > 0$.

Here 'if e then h' is symbolized as '$e > h$', which as we shall see, is not a relevant conditional.

It might seem reasonable to claim also that the converse of (1) is true. Indeed, it might even seem reasonable to make the stronger claim that the values of the two support functions are equal, that is:

(1′) $p(h/e \cdot f) = p(e > h/f)$, where $p(h/e \cdot f) > p(h/f)$.

This is not to be faulted by claiming that the left side of the equation presupposes the truth of e whereas the right side does not. For one can speak of the support an hypothesis has relative to certain evidence both when the evidence has actually been observed and when it is merely assumed. The meaning of the support claim is the same in each case.

Moreover, it is not to be faulted by considering the case in which an assumed, but actually false, e is incompatible with f. In such a case it might be argued that since e and f are incompatible, they together validly imply anything, and in particular h. Holding this implication to be not just true but valid, one reaches the undesirable result that, since the value of the left side of equation (1′) is unity, the value of each side of equation (1′) must be unity.[7] However, if the expression "validly implies" means the same as "validly relevantly implies," it is surely false that e and f validly imply h simply on the basis of their incompatibility. Their incompatibility alone does not guarantee that they relevantly imply h. Still, however solid (1′) might be, I shall need only the weaker claim (1).

In taking this first step, one is already moving away from the kind of thinking that treats the world as a multiplicity of disjointed entities. One is already thinking in terms of connections. Data fail to support hypotheses where there are no chances of connections, where there are merely associations. Suppose the conditional $(e > h)$ is no more than the material conditional $(e \supset h)$, for which, as we saw, both $(h \supset (e \supset h))$ and $(\sim e \supset (e \supset h))$ are valid. Then, the consequent of (1) would automatically be satisfied provided either $p(h/f) > 0$ or $p(\sim e/f) > 0$. But I shall show that $(e > h)$ is true, unlike $(e \supset h)$, only when e makes h true.

If e supports h, or makes h likely, in respect to f, then there will be a chance, in respect to f, that, when true, e makes h true. To make something likely is to stand a chance of making it true. Suppose the individuals that e is about are both F and G and that e says of them that they are both F and G. Hypothesis h projects the conditional property, G if F, to other individuals. Could we still say that e supports h if it were certain that e does not make h true?

If it were certain that e does not make h true, then it would also be certain that the having by individuals that e is about the having of properties similar to those of other individuals, where the similar properties are those signified by 'F', would *not* influence the latter individuals to have G. For if the similarity in regard to F were to influence the unobserved individuals favorably for having G, then there would be a chance of circumstances in which this influence would make these individuals have G. But assume that the similarity in regard to F is a basis for a chance that the unobserved individuals will be made to have G. Then, that the evidence individuals are both F and G stands a chance of making other individuals G if they are F. So if the similarity in regard to F is a basis for a chance of making individuals have G, e has a chance of making h true. But if the similarity in regard to F in no way influenced unobserved individuals to have G and hence gave no basis for a chance of making individuals have G, then e would certainly not make h likely. In short, if e did not have a chance of making h true, it would not make h likely, which it does merely if it supports *h*. Clearly, then, $(e > h)$ is more than a material conditional since it holds only if, when true, the antecedent makes the consequent true. It can naturally be called a "factive" conditional.

Two things are important to note about the factive conditional. First, it is not necessarily a causal conditional, even though it has been described in terms of the idea of making something true. Suppose what a grain of salt does when it is put in water happens just because it is a grain of salt. Then a true proposition about what it does can be said to make true a proposition about what another grain of salt would do if immersed. The truth-making lies in the fact that both propositions are about grains that behave the same way in water because they are salt. It does not lie in the fact that one grain acts causally on the other. Second, *e* may make *h* true, and thus factively imply *h,* even though under different circumstances it might not make *h* true, and thus not factively imply *h*. In general, factive implication will be context dependent. It may depend for its truth on matters beyond its antecedent and consequent. Thus one can agree with C. I. Lewis when he said that "real connections" need not be necessities.[8] When *e* is true, it may make *h* true only because certain favorable circumstances happen to be true. When *e* is false, and we are thus dealing with a counterfactual conditional, *e* makes *h* true only because in a selected possible situation in which *e* is true there are circumstances that allow *e* to make *h* true.[9] On the other hand, our relevant conditional differs from the factive conditional in not being context dependent.

§4. *Necessities for Evidence Individuals.* The second step in the argument characterizes the connection that holds when a factive conditional is true as one with a modal condition. The connection holds only if some necessity holds. Nonetheless, the connection itself is not a necessity.

Among the propositions comprising the evidence for an hypothesis there will be singular propositions such as ϕa. If ϕa can increase support for *h,* then *a* is an "evidence individual" in respect to the evidence *e* and hypothesis *h*.

It would be convenient to have a unified conception of the features projected by inductions, even when the inductions are to quite different kinds of proposition. An induction to a universal claim of the standard sort indicated in §2 projects onto any entity the feature $(F\_ \rightarrow G\_)$. That projected by a statistical claim is the feature $\left(F\_ \rightarrow \frac{m}{n} G\_\right)$. Inductions to instantial claims can be brought into line with these cases by using the idea behind (1). That is, we shall simply assume that an induction to *Gb* from *Fb* and *e* could be replaced by an induction to $(Fb > Gb)$ from *e*. One then projects onto *b* the feature $(F\_ > G\_)$. It will be true in all three cases that if the inductive conclusion is true then each of the evidence individuals will have a chance of having the projected feature. This might not seem to be the case when one infers *Gb* from *Fa* and *e*, for there may be no chance that *a* have *G*. But if such an inference is replaced by one to $(Fa > Gb)$ from *e*, then the projected feature is $(F\_ > Gb)$, which the evidence individual *a* has a chance of manifesting.

Not only will the evidence individuals have a chance of having the projected feature, but also they will have a chance of having it necessarily. It is by consideration of the factive conditional that this additional requirement emerges. It is because there is a chance of $(e > h)$ that each evidence individual will have a chance of having the projected feature of necessity. So:

(2) If $p(e > h/f) > o$ then, where x is any evidence individual in respect to e and h and H is the projected feature corresponding to h, $p(\Box\, x(Hx)/f) > o$.

This is the second step of my argument. It can be justified if it can be shown that to have the sort of connection introduced in the first step between evidence and hypothesis, each evidence individual will have, of necessity, the feature projected onto other individuals by the hypothesis.

But before justifying (2), let me contrast the view about the world implied by (1) and (2) with a familiar view about order in the world. This is the view that for hypotheses to be supportable by data it suffices for the world to be orderly. That is, it suffices for there to be a great number of simple regularities, universal and statistical, though all of these are matters of the sheerest contingency. Given a great number of universal regularities, observed exceptionless regularities will support universal hypotheses. Given a great number of statistical regularities, observed statistical regularities will support corresponding statistical generalities. Now why will such a cosmology of contingent orderliness not do? It would do if $(e > h)$ were true simply by h being true. For to assume order is only to assume that a great number of simple hypotheses are true. Thus if the assumption of order is to suffice, it must suffice to make $(e > h)$ true in a great number of cases. It will do this only if $(e > h)$ is merely a material conditional. But if e is to give support to h, a connection stronger than material implication is required. In view of (2), I am also claiming that this connection holds only when certain entities have certain features by their natures. Mere order has to be supplemented by necessities, and hence by natures, to arrive at an adequate cosmology for induction.

How is this claim to be defended? Assume the evidence individuals relative to e and h have the projected feature corresponding to h in only a contingent fashion. Could $(e > h)$ be true? There will be types of circumstances in which the evidence individuals would not have the projected feature. This leads us to consider two cases. First, there is the case in which the evidence individuals are such that the context for which $(e > h)$ is to hold is incompatible with circumstances in which an evidence individual would lack the projected feature. Second, the evidence individuals allow that this context is compatible with circumstances in which an evidence individual would lack the projected feature. In each case, $(e > h)$ must be rejected unless a requirement of necessity is recognized.

In the first case, though the evidence individuals have the projected feature contingently, they have of necessity the conditional property that if they are in the context supposed by $(e > h)$ then they have the projected feature. For they are such that this context excludes circumstances in which an evidence individual might lack the projected feature.

In the second case, the evidence individuals allow that the context supposed for $(e > h)$ is compatible with circumstances in which an evidence individual would fail to have the projected feature. But then we are faced with a grave difficulty. An evidence individual does not have the projected feature of itself, since it has it only contingently. So it will not be because of what the evidence individuals are of themselves that e will make h true. Will, then, e

make *h* true because of what the evidence individuals are in the supposed context? Not at all; the context is compatible with circumstances in which the evidence individuals do not even have the projected feature. Nothing is fixed about the unobserved individuals with which the hypothesis is concerned since they may be in precisely those circumstances that would exclude the projected feature. In this case, then, there is no obvious way that, when true, *e* could make *h* true. In this case, $(e > h)$ holds only if the evidence individuals have the projected feature of necessity.

The conclusion to be drawn from taking these cases together involves a qualification on my original (incautious) way of putting the second step. One should not say simply that, when $(e > h)$, the evidence individuals will have the projected feature of necessity. Rather, one must say that, when $(e > h)$ holds for a certain supposed context, the evidence individuals will have of necessity either (1) the conditional property that if they are in this context they will have the projected feature or (2) the property that is the projected feature itself. In either case, there is a necessity, and we have thus uncovered at least one way that action based on prior experience involves necessity. Nothing essential will be changed if, now that we have reached a requirement of necessity, we ignore the qualification introduced here and return to our incautious way of putting the second step. This means ignoring the context dependent character of the factive conditional.

A third step is still needed. All that is required so far is that there be a *chance* that any evidence individual have the projected feature of necessity. Does this mean that there will be any necessities? And if so, will they be necessities of the evidence individuals? My answer is affirmative to both questions. Thus, where *f* is in fact true:

(3) If, where *x* is any evidence individual in respect to *e* and *h*, and *H* is the projected feature corresponding to *h*, $p(\Box\, x(Hx)/f) > 0$, then each evidence individual will have some properties of necessity.

The net effect of (1)–(3) is vastly different from saying that an induction presupposes that there be some necessities or some laws. It is, rather, the more specific claim that an induction presupposes that *the evidence individuals* have some properties of necessity. The properties that they in fact have of necessity need not be the projected features. Moreover, on this account, determinism is not required for induction. It is not required that each evidence individual have each property either of necessity or because of some cause. As far as (3) is concerned, the evidence individuals can have many contingent properties. Moreover, the idea of causation is not even introduced by (3).

Let me consider two objections to (3). First, there are many combinations of properties an individual might have. Each combination is a possible over-all state of the individual. The property red might belong to some of the combinations for the individual *a*. If, all told, there are a finite number of combinations for *a*, then it will stand a chance of being red. Likewise, if *a* is to have a chance of being necessarily red, then the property necessarily-red —if there could be such a property—will have to belong to one or more of the combinations. But the combinations of properties to which it belongs may all be different from the combination that *a* actually has. And, indeed, there need be no property involving necessity that *a* actually has. So to stand a chance of having a certain property of necessity does not—as (3) claims it does—imply having any property necessarily.

This objection is incompatible with the notion of necessity developed in Chapter II, §4. And that notion was precisely the notion of real necessity required in a discussion of induction. If, in one of the combinations of properties, we find necessarily-red, then *a* is *possibly* necessarily red. But then *a could* have a nature that supports red. If it could have such a nature, it actually has it. For, otherwise, if its actual nature were not the same as the nature it could have, we would no longer be speaking of the same individual. So it would be *b*, not *a*, that is possibly necessarily red. But we had assumed that the combinations of properties were possibilities for the same individual. Only if the evidence individual has the projected feature necessarily will there be a chance that it has it necessarily. But this is clearly too strong, so some other method of accounting for the chance of necessity should be sought.

Second, an individual has a certain chance of having a specified property when considered as a member of a reference class in which the proportion of members with that property is equal to that chance. On this premiss the objection will be raised that the chance of an evidence individual having the projected feature of necessity does not imply that *this* individual has a necessity but only that some proportion of the individuals in the appropriate reference class has the projected feature of necessity. But what reference class? All individuals? Certainly not, for only a vanishing proportion of them will have the projected feature of necessity. Then perhaps all evidence individuals? Suppose, though, there is only one evidence individual. On this account it will be a certainty it has the projected feature of necessity. But this cannot be, since there are cases in which single instances provide support, even though it becomes clear later that they manifest the projected feature only contingently if at all. In the absence of other likely alternatives for a reference class, I conclude that an entirely new picture of the matter is called for.

The idea of possible combinations of properties was unsatisfactory, and so is that of a reference class of actual individuals. Neither accounts for the chance of having the projected feature of necessity. In their place I propose the following. An individual has certain properties, and among these are some it has of necessity. How can there be a chance that it has one of its properties with necessity? This is possible if within the individual there is an appropriate mixture of necessary and contingent properties. The details of this proposal will be worked out in the following chapter. All that is important now is that for there to be such a mixture the individual must have some properties of necessity.

§5. *The Possible-Histories Approach.* The above argument for necessity as a presupposition of induction is, in one crucial respect, less vulnerable than the more familiar one that sets out from the notion of possible histories. The latter argument can be summarized as follows.

Suppose Hume is right in adopting an ontology without anything that would support a real physical necessity. What are the implications of this for inductions to, say, universal claims, such as that all F are G? The observed regularity that is the evidence for this claim is compatible with an infinity of courses of subsequent events. With logical consistency as the only constraint, the number of possible histories that contain the observed regularity and that do not violate the universal claim is insignificant by comparison with the total number of possible histories that contain at least the observed regularity.

If the possible histories containing the observed regularity are treated as equiprobable, then the observed regularity would not support the universal claim, for there are an overwhelming number of possible histories with which the latter is incompatible. On the one hand, it might be said that the possible histories are not themselves equiprobable. It is rather, say, types of possible histories that are equiprobable; a history has an equal chance of being of that type in which one-half of the *F*'s are *G*'s as it does of being of that type in which three-fourths of the *F*'s are *G*'s, even though there may be more histories of the former type than the latter.

Thus Joseph—an advocate of the possible-histories approach to necessity—says, "But if, as the empiricist insists, all things are antecedently equally possible, then all proportions of regularity to irregularity in the world are equally possible antecedently."[10] However, Keynes—an advocate of necessity, though not of the possible-histories approach—holds that the individual histories are equiprobable.[11]

Keynes' point is that equiprobable hypotheses ought to be of the same logical complexity. Yet the hypothesis that one-half of the four balls in an urn are black and the rest white is equivalent to a disjunction of six compositions for the urn, whereas the hypothesis that one-fourth are black is equivalent to a disjunction of only four compositions. Being disjunctions of six and four basic possibilities, respectively, the hypotheses are of different logical complexity and hence are not equiprobable.[12]

But even if types of possible histories, rather than individual possible histories, are assigned equiprobability, the observed regularity would not support our universal claim. For there are innumerable types of possible histories that are unfavorable, and only one type that is favorable to the universal claim. So the above objection can be ignored here.

On the other hand, it will be objected that it is illegitimate to introduce probabilities at all when we have considered only possibilities. "How probable it is that these logical possibilities are realized in a balanced or unbalanced way can be estimated," says Ayer, "only in the light of experience."[13] For Ayer there is no connection between few favorable possibilities and improbability, or between many favorable possibilities and likelihood. It is not counting possibilities but counting observed frequencies that is relevant to estimating probability. In particular, it is the observed regularity and not the overwhelming number of unfavorable possible histories that is relevant to the question of whether there is support for our universal hypothesis. But if counting possibilities is irrelevant, how is counting frequencies relevant? If counting frequencies is to be relevant to judging the support for an hypothesis, must it not already have been agreed that there is a significant proportion of favorable possibilities?

How might our anti-possibilist respond? There seems to be no way of showing, by relying solely on the probability calculus, that observed instances support hypotheses. It has long been recognized that Laplace failed to show this by his inversion of Bernoulli's theorem to get the so-called inverse law of maximum probability.[14] If such purely formal attempts are unavailing, what recourse is there? There remain the pragmatic and conventionalist arguments referred to in §1. Based on considerations internal to inductive practice, these arguments attempt to show that frequencies, but not possibilities, are relevant to support. The pragmatic argument leads to the reasonableness of using the uniformity rule to assign support. For even if some other rule successfully predicts events in the world, the uniformity rule would be successful at least in predicting the success of this other rule. Since, in general, our practice is to project the frequencies that we have actually observed, the conventionalist argument also leads to the reasonableness of the uniformity rule to assign support.

One is tempted to reply that a healthy realism seems to make it obvious that possibilities at least partially determine support. So the pragmatist and the conventionalist must already be assuming that the possibilities have been reduced in number from the Humean logical possibilities to the necessitarian's physical possibilities. Now, though it is obvious to Kneale and Carnap that possibilities are to be considered in determining support,[15] this obviousness to them is no answer to the anti-possibilist. At this point, the possibilist might resort to pointing out some of the difficulties of the pragmatic and conventionalist arguments. Is there only *one* rule such that, if any rule is successful, this one rule will be?[16] Does our common inductive practice fit only *one* inductive rule, or are there many that can be used to represent it? But the possibilist has no way of showing that these difficulties are insuperable. He cannot deny that reasons could be given from inside inductive practice for using a rule that accords support without regard to possibilities. So there appears to be a stalemate.

Nonetheless, the possibilist wants to retort that whatever the internal reasons might be for according support without reference to possibilities there are, in a Humean world, simply too many equiprobable alternatives. So in such a world, the uniformity rule cannot be held to be successful, for it would be unreasonable to hold that any rule would be successful. But how can the possibilist make such a retort here? The context of the debate is that the anti-possibilist challenged his right to say *a priori* that the alternatives have probabilities, whether equal or unequal. Yet here he has supposed they are equiprobable precisely in order to attack the anti-possibilist's assertion that frequencies determine support through a rule that makes support insensitive to possibilities.[17] In short, the possibilist is unsuccessful in showing that pragmatic and conventionalist arguments for the reasonableness of assigning support by certain inductive rules fail in a context where the logical possibilities are not cut down by physical necessities. It does not help the possibilist to allow him to distribute the probabilities unequally among possibilities, for the question is not whether the probabilities are equal or unequal but whether possibilities have any probabilities *a priori*.

The argument for necessity in §3 and §4 avoids the stalemate facing the possible-histories approach. The former does not depend on the association of probabilities with possible histories. Rather, by following up the consequences of the correlation between conditional support and support for a conditional, we were forced to grant that the evidence individuals had some properties of necessity. This of itself does not limit possible histories containing the evidence, since it concerns only the evidence individuals. It does limit these histories when it is assumed that there are future individuals with the same necessities.

Whether this or a related assumption about the future is needed will be the subject of part of the next chapter. But even at this point, it is established that any purely enumerativist approach to induction is a mistake. That is, in addition to the data enumerated one needs the assumption that the individuals involved in the data have some physical properties of necessity. Otherwise, the data cannot support an hypothesis. But this conclusion has not been reached by an argument from the multiplicity of possible histories.

It remains to be pointed out that the argument for necessity in Sections 3 and 4 is not one that ties us down to any particular inductive rules. In particular, it does not tie us down to the uniformity rule.

(a) Suppose on the evidence that $\frac{m}{n}$ *F* are *G* there is support for the hypothesis that $(x)(Fx \rightarrow \left(1 - \frac{m}{n}\right) Gx)$. Even though the evidence itself fails to show a ratio of *G*'s to *F*'s equal to the projected chance, it may nonetheless be the case that each evidence individual has a $\left(1 - \frac{m}{n}\right)$ chance of being *G* if it is *F*. Indeed, given that the evidence supports the above hypothesis, each evidence individual has some likelihood of necessarily having the property of having a $\left(1 - \frac{m}{n}\right)$ chance of being a *G* if it is an *F*.

(b) Suppose on the evidence this emerald is green there is support for the hypothesis that anything is either green if it is an emerald observed before 1975 or blue if it is an emerald not observed before 1975. In short, it supports the hypothesis that all emeralds are "grue" (that is, green and observed before 1975 or blue and observed after 1975). Again, in order for there to be such support, this emerald, which I observe in 1971 to be green, will have to have a chance of being necessarily grue, assuming it is an evidence individual.

There might well be reasons for rejecting such odd inductive rules as the ones assumed in (a) and (b). But I am not concerned here with their acceptability. What is important is that the requirement for necessity depends on the notion of support and not on the kind of rule from which support is inferred. This is important because the notion of action on prior experience does not limit one to rules of certain kinds. So one can now say that the practice of acting on the basis of prior sense experience would be incoherent with a denial of real physical necessity.

CHAPTER V

The Structure of Physical Individuals

§1. *Limited Independent Variety.* Whether a claim is supported by data depends on what data there are and, as importantly, on what necessities there are. Where the only necessities are the logical necessities, there can be no support, however reassuring the data may appear. So, if support is to be given to claims by data, there must be necessities other than the logical ones. Up to this point, we have only hinted at how extensive such a realm of physical necessity must be. It is plain from Chapter IV that it must be extensive enough for evidence individuals relative to any hypothesis to have a chance of having the projected property corresponding to that hypothesis of necessity. But to satisfy this and other relevant demands, must one adopt the doctrine that in any individual no two properties are independent of one another? If such were the price, one might be willing to conclude that the only way to make inductive practice reasonable is to adopt an inherently unreasonable ontology. Is there a way short of this extreme necessitarianism? A modification of Keynes' principle of limited independent variety does, I wish to show, provide a way. It will indicate the sort of mixture of necessary and contingent properties that evidence individuals must have.

The emphasis here is on the properties of individuals rather than on properties considered as entities apart from individuals. And Keynes' strategy is precisely to concentrate on individuals. He imposes no limitation on the number of properties considered as separate entities; rather, the limitation concerns the properties a given individual can have. It is assumed that the properties in question are physical. According to Keynes, "We seem to need some such assumption as that the amount of variety in the universe is limited in such a way that there is no one object so complex that its qualities fall into an infinite number of independent groups."[1] Thus, finite independent variety in individuals does not preclude an infinity of individuals, each with, say, a different temperature. Infinite independent variety among individuals is allowed by finite independent variety in individuals. It will not suffice here to assume merely that there is a chance an individual will have limited independent variety. For then an evidence individual might have infinite independent variety. But without limited independent variety, one will be unable to show that the individual has a chance of having the projected feature of necessity.

Keynes understood independence in a modal fashion. What he called "laws of necessary connection" were the basis for the limitation of independent variety.[2] Thus, if F and H are independent properties, then, for any individual x, it is not a necessity of x that if it is F then it is H, or conversely that if it is H then it is F, and it is not a necessity of x that if it is F then it is not H, or conversely that if it is not H then it is F. So independence or dependence holds between properties, not just for individuals of special natures, but for individuals generally.

The principle of limited independent variety asserts that:

(I) The number of properties in the set B_a of basic properties of an arbitrary individual a is greater than zero and less than some given finite number.

The requirement that the number of B_a be less than a given finite number rather than merely finite was noticed by Nicod rather than Keynes.[3] "Basic" properties are not just underived; together they suffice for the derivation of all other relevant properties. The set of all relevant properties of a, P_a, has already been limited to physical ones, and will soon be subject to two more restrictions. So a member of B_a is underived from any other properties of P_a, and any member of P_a is derived from a subset of B_a. H "derives" from a property or set of properties F when any individual is necessarily such that if it is F or has all the properties of F then it is H. Notice that basic properties need not themselves be necessary. Indeed, the basic-derived distinction cuts across the necessary-contingent one.

Let us call the subsets of B_a "groups." If a has limited independent variety, then it has only finitely many groups. But even if there are only finitely many groups, there may be an infinity of different properties in a. This is possible if there are necessary connections making the groups sufficient for an infinity of properties.

Suppose properties of the set G and the property H belong to P_a. Suppose further that H is derived from G. Is the "derivational property" $(G\_ \rightarrow H\_)$ itself to be listed among the basic and derived properties of a? If P_a is infinite and B_a is finite, a has infinitely many such derivational properties. Only a finite number of these could be basic. It might then seem convenient to treat them all as properties derived from their own antecedents. After all, it might seem that if having G is sufficient for having H, then, just as a matter of logic, having G must be sufficient for this connection between G itself and H. But not only is this not logically true for relevant implication but also it fails to determine the status of $(G\_ \rightarrow H\_)$ for any individual that lacks G. Yet if the connection is a true derivation, all individuals will have $(G\_ \rightarrow H\_)$ whether or not they have G. It will not do to say that the derivational property is basic in individuals lacking G. For, again, there will be an infinity of such properties in any non-G. It is then imperative to exclude derivational properties from among those considered by Keynes' principle. Thus P_a includes properties between which derivations hold, but no derivational properties.

To make things relevant to induction, imagine that we observe a to be both F and H. Let this observation support the hypothesis that all F are H. The projected feature is then $(F\_ \rightarrow H\_)$. There are now two questions. First, can (I) account for there being a chance that a has this projected feature of necessity? Second, can (I) help to explain how individuals other than a have a chance of having the projected feature? (I shall deal with this question in the next section.) To begin to deal with these questions, let us define any group B^F_a as follows. On the one hand, any such group is a subset of B_a from which F is derived. On the other hand, F is derived from no proper part of B^F_a. In Keynes' terminology, *F* "specifies" any of the B^F_a. Since there may be several such groups even in a single individual, *F* may specify a "plurality of generators" in *a*.

Regarding the first question, it is clear that, with only finitely many groups in *a,* the possibility that *H* derives from a group in *a* specified by *F* is one among a finite number. For *H,* being a property of *a,* will derive from some group of *a*. And this group may be a B^F_a. Since this possibility is one among a finite number, may we say that there is a chance that *F* and *H* derive from one and the same group of *a*? One might object that, in Chapter IV, §5, we seemed to argue that chances are not based on possibilities. The way seems blocked.

However, two things are to be recalled. First, it was not argued that chances could not be based on possibilities. It was argued only that the possible-histories approach to necessity had no way of justifying, against an enumerativist like Ayer, its assumption that chances can be based on possibilities. Second, without assuming at the start that chances can be based on ratios of favorable to all possibilities, we arrived at the conclusion that evidence individuals must have a chance of having projected features necessarily. Immediately, the question arose as to how there can be such a chance. Several proposals were quickly rejected, and we drew the conclusion that such a chance depends on the way individuals are structured out of necessary and contingent properties. But inevitably this means that such a chance depends on ratios of possibilities within the structure. Rather than assuming, as in the possible-histories approach, that chances are based on possibilities, our argument led to this claim through a sequence of presuppositions of induction. So, despite the criticism we made of the possible-histories approach, we are free to claim here that if one among a finite number of alternatives is that *F* and *H* derive from the same group of *a,* then there is a chance that *F* and *H* derive from the same group of *a*.

But clearly we are in search of a stronger conclusion. To say there is a chance that *a* has a common source for *F* and *H* is not to say there is a chance *a* is necessarily such that if it is *F* then it is *H*. Of course, if *H* is necessarily implied by the B^F_a *G* and *G* is necessarily implied by F, then indeed F would necessarily imply H. The difficulty is that though G necessarily implies F when F specifies G, the converse does not hold in general. For there may be another B^F_a besides G, and thus a could be F without being G.

Consider for a moment, though, the consequences of assuming that a group F specifies, say G, contains only properties that a necessarily has. I shall call such a group a "necessary group" of a. So a's appearance as F points back not just to basic properties a happens to have but to basic properties that are essential to a. Since F specifies G and since G is essential to a, a will necessarily be such that if it is F then it is G. The idea is that, in a, F must have G as a necessary condition provided that F derives from G, but no proper subset of G, and that a could not be without G. Adding this new principle to the premisses that (1) G is a necessity of a, that (2) G is specified by F, and that (3) H derives from G we have, where G' is a proper subset of G, the following proof:

(1) $\Box\, a(Ga)$
(2) $\Box\, a(Ga \rightarrow Fa) \cdot {\sim}\Box a(G'a \rightarrow Fa)$
(3) $\Box\, a(Ga \rightarrow Ha)$
(4) $(\Box a(Ga \rightarrow Fa) \cdot {\sim}\Box\, a(G'a \rightarrow Fa)) \rightarrow (\Box\, a(Ga)$
$\rightarrow \Box\, a(Fa \rightarrow Ga))$
$\therefore$ (5) $\Box a(Fa \rightarrow Ha)$

This conclusion is indeed the one we were searching for.

Objections to our new principle (4) will arise only if one mistakenly reads a necessary relevant implication as a derivational claim. In (4), $\Box\, a(Fa \rightarrow Ga)$ might be the claim that a is necessarily such that if it is water soluble then it has an ionic crystalline structure. But this does not mean that the structure is due to the solubility. Nor does it mean that the structure of the individual is the only thing that could account for its solubility. There might be multiple generators in a. Rather, this necessary implication is adequately supported by the fact that the solubility of this individual cannot help but be accounted for by, among other things, its crystalline structure.

Also, when 'Ga' is replaced in (4) by '$Ga \cdot G'a$' and 'Fa' is replaced by '$(\exists x)Gx \cdot G'a$', we get from $\Box\, a(Fa \rightarrow Ga)$ the claim that $\Box\, a(((\exists x)Gx \cdot G'a) \rightarrow (Ga \cdot G'a))$. This claim seems false when we require for its truth that its consequent be derived from its antecedent. However, this necessary implication is adequately supported by the fact that *a*'s satisfying $((\exists x)Gx \cdot G'a)$ cannot help but be accounted for by *a*'s having G and G'. It cannot help but be accounted for in this way since, as the analogue to (1), one has that *a* is necessarily G and G' and, as the analogue to (2), one has that $Ga \cdot G'a$, but no part of it, necessarily implies $(\exists x)Gx \cdot G'a$.

Keynes' principle is not adequate for the claim that there is a chance that (5) is true. His principle, (I), gives premisses (2) and (3) a chance of being true. Premiss (4) was just argued for as being true. But for there to be a chance that (1) is true we also need the claim, not made by Keynes, that I shall call the principle of necessary basic properties:

(II) Any basic property of an individual has a chance of being a necessary property of that individual.

Since groups are, by (I), finite, it follows directly that any group had by an individual has a chance of being a necessary group of that individual. So there is a chance that (1) is true. (I) and (II) jointly provide that an evidence individual has a chance of having the projected feature of necessity.

Let us assume for the moment that (I) and (II) are not only adequate but also indispensable. Thus, they not only imply a finite chance for (5), but are also implied by a finite chance for (5). This will lead us to see that if evidence individuals do have a chance of having the projected properties of necessity then each evidence individual has some properties with physical necessity. (We will then have a direct proof of (3) of Chapter IV, §4, in addition to the indirect proof given there.)

This can be seen as follows. On the one hand, the principle of necessary basic properties requires for its truth that each individual have at least one property that is necessary, if as (I) guarantees, it has at least one basic property. This would not be required were it assumed that there are many individuals of which a fraction have necessary basic properties. For then, even though some may lack necessary basic properties, each would have a chance of at least one necessary basic property. Since there would be no reason to distinguish among basic properties, each basic property would, as (II) states, have a chance of being a necessary one. The difficulty with this is the assumption that there are many individuals.

The view of evidence individuals developed here needs to be independent of whether there are many evidence individuals and of whether there are unobserved individuals. That is why we must rely solely on the structure of any given evidence individual. We cannot assume a multiplicity of individuals in trying to justify the claim that an evidence individual has a chance of having a feature necessarily. For the claim that such a feature might be projected if there were other individuals to project it on is a claim that is true or false of the individual in question, and it does not change its truth value if other individuals cease to exist.

On the other hand, the principle of limited independent variety requires for its truth that each individual have its derivational properties of necessity. Suppose these derivational properties all hold of logical necessity. But we are interested solely in the real physical necessities. The possibility of making inductions to physical hypotheses requires that there be a chance that two logically independent properties are connected by necessity. Such a connection will not then be logical, and hence (I) is irrelevant unless it is taken to assume that there are *physical* derivational necessities.

Thus individuals understood in the light of (I) and (II) are seen to have a mixture of necessary and contingent properties. The mixture contains a finite ratio of necessary basic properties to all basic properties. It also contains some derived properties that are connected to basic properties by physically necessary connections. The necessary basic properties are physically necessary since they are physical properties.

§2. *Natural Kinds and the Multiplicity of Generators.* The second question takes us beyond evidence individuals to unobserved ones. Is there a chance that in addition to *a* all other individual *F*'s have $(F\_ \rightarrow H\_)$ of necessity? If so, the datum that *a* is *F* and *H* would support the claim that all *F* are *H*. (When I speak of two *F*'s, I am speaking of two individuals with two similar properties, not with one shared property.) But the chance that *a* has $(F\_ \rightarrow H\_)$ of necessity depends on the chance that *H* derives from one of the groups, say G, that F specifies in a and on the chance that this group is necessary to a. So the most one can say is that there is a chance that every other F for which F specifies G has $(F\_ \rightarrow H\_)$ of necessity. And so the given data support only the qualified claim that all F for which F specifies G are H.

The reason for this qualification is recognized by Keynes as the possibility of a plurality of generators as between individuals.[4] In another F, G may not be among the groups specified by F. If this individual is b, then it may be that b is F but not H. For, though H was derived from G in a, it may not be derived from any group in b that F specifies.*

Suppose the evidence individual a—which is F and H—has a chance of having the projected feature $(F\_ \rightarrow H\_)$ of necessity. But suppose further there is no chance that all other F's have this feature. Then clearly there would be no chance that $(e > h)$, that is, that a's having F and H factively implies that all F are H. It is for this reason that a chance must be secured for all other F's having the projected feature. The reason is not the one Keynes adduced. He wanted a prior probability for the hypothesis so that, by Bayes' Theorem, evidence could increase its probability. However, my reasoning here does not rely on Bayes' Theorem and, to that extent, is not Bayesian. Rather, I am insisting that there be a chance that all other F's have the projected feature $(F\_ \rightarrow H\_)$ for the reason that otherwise there would be no chance that $(e > h)$. There would be no chance that $(e > h)$ since, with the evidence in, e would be true even though there would be no chance that h is true. The need for h to have a chance to be true is based on the need for $(e > h)$ to have such a chance and not on the need for a factor greater than zero in the numerator of Bayes' Theorem.

As Keynes himself points out, an additional principle is needed. It can take either of two forms. Suppose it has the form:

(III) An arbitrary property F has a finite chance of specifying a common group wherever it occurs.

Call this the principle of the common generator. From (III) and (II) it follows that an arbitrary property has a chance of specifying

*It is to be emphasized that here we have had to treat the universal claim that all F are H as a claim about F's rather than about any individuals whatsoever.

a common necessary group wherever it occurs. If there is support for the qualified universal claim that all *F* for which *F* specifies *G* are *H* then, since there is a chance *F* specifies *G* everywhere, there is support for the unqualified claim that all *F* are *H*.

Suppose, however, the principle has the form:

(IV) For an arbitrary property *F* there is a chance that there is a finite set of groups such that *F* specifies some member or other of this set wherever it occurs.

Call this the principle of limited sufficient generators. It is compatible with *F* specifying an infinity of groups. It requires only a chance of a finite core of groups specified by *F*, where some member or other of the core shows up in every *F*. Under (IV) one abandons the possibility of supporting unqualified universal claims. For the chance that the *F*'s in larger and larger classes of *F*'s have the same generators tends to zero. The possibility of supporting instantial claims is retained. For, if *F* specifies *G* in *a*, there is still a chance it specifies *G* in another *F*, say *b*, since there is a chance that the *G* in *a* belongs to a finite core of groups.

Keynes' problem of the multiplicity of generators is related to the old question as to whether there are natural kinds. It turns out that the principle of the common generator, (III), is equivalent to the claim that there are natural kinds, in the context of (I) and (II). This establishes a link between Keynes' (III) and Broad's claim that induction is warranted only where it has to do with individuals identified as members of natural kinds.[5]

In the strong sense, a natural kind was defined as a class in which all members are physical individuals of exactly similar natures. In the weak sense, a natural kind was defined schematically as a class of physical individuals, whose natures support certain exactly similar necessities. Precisely what necessities are to be similar here? Now the collection of necessities associated with a group *G* of *a* divides into two parts. First, there are the necessities *a* is under to have certain basic properties of *G* and to have all the properties derived directly from these basic ones. This division may be empty. Second, there are the necessities *a* is under to have all the derivational properties ($F_{-} \rightarrow H_{-}$), where *F* is derived from *G*. I call these two the divisions of basic and derivational necessities of *G*.

I now make the notion of a natural kind definite by requiring that every member of a "natural kind" have one set of properties, comprised of necessary basic properties, that is exactly similar to some set in every other individual of the natural kind such that the properties of this set are still necessary basic properties of its individual. In Platonic terms, members of a natural kind have a common necessary group. Common necessary derived properties do not suffice; they may be derived from dissimilar groups in distinct individuals. Both Jones and his computer may be necessarily rational, but if the bases for rationality in the two are dissimilar groups, it is not established that they belong to the same natural kind.

Further, a common contingent group would suffice for common derivational necessities. But derivational necessities hold for individuals generally, not just for those with a given group in common. So a group cannot be the basis for a natural kind due to its division of derivational necessities. Nor can the divisions of derivational necessities associated with different groups define natural kinds. For the members of each such division apply to all individuals. We are led, rather to associate natural kinds only with those groups whose divisions of basic necessities include all their properties.

Keynes' (III) was needed for inductions to universal claims. I shall now show that, in the context of (I) and (II), it is equivalent to the claim that an arbitrary property has a chance of being coextensive with a natural kind. Even induction to universal claims does not, then, require appeal to natural kinds in the strong sense of individuals with similar natures.

Suppose there is a chance that *F* specifies the same necessary group wherever it occurs. There is, then, a chance that there is a necessary group common to all the *F*'s. So there is a chance that the *F*'s make a natural kind.

Conversely, suppose there is a chance that the *F*'s make a natural kind. There is, then, a chance that (i) there is a necessary group common to all the *F*'s. Also, there is a chance that (ii), when some group is a necessary group common to all the *F*'s, *F* specifies that group in all the *F*'s. Since there is a chance that (i) and a chance that (ii), it follows that there is a chance that *F* specifies a common necessary group in all the *F*'s. Thus (III) is satisfied.

How though are we sure there is a chance that (ii)? Here we rely on (I) and the fact that derivational properties hold universally. In view of the finitude of groups, there is a chance that, when some group belongs to an *F*, the property *F* specifies that group. If the group that *F* specifies in this individual is common to all the *F*'s, then, in view of the universality of derivational properties, *F* specifies that group in all the *F*'s. So, there is a chance that, when some group is a necessary group common to all the *F*'s, *F* specifies that group in all the *F*'s.

Keynes' principle of limited sufficient generators (IV) suffices to provide support for instantial claims. Natural kinds are then superfluous. Still, in the context of (I) and (II), Keynes' (IV) is equivalent to the assumption that there is a chance that any two members of the set of *F*'s share a group whose properties are basic and necessary for each. Any two members may, of course, share a necessary group when there is no necessary group common to all. The group that *a* and *b* share may not be the one *b* and *c* share. If any two members of a class share a necessary group, then I shall call the class a "family kind." Human family resemblances do not require a single obvious common and distinguishing feature in all members of the family, but generally any two members have some distinguishing point in common—the shape of the nose, the texture of the skin, or the shape of the mouth. In a family kind there is not only no single nature shared by all, but there is also no need for a common necessary group.

Assume there is a chance that there is a finite set of necessary groups such that, among the groups specified by *F* in any individual, there is one from among this finite set of necessary groups. This is just (IV) combined with (II). There will then be a chance that, between any two individuals that are *F*, the property *F* specifies the same necessary group. Thus there is a chance that *F* is coextensive with a family kind.

Conversely, assume there is a chance that the *F*'s make a family kind. If there is such a kind, let *a* be a member of it. By (I), *a* has only the finite number of groups $G_1, G_2, \ldots, G_n$. By definition, *a* has a group in common with any other member of the family kind coextensive with *F*. Indeed, it has a common necessary group. All individuals in this kind can be put in the finite number of possibly non-disjoint classes $\{G_1\}$, $\{G_2\}$, . . . , $\{G_n\}$, where $\{G_i\}$ is the class of all individuals in the kind sharing G_i when G_i is a common necessary group. Since a given G_i need not be a common necessary group, some of these classes might be empty.

By (I), there is a finite chance that F specifies any G_i in a. Since there is a chance that G_i is one of the necessary groups of the family kind, there is a chance that individuals with G_i form $\{G_i\}$. Moreover, if F specifies G_i and the individuals with G_i form $\{G_i\}$, then F specifies a necessary group G_i throughout $\{G_i\}$, since derivation holds universally. Therefore, there is a finite chance that F specifies a necessary group G_i in every individual in $\{G_i\}$. But then there is a finite chance that F specifies either G_1, G_2 . . . , or G_n in any individual F and that each of these is a necessary group. Hence there is a chance that there is a finite set of necessary groups such that among the groups specified by F in any individual there is one from among this set.

Earlier, in Chapter III, §3, I noted that the practice of action on prior experience does not depend on assuming the existence of classes whose members have the same nature. I noted that at most the assumption of natural kinds in the weak sense was needed. Now it appears that the assumption of natural kinds, even in the weak sense, is needed only when we assume that induction to universals is an essential part of inductive practice. If, however, we content ourselves with induction to instantial claims, we see that the assumption of natural kinds in the weak sense is unnecessary. All that is needed is family kinds. The assumption that there is a chance that any property is coextensive with a family kind would seem to be the weakest assumption that would still allow inductive practice.* It cannot then be claimed that natural kinds are part of the required ontology.

If universal hypotheses are formulated explicitly in terms of natural kinds, then not only is Keynes' assumption (III) about multiple generators superfluous but so is my assumption (II) about necessary basic properties. This is obvious since F's being coextensive with a natural kind was just seen to imply F's specifying a common necessary group. Suppose the hypothesis is that

*This anticipates the fact that statistical induction requires no weaker assumption.

$(x)(Nx \rightarrow (Fx \rightarrow Hx))$. Recalled that '*N*', as a natural-kind term, signifies a property, the kind property, that belongs to each *N* necessarily. Though (I) is needed if there is to be support for this hypothesis, (II) and (III) are not. This may be shown as follows.

The evidence individual *a* is, we suppose, an *N* and has $(F\_ \rightarrow H\_)$. Now let the kind property signified by '*N*' be *J*. There is a chance, in view of (I), that $(F\_ \rightarrow H\_)$ derives from a group, *G*, specified by *J*. Since *a* has limited groups, *G* has a chance of being the necessary group common throughout *N*. So there is a chance that $\Box a(Ga)$ holds. In view of (1)–(5) of §1, there is a chance that $\Box a(Na \rightarrow (Fa \rightarrow Ha))$.

What is the prospect for generalizing this? Instead of assuming (III) at this point, one merely notes that, by definition, members of a natural kind have a necessary group in common. In view of limited independent variety in *a*, there is a chance that *G*, the necessary group specified by the kind property *J* in *a*, is the common necessary group. Thus not only is there a chance that *G* is necessary in every *N*, but also there is a chance that $(F\_ \rightarrow H\_)$ is derived, in any *N*, from a group that the kind property of *N* specifies in that member of *N*. That is, there is a chance that $(x) \Box x(Nx \rightarrow (Fx \rightarrow Hx))$, which by the Principle of Essentialism is interderivable from $(x)(Nx \rightarrow \Box x(Fx \rightarrow Hx))$. This last we called a kind-specific necessity. Universal inductive hypotheses characteristically have this form, or at least the implied non-modal form. So without kind-specific hypotheses, or ones implied by them, induction requires the strong principles (II) and (III). The Principle of Essentialism transforms a kind-specific necessity into the full necessity that is given support by (I) alone in the above argument.

§3. *Relations and Limited Variety.* Among the properties of an individual are its relational ones of being spatially apart from each of the other individuals in the world. In addition, there are its relational properties of being darker than, cooler than, larger than, slower than, and heavier than various individuals in the world. Now how is it possible to contend that any individual has a limited number of independent properties in view of these facts? Being distant from Sirius and being distant from Spica would seem to be independent properties of an earthling. Being darker than this flower and darker than that leaf would seem to be independent properties of a color sample. So it would seem that either there is no limited variety in individuals or there is only limited variety for non-relational properties. On the first alternative, no claims are supportable that go beyond the observed. On the second, only those claims are supportable that do not involve relations between individuals.[6]

Suppose the color sample is darker than the flower. There will then be the two relational properties, *darker than the flower* and *lighter than the color sample*. As I shall show in Chapter VII, there cannot be relational properties without certain foundations. In other words, for the color sample to have the relational property *darker than the flower,* it is requisite that two conditions be satisfied. First, the color sample must have a certain shade of color; second, the flower must have a certain shade of color. So there are two distinct property foundations for any one relational property. The situation for a purely spatial or temporal relational property is more subtle. Action, which is also a component of individuals, is the foundation for both temporal and spatial separation, as I shall argue farther on.

Many relational properties of a single individual have the same foundation in that individual. Yet they will have distinct foundations in other individuals. The shade of the color sample is the foundation for its being darker than any number of other individuals. So with only a finite number of independent properties other than relational ones, an individual may still have an infinity of independent relational properties. But the important thing is that those finite independent non-relational properties can include directly or by derivation all the foundations in that individual for the infinity of its independent relational properties. This is possible since each of those relational properties also has a foundational property outside the individual.

In view of this, it becomes clear how the principle of limited independent variety can be restricted to non-relational properties of an individual without losing its applicability to all hypotheses, including relational ones. The set P_a of properties of a that are relevant to limited variety are then physical, non-derivational, and non-relational. Consider the relational claim that electrons are lighter than protons. The claim is true if any electron has a foundational property from a certain range, a range of masses, and protons have masses from another range. So there is support for the relational claim if there is support for the two non-relational claims about foundational properties. The principle of limited independent variety is applied to protons and electrons separately. One is not forced to apply it to artificial entities, each containing an electron and a proton. It still remains to deal with the more complex problem of allowing for inductions to claims asserting temporal posteriority within the context of limited variety. I shall return to this problem in Chapter VIII, §1.

§4. *Levels of Limited Variety.* Keynes' principle of limited independent variety, (I), is not required by inductive practice. A more general principle—the principle of levels of limited variety—can do the job that needs to be done. A view of individuals that incorporates it still requires real physical necessities.

Formally speaking, a level is merely a class of properties of an individual. Levels of the same individual are disjoint. There is no limit to the number of levels an individual may have. The formal notion of level gains some content only under the restrictions of the principle of levels. The first restriction is that each level in an individual must be characterized by limited independent variety relative to the properties at that level, and that some finite number is larger than the amount of independent variety at any level. A property that is basic relative to a level is simply one at this level that is not derived entirely from properties at this level. It may have a derivation that involves a property of a different level and thus not be basic, absolutely speaking. Suppose F and H belong to one level and J belongs to another. Conceivably, H could be derived from F with an assist from J. Still H would be basic at its level if it were not derived entirely from any other properties at its level. The second restriction is that between any two levels there must be a connection in the sense that having the properties of some group at the one level necessarily implies having the properties of some group at the other level. Here, of course, a group is relativized to a level and is thus defined as a set of properties that are basic relative to a given level.

The principle of levels of limited independent variety says:

(I*) There is a set of levels of the properties of an arbitrary individual such that there is limited independent variety at each level, and there are connections between any level and each of the others.

I shall now speak of a set of levels satisfying both restrictions of (I*) simply as a set of levels.

The properties of an individual divide up in various ways. Thus to say they can belong to the levels of a specified set is not to say they cannot belong to another set of levels. Whether a person's weight, blood type, and intelligence quotient all belong to the same level or not depends on factors beyond the principle of levels. If there are several sets of levels, all of these properties may belong to one level in one set, and each may belong to a distinct level in another set. And even if there should be a unique set of levels in an individual, (I*) does not specify which properties belong to which levels.

Now an individual with a set of levels may have an infinite number of absolutely basic properties. Suppose the individual has infinitely many levels, and that two properties are basic in respect to each level. If one of these properties at each level is not connected with any property at any other level, then it is basic in an absolute sense. A universe containing some such individuals would violate Keynes' principle, (I), but would still satisfy the levels principle, (I*). Such individuals might seem strange since one property at each level is shielded from all other levels. They fit neither a reductionist nor an emergentist world view. But this is no objection here since the practice of action on prior experience does not require either a reductionist or an emergentist ontology. Typically, the reductionist would think in terms of a single level. The emergentist would think of all properties of at least some levels as derived from, though not reduced to, those of other levels. This case of an infinity of absolutely basic properties is not the only one that conflicts with Keynes' (I). For (I*) does not require that there be any absolutely basic properties at all.

Does the principle of levels provide a basis for saying that an evidence individual has a chance of having the projected feature of necessity? Let the evidence individual, *a,* be *F* and *H* and the projected feature be ($F\_ \rightarrow H\_$). Now *a* may have several sets of levels. But nothing in our argument will depend on the peculiarities of any one set. In any set of levels, *F* will specify a group at some level, say *i*, and *H* will belong either to *i* or to some other level *j*. On the one hand, if it belongs to *i*, the possibility that *H* derives from a group specified by *F* is one among a finite number of possibilities, there being only finitely many groups at *i*. On the other hand, let *j* be the level at which *H* is derived. Since levels are connected, one group at *i* necessarily implies some group at *j*, or conversely. If *i* has *m* and *j* has *n* groups, the possibilities that a group specified by *F* and one specified by *H* are connected is one out of—at most—$m \cdot n$ possibilities. So the possibility *H* is derived, through inter-level connection, from a group specified by *F* is one out of—at most—$2(m \cdot n)$ possibilities. Even with an infinity of levels, the connections among levels secures a chance that *F* and *H* have a common source.

This is not yet what we want. Is there a chance that, for *a*, *F* necessarily implies *H*? For this to be the case we need to assume:

(II*) Any individual has some level at which any property that is basic at that level has a chance of being a necessary property of that individual.

But since there are connections among levels and since the connections stand an equal chance of running in either direction, any group at any level has a chance of being necessary. Suppose, then, *F* specifies the group G^i at level *i* and that *H* derives from G^j. By the interconnection of levels, G^i may necessarily imply G^j. So by (II*) there is a chance *F* and *H* derive from the same necessary group G^i. And by the argument (1)–(5) of Section 1, there is a chance that, for *a*, *F* necessarily implies *H*.

Of course, to project ($F\_ \rightarrow H\_$) in a universal claim, there must be either an assumption regarding the plurality of *F*'s generators or a use of '*F*' as a natural-kind term. The assumption would be:

(III*) There is a set of properties *G* such that for any individual that is an *F* there is a finite chance that *G* is a group relative to some level in that individual and that *F* specifies *G*.

We cannot say simply that there must be a chance *F* specifies the same group at the same level. For we have given no sense to the idea of sameness of level in individuals that differ in some properties. As before, (III*) in the context of (I*) and (II*) is equivalent to the claim that there is a chance the *F*'s constitute a natural kind. A natural kind is now a class in respect to which there is a set of properties *G* such that, in any individual in the class, *G* is a group relative to some level of that individual, and the properties of *G* are necessary for that individual.

There is an analogy between what I have called levels of limited independent variety and levels of scientific inquiry, such as physics, chemistry, biology, psychology, and the various levels within each of these. The levels of limited independent variety may be infinite in number, and Bohm has suggested that the levels of scientific inquiry are infinite.[7] The important thing about an infinity of levels of independent variety is that an infinity of levels allows that properties may be basic only relative to given levels, and not absolutely so. Keynes' principle, however, requires that all individuals have absolutely basic properties. Bohm and others argue that it is out of keeping with the scientific spirit to posit, as Keynes does, an ultimate level, that is, a level of properties that are absolutely basic.

I am not concerned here with this aspect of the scientific spirit, but only with the question of whether induction requires an ultimate level. I am saying that a universe of the sort Bohm thinks the scientific spirit posits—a universe in which individuals have no ultimate level—can contain the proper allotment of necessity to make support for hypotheses possible. Induction does not require absolutely basic properties, as Keynes thought it did. Bohm denounces as "mechanistic" any natural philosophy involving "the assumption that the possible variety in the basic properties and qualities existing in nature is limited."[8] However, my objection to such a natural philosophy is only that its assumption is not the most general one that allows induction to be reasonable. Induction allows for—though does not require—infinite levels.

Levels of scientific inquiry are generally assumed to be serially ordered, but no requirement of order is imposed by the principle of levels. Bohm's levels, for example, are ordered by the fact that each one is only approximate as judged by reference to the ones below it, the latter taking into account factors the former leaves out. In addition, levels of scientific inquiry are distinguished by distinctive types of properties such as physical properties and biological properties. Mass and distance belong to the physical level since they are properties of the physical type. Properties of the same level in individuals with different properties are simply properties of the same type. But the levels of (I*) are distinguished by the individual properties they contain, not by the types of these properties.

The levels principle provides an interesting perspective from which to view Goodman's "new riddle of induction."[9] We used the predicate 'grue' to apply "to all things examined before *t* just in case they are green but to other things just in case they are blue." Now the property signified by this curious predicate—if indeed there is such a property—is not derived from the property green, and conversely green is not derived from it. For there are green things that are not grue (green things not examined before *t* are not grue) and there are grue things that are not green (blue things not examined before *t* are not green). So green and grue do not specify the same group.

Now 'grue' is only one of the predicates we can think up alongside 'green'. There is also 'gred'—the corresponding blend of green and red—and a host of others. Assuming they signify properties, observations before *t* on emeralds that indicate they are green are also observations that indicate they are grue and gred. Thus the conflicting hypotheses that all emeralds are green, that all emeralds are grue, and that all emeralds are gred have the same observed positive instances. Yet one would instinctively suppose that not all these hypotheses are equally supported by these observations. The problem is, why not?

The principle of levels allows for many sets of levels in the same individual. But in empirical practice some set of levels comes to be thought of as *the* set of levels. Thus the physical, chemical, and biological levels are thought to be in the set of levels of living things. Similarly, if one admits grue-type properties, one might segregate them into a level other than that at which properties like emerald and green are located. This would mean that one could speak of an emerald-green level for common-sense properties and of an emerose-grue level for any grue-type properties. ('Emerose' applies to all things examined before *t* that are emeralds and to all other things that are roses.) I wish to suggest that it is in terms of a segregation into these levels that our feeling that hypotheses crossing these levels have less support is to be accounted for.

At a given level we look for the chance that two properties are derived from the same group. Between levels we look for the chance that the groups specified by the properties of the two levels are connected. I shall try to show that, in general, the intra-level chances outweigh the inter-level chances. In particular, this will be the case when some of the groups at one level are not connected with those at the other level.

Is there a group at the emerald-green level that is not connected with a group at the emerose-grue level? A group specified by green does not necessarily imply a group specified by grue. Conversely, a group specified by grue does not necessarily imply the group specified by green. Assuming that the property of being examined before *t* belongs to the emerald-green level, then not only will green not be connected with grue, but it will not be connected with any group at the emerose-grue level. Perhaps this proves too much; perhaps it shows that there are no connections at all between groups at the two levels. We would not then have levels in the sense of (I*). But clearly there are some connections. A group specified by green-and-examined-before-*t* necessarily implies one specified by grue in any individual, as does a group specified by blue-and-not-examined-before-*t*.

Suppose then that there are *m* groups at the emerald-green level, *k* of which are connected with some of the *n* groups at the emerose-grue level. On the one hand, at the emerald-green level there is a $\frac{1}{m}$ chance that a group specified by emerald gives rise to green. At the emerose-grue level there is a $\frac{1}{n}$ chance that emerose is similarly related to grue.

On the other hand, the inter-level situation is more complex. What is the chance that a group specified by emerald necessarily implies a group specified by grue? Any group emerald specifies has a $\frac{k}{m}$ chance of being necessarily connected to some group at the emerose-grue level, and hence a $\frac{k}{2m}$ chance of necessarily implying some such group. But any group grue specifies has a $\frac{1}{n}$ chance of being a group necessarily implied by a group that emerald specifies. So there is a $\frac{k}{2(m \cdot n)}$ chance that a group specified by emerald also generates grue. It was shown that $k < m$ by indicating that there were inter-level lacks of connection. Now n is at least as great as m because there are multiple counterparts at the emerose-grue level for most properties at the emerald-green level. Therefore, support for the hypothesis that emeralds are grue is significantly less than that for the hypotheses that emeralds are green and that emeroses are grue.

Introducing grue-type properties does not destroy limited independent variety on the levels model, though it would if there were no levels. If there is limited variety at the emerald-green level, there will be limited variety at the emerose-grue level. For the properties at the emerose-grue level will then correspond to combinations of properties based on finite variety. The major difficulty is that we can use different critical times to determine the corresponding properties. Given an infinity of times, the emerose-grue level becomes a level of infinite independent variety. There would then be a grue for which the critical time is t_0, one for which the critical time is t_1, and so on. To counter this difficulty, each critical time must be associated with a different level. There would then be an emerose-grue-t_0 level, an emerose-grue-t_1 level, and so on.

§5. *The Statistical Case and Limited Variety.* Limited variety is also important in regard to the support of statistical claims by observed frequencies. The statistical hypothesis that all F have an $\frac{m}{n}$ chance of being H is supported by some ratio—not necessarily the projected ratio of $\frac{m}{n}$—of H's to F's in a sample. Assume the properties of the individuals in the sample are segregated into levels of limited variety in the sense of (I*). In each sample individual, the property F will specify a group at some level. If a sample individual has the property of having an $\frac{m}{n}$ likelihood of being H—

that is, the property $\frac{m}{n}H$—then either this property is at the level of *F* or at another level.

In asserting the statistical hypothesis on the basis of the sample, it is already believed—though, as I shall claim, not on the basis of a prior induction—that each sample individual has $\frac{m}{n}H$. For there to be support, each sample individual must have a chance of having the projected feature $\left(F\_ \rightarrow \frac{m}{n}H\_\right)$ necessarily. Thus, in any individual in the sample, either the property $\frac{m}{n}H$ follows from a group at the level of *F* or from a group at another level. With finite variety at each level and with connections among levels, there is a significant chance a group specified by *F* in each sample individual generates $\frac{m}{n}H$ in that individual. Given (II*), there is a significant chance that each sample individual has the projected feature of necessity. Where '*F*' is not a natural-kind term, induction beyond the sample requires a limitation on multiple generators for *F*. (III*) suffices for this.

Two consequences of this treatment of statistical induction may seem to weigh against it. First, when one considers whether a group that *F* specifies is a group that generates $\frac{m}{n}H$ in the sample individuals, it is assumed the sample individuals have $\frac{m}{n}H$. But the limited-variety model provides no account of how the fact that, say, $\frac{i}{j}$ *F*'s in the sample are *H*'s supports the claim that each sample individual has an $\frac{m}{n}$ chance of being *H*. In effect, then, my account treats $\frac{m}{n}H$ as a directly ascribed, rather than an inductively inferred, property of the *F*'s in the sample where $\frac{i}{j}$ *F*'s are *H*.[10]

Some will find this strange indeed. They will reason that, since one can be in error about the chance of being *H* while correctly noting the proportion of *H*'s in the sample, the chance is inductively inferred from that proportion. But by the same logic, they should object to treating the non-statistical properties emerald, green, and spherical as directly ascribed rather than inductively inferred. For, when one has limited acquaintance with a physical thing, one can be in error in ascribing to it one of these physical properties even while correctly describing one's sensations of it. Again, on the limited-variety model, there is no account of how sensations provide support for a claim that a thing has a certain physical property.

In general, the limited variety model is applicable only when evidence individuals can be supposed to have the properties mentioned in the corresponding hypothesis. But this is no objection if a distinction between conceptual interpretation and inference is granted. One conceptualizes a sample of a certain composition as made up of individuals with a definite chance of having a certain property. One conceptualizes an object of sensation as one with certain physical properties. Our mental pathways are such that, after having certain kinds of sensations, we say a thing is an emerald. Likewise, on observing a sample in which $\frac{i}{j}$ F's are H, we ascribe $\frac{m}{n}H$ to each of those F's, where normally the two ratios are equal. Described in this way, the matter does not require that our observations be converted into premisses for inductive inference. Since this description is available, it is not objectionable that the limited-variety approach to statistical induction treats the chances sample individuals have as non-inductively ascribed.

Second, in our account statistical properties are grounded in non-statistical properties. Thus $\frac{m}{n}H$ is grounded in, say, the group the reference property F specifies. But in familiar cases, it is not a group of properties specified by the reference property but chance variations in certain properties among individuals that are the source of a statistical property. The chance of one-half that a coin has to land on its head is not derived from a group specified by the property of being a tossed coin.[11] If it were, it would be impossible to devise a physical tossing device that controlled the initial conditions in such a way that the coin had to land heads up. Rather, the chance of one-half for heads depends on variations of the initial conditions from toss to toss. It depends, in effect, on the distribution of possible initial conditions, that is, on the chance that each one of various sets of initial conditions has of prevailing. On the other hand, the situation is quite different for an orthodox quantum entity. Such an entity does not depend for all of its statistical properties on chance variations in experimental set-ups. The chance that a radioactive nucleus will decay in a certain period is grounded in its internal structure, not in chance variations in circumstances.

Statistical induction, properly speaking, is, then, severely limited in extent. Suppose a sample does support an hypothesis. The hypothesis projects a statistical property, $\frac{m}{n} H$, over the reference class coextensive with F. It would then be incoherent to hold that this statistical property has no chance of being derived from a group specified by the reference property in a sample individual. For if there were no chance of this, there would be no chance that the individual has $\left(F\_ \rightarrow \frac{m}{n} H\_\right)$ of necessity. So if the statistical property is grounded only in the chance variations of circumstances into which individuals with the reference property enter, the sample does not support the hypothesis. It follows then that there can be statistical induction for uranium decay but not for coin tosses.

For consolation, one can complicate statistical hypotheses by adding antecedents to them that posit distributions of initial conditions. From a sample one can infer the hypothesis that any tossed coin has a one-half chance of landing heads up *provided* there is a uniform distribution of initial conditions. However, this is possible only if the sample individuals can be assumed to have the chance properties assigned by such a distribution. In many interesting cases, the distribution assumed on the basis of prior observation is doubtless false. The distribution assumed for a statistical political claim would, if correct, lock people into an eternal pattern of response to changing circumstances that is in fact only a reflection of the way current society has conditioned them to respond.[12] This is to assume a passive populace, whereas some "political action aims precisely at raising the multitudes out of their passivity."

Even so, only those statistical hypotheses with assumptions about chance variations of conditions built into them can be inductively inferred in a world in which the only properties derived from non-statistical ones are other non-statistical properties. Such a world need not be deterministic, for to say that being $\frac{m}{n}$ H is not generated by being F is not to say that being H is generated by being F. On the other hand, simple statistical hypotheses, which do not have assumptions about chance variations built into them, can be inductively inferred only in a world in which some non-statistical properties generate statistical ones. Such a world will indeed be non-deterministic. Since inductions to simple statistical hypotheses are not needed for the practice of action on prior experience, the fact that induction to simple statistical hypotheses requires a non-deterministic world does not imply that the required ontology is non-deterministic.

Statistical properties derived from non-statistical ones will, in Chapter X, be interpreted as dispositions for frequencies. Statistical properties depending on chance variations in conditions lack at least one feature of most genuine properties: they cannot be inductively projected. Thus claims apparently involving them are best viewed not as ascribing genuine statistical properties to individuals, but as saying what proportion of individuals in the reference class have a certain property.

CHAPTER VI

Analytic and a Priori

§1. *Truth and Rules of Meaning.* The view that the necessities required by induction are real stands in contrast with the view that whatever is necessary is so precisely because it is analytic. Moreover, the necessities important here need not be—as necessities are often supposed to be—*a priori*. To make the notion of real *a posteriori* necessity less mysterious requires a fresh look at the interrelation of the notions of the necessary, the analytic, and the *a priori*.

The necessity of a grain of salt to be water soluble and the necessity of the grain to be the same as itself are not different modalities. As was argued in Chapter II, §1, the necessity of a physical and that of a logical condition are identical. Of course, the conditions that are necessary—the necessities—are not identical, and the propositions—also called the necessities—made true by these conditions are not identical. It is widely thought that analyticity is the nature of the necessity of a logical truth.[1] Such a truth holds in all possible situations if and only if it has a form that makes it undeniable. But if the necessity of a physical truth and that of a logical one are not different—that is, if the univocity thesis holds—then analyticity is the nature of the necessity of a physical truth, and thus a necessary physical truth is necessary because it is analytic. In particular, the necessities required by induction are necessary, not because of what entities are, but because of linguistic rules. We cannot avoid this result by abandoning the univocity thesis.

For, as we saw in Chapter II, without it one can no longer claim that there is a genuine concept of physical necessity.

To illuminate the notion of real *a posteriori* necessity will involve two projects. First, to avoid putting analyticity at the basis of physical necessity, I shall try to show that analytic propositions may even be false. Mere form is no guarantee of truth. But if this is so, then analyticity cannot be at the basis of the necessity of a logical truth either.

The chief reason for holding that analyticity is at the basis of logical necessity is that the necessary truths of logic are thought to be vacuous. They are "vacuous" if there are no specific features that entities must have for them to be true. Now an analytic claim cannot be denied without a violation of rules. But despite this, may not what it claims misdescribe entities? Yet if the claim is vacuous this difficulty is blocked. For then it cannot misdescribe anything. So in view of their vacuity, logical truths can have a necessity whose nature is analyticity. But if analyticity is the nature of logical necessity, then analyticity is at the basis of physical necessity, according to the univocity thesis. An important part of the first project will, then, be to reject the view that logical necessities are vacuous.

Second, if a physical truth is necessary because it is analytic, then physical necessity would be intentional rather than real. The necessity of a physical proposition would imply that it had a certain relation to consciousness and not that the physical condition making it true results from the nature of the entities with that condition. But if the necessity is real, it not only does not come from analyticity but does not imply analyticity. So the view that physical necessity is real seems to commit me to the view that at least some necessary physical truths are synthetic *a priori*. For it is an old and respected doctrine that the necessary is also the *a priori*.

The logical empiricist philosopher will predictably recoil from this consequence.[2] But whether or not there are persuasive arguments against the synthetic *a priori*, it is well to point out that the dogma of the *a priori* nature of necessities is unsupportable. Once we reach this point we see that any one of the unspecified necessities called for by inductive practice may be at once necessary in the way a necessary truth of logic is necessary; synthetic in the way a claim that an entity has a certain definite condition is synthetic; and *a posteriori* in the way contingent claims about the world are *a posteriori*.

In carrying out the first project, I need to show that analyticity does not imply truth in the correspondence sense. The fact that it does not imply truth in the correspondence sense is at the basis of Quine's attack on the analytic-synthetic distinction. If we suppose there is such a thing as a rule of meaning for a term, as opposed to a rule of liturgy or a rule of clean speech, then an "analytic" proposition is one expressed by a sentence that cannot be negated without violating a meaning rule for one of its terms.* Now, by denying that a proposition will be true just because a sentence expressing it cannot be negated without violating a meaning rule for one of its terms, I am denying at least one sort of analytic-synthetic distinction. For I am denying that any proposition is guaranteed correspondence with entities just by its form or by rules for terms used to express it.[3]

Let us say a proposition is "ontically" analytic if it is expressed by a sentence that cannot be denied without violating a meaning rule *and* it corresponds to what entities are precisely because it is expressed by such a sentence. But how could linguistic constraints ever suffice for correspondence? Suppose, however, one switched from linguistic to conceptual constraints. An analytic proposition would be one whose denial involved a confusion about the concepts composing it. This does not help since concepts, like words, are inventions that may inadequately reflect the realities they stand for. So neither terms nor concepts can of themselves guarantee truth.

It might be objected that the defenders of analyticity never intended to claim that meaning rules generate truth in a correspondence sense. But if this objection were sound we could expect to find some alternative account of truth for analytic truths put forth by the defenders of analyticity who were attacked by Quine. There

*I purposely leave open the question of whether, if this is true of one such sentence expressing an analytic proposition, it must be true of any sentence expressing the same proposition. For the only reasonable way for this to be true would require a debatable dependence of propositional sameness on sameness of meaning rules.

is, however, rather general agreement among these defenders that no such account was needed. Indeed, an account along the lines of Tarski's semantic conception of truth[4] was adopted for logical truths, which were deemed the core of analyticity. In this account, the logical truth that *either Jones is tall or he is not tall* is true since, in this world of ours, Jones has the condition of being tall. Of course, it would also have been true had he been short. But the important thing for the defender of analyticity is that, by virtue of the meaning rules for the logical particles, the proposition is true in the sense that it corresponds to Jones's actual condition. Indeed, by virtue of these meaning rules the proposition would be true in any circumstances and is thus vacuous in the above sense. This does not mean that it corresponds to no condition of Jones. Rather, it means it would correspond to whatever condition—whether it is being tall or being short—Jones would have in any given circumstances.

One who denies a distinction between synthetic propositions and ontically analytic ones—because of denying that there are any ontically analytic propositions—may still hold that indeed there are propositions expressed by sentences that cannot be negated without violating meaning rules. Let us say a proposition is "neutrally" analytic if it is expressed by a sentence that cannot be negated without violating a rule of meaning for one of its terms. Now Quine has suggested a reason for rejecting even an analytic-synthetic dichotomy for neutral analyticity. He has challenged others to give an account of the notion of rule of meaning that does not rest on the notion of ontic analyticity. If the challenge cannot be met, the notion of a meaning rule is essentially empty since there is no ontic analyticity.[5] In effect, if by rules of meaning you must mean rules that of themselves can generate truth, there can be no such rules since it is wrong to think that there are truths generated by rules.

The mistake here is the supposition that a rule of meaning must be treated so that it is the sort of truth-generator required by ontic analyticity. Once we see that the role of rules of meaning is to establish fixed points of reference from which progress can be made in conversation and inquiry, the rules cease to depend on the possibility of their generating truth. Quine himself recognizes neutral analyticity and, consequently, rules of meaning in this non-truth-generating sense when he speaks of "analyticity intuitions."[6] Such intuitions, and hence the existence of the neutrally analytic, do not justify a "dichotomy between analytic truths as by-products of language and synthetic truths as reports on the world."

That there can be no justification for such a dichotomy should be evident from the frequent reminders we have that our language is not fully adequate to deal with the subject matters for which it was developed. We grope our way to more adequate concepts and to less misleading associations for corresponding terms. The following account for getting at this notion of adequacy for a certain subject matter is the basis for my contention that there may be false analytic propositions.

§2. *Reference and Inadequate Concepts.* Meaning rules, as I have just described them, relate term to term. But any full account of usage must consider the way terms relate to the world. One meaning rule will lay it down that 'fox' is not to be denied of anything 'vixen' applies to. Another will lay it down that 'green' is not to be affirmed of any surface to which 'red' applies to every part. But to what does 'vixen' or 'red' actually apply? Here one might appeal to other meaning rules; one might say these terms apply precisely where certain other terms apply. But the question of application continues to arise. There must then be an element in the usage of some terms that is independent of the linguistic relations posited by meaning rules. Such an element will enter into the account of how it is that humans use terms consistently, that is, apply them to or withhold them from roughly the same entities. It is part of such an account that the entities to which a term is generally agreed to apply will have similar components.

But this of itself is insufficient, since to account for the consistency of usage one must appeal to the fact that humans interact with some of these entities. Not any kind of interaction will do; it must be one yielding an experience. And the experience must be an experience of a condition of one of the entities to which a term is generally agreed to apply. The condition experienced must be a condition of having a component that is similar to components of the other entities to which the term is generally agreed to apply.

But, as was noted in Chapter I, §3, an experience need not be, nor need it involve, a judgment. Thus to appeal to experience in order to account for usage is not to introduce the conceptual apparatus of judgment. In particular, an experience of a condition need not be conditioned by having learned any meaning rules. Rather than involving a judgment, an experience is required to account for consistency in judgments.

This discussion complements that of signification in Chapter III, §3. There the signification of a term was said to be a collection of components of entities to which it applies. 'Red' signifies the rednesses of all the red entities. The components in the signification are, then, similar entities. (A fuller account would consider terms whose significations contain components that, though not all similar, all resemble one another in some way.) For simplicity, I shall speak in a Platonizing fashion of the red of all red entities, rather than more correctly of the collection of rednesses, as the signification of 'red'.

This tells us that the significations are components but not which ones they are. Clearly, a term's signification has something to do with its consistent usage. Indeed, in applying a term, without relying on inference or habitual expectation, to an entity with which one is presented, one generally experiences the condition of the entity's having the component the term signifies. This component is often a property, but it may be an action or even a physical part. I have not said that one applies the term because one reasons that, if the presented entity has the condition one experiences, then the term applies to that entity. Rather, the experience is part of the very application of the term. It is not a premiss from which the language user infers that the term applies. Similarly, between the objects of such experience, there is a basis for consistent usage of the term. Of course, a term is often applied to entities too far removed to be objects of experience or to entities which, though present, do not reveal all of their conditions directly. Nonetheless, to account for the consistent usage of such a term it will be essential to appeal to an experience of the relevant condition in at least some of the entities with the term's signified property.

Let F be a term and ϕ and ψ properties. Now one might apply F

directly on experiencing the having of ϕ. Thus *F* would signify ϕ. But what if one also applies *F* on experiencing the having of ψ? If one does this directly, then *F* signifies, in addition, ψ. But suppose one does it indirectly. That is, suppose one applies *F* to an entity on experiencing the condition of its having ψ, only because one has the belief that whatever is ψ is ϕ. Does *F* then signify ψ in addition to ϕ? Or suppose one applies *F* to an entity on experiencing the condition of its having ψ only because one accepts the meaning rule that *F,* which signifies at least ϕ, cannot be denied of an entity of which *G,* which signifies ψ, is affirmed. Experiencing the entity's condition of being ψ does not account directly for applying the term *F.* The application is mediated by transformations depending on general beliefs or meaning rules that relate several properties or several terms. But we want a signified property to be one that accounts for the application directly. The experience of a condition of having the signified property is a facet of consistent usage that involves a relation to the world that is not mediated by beliefs relating several properties or several terms. So in the above case it is ϕ, not ψ, that *F* signifies.

Ignoring terms with multiple significations, we have:

(1) A component ϕ is the "signification" of the term *F* if and only if (i) users apply *F* to roughly the same entities; (ii) a basis for this consistent usage is that (a) ϕ is common to those and only those entities to which *F* would generally be applied and (b) some users of *F* experience some of these entities' condition of being ϕ by interaction with them; and (iii) this experience is not a basis for consistent usage just because the users accept meaning rules for *F* or have beliefs in regularities for ϕ.

The signification is not just a common component, for there may be many such components. It is rather a common component that is a basis for consistent usage. Since signification is a matter of the relation of a term to the world and not of a term to other terms, there is nothing paradoxical in the idea that one could vary the meaning rules for a term without varying its signification. Suppose it becomes a violation of usage to say that *F* applies to that to which the term *G*—signifying ψ—applies, whereas previously *F* and *G* were unrelated by meaning rules. All that has happened is, doubtless, that a connection between ϕ and ψ that was already believed to hold has come to be taken as a settled matter. The property signified has not been replaced by a new one just because the term for it has come to be connected by a rule with another term. This is not to deny that a change of meaning rules can so alter the application of a term that in time it does come to signify a new property. But even when we alter radically our view as to which connections between a property signified by a term and other properties are to be taken as matters beyond further investigation, we may continue to use that term to signify the same property.

If, then, a meaning rule does not contribute to signification, to what does it contribute? I shall say it contributes to intension:

(2) The "intension" of a term is the collection of components of entities signified by the terms to which it is related by meaning rules for it.

The kind property signified by 'fox' and the property signified by 'female' are members of the intension of 'vixen'. The intension, though, divides into those properties deemed sufficient for the application of the term, those deemed necessary for its application, and those deemed exclusive of its application. Thus even greenness is in the intension of 'red' since 'green' cannot apply to that to which 'red' applies everywhere.

A term can have an intension without a signification. Suppose it is a recently coined term. Even though its application will involve the judgment that a certain property is present, this application will be indirect since it will depend on a meaning rule leading from the term for this property to the coined term. Until the term becomes familiar, it will not become associated with any property that is its own signification.

Do theoretical terms of science have, then, intension without signification? Nothing in the concept of experience I am using limits us to everyday, non-laboratory experience. The requirement of experience in the definition for signification can be met, in principle at least, for conditions of microparticles. Observing a diffraction pattern obtained by rebounding electrons from a metal grating may in some cases be an experience of the electrons' having a wave character. Davisson and Germer, who first made this observation, doubtless reasoned from it back to the wave character of electrons. But the observation of the pattern could become an experience of the wave condition; such an experience need not conceal an inference from a differently described experience by a meaning rule or an assumed regularity.

As regards signification of scientific terms, there are two separate questions. First, it might be wondered whether the consistent usage of scientific terms could be based on nothing more than their connections among themselves and to pre-scientific terms with their own signification. There is no obvious obstacle to saying this should be possible, that is, to saying that their having intensions alone would suffice for their consistent usage. Second, it might be wondered whether the terms, if they lack signification, can be used to make true or false claims that entities in the world have certain conditions. In the next section I shall try to show that without signification of their own these terms could not be used to make true or false claims. Kant expresses this view when he says that "knowledge of an object" requires that the object be signified and that this in turn requires that the object be experienceable.[7] "If we abandon the senses, how," he asks, "shall we make it conceivable that our categories . . . should still continue to signify something, since for their relation to any object more must be given than merely the unity of thought—namely, in addition, a possible intuition to which they may apply."[8]

Not only may a term have intension without signification, but it may also happen that a term may have a signification without an intension. It can come into use on the basis of the recognition of an associated property without any rule relating its application to that of other terms with signification. Indeed, two terms might signify different properties but have the same intensions. For, though they have come to be used on the basis of experience, no meaning rules may have been laid down to indicate that, say, the two terms exclude different properties. And even if they are finally differentiated by such rules, they may continue to signify the properties they did before.

Corresponding to the notions of signification and intension are those of reference and extension:

(3) The "reference" of a term is the class of entities having the component it signifies.

Just as reference is based on signification, extension is based on intension. But some complication is involved in considering the class determined by an intension. I shall mean by the class "determined" by the intension of a term that class of entities in which each member, first, has the components that, according to the meaning rules of the term, are needed for the term's application; second, lacks those components that, according to the rules, must be absent for it to be applicable; and, third, has any one of the components, if any, that, according to the rules, suffice for its application. So:

(4) The "extension" of a term is the class determined by the intension of the term when the intension provides at least one sufficient condition for the term's application; otherwise, it is the null class.

Clearly, reference and extension will not always coincide. (i) The reference of *F* might be included within its extension. This might happen when there is a meaning rule saying that whatever the term *G* applies to the term *F* applies to. For, in actuality, the presence of the property signified by *G* may simply not guarantee that of the property signified by *F*. In short, the meaning rule is misleading as to the real connections among properties. (ii) The reference of *F* may lie partly outside its extension. This would happen if there were a property that implies that signified by *F*, but there were no meaning rule taking this to be a settled matter. (iii) The reference of *F* may lie totally outside its extension. For the meaning rules may posit a necessary condition for *F* that is, in fact, only thought to be present when the property signified by *F* is present.

We can grasp the notion of adequate terminology in terms of the notion of signification. To enforce a meaning rule is to attempt to have language users treat a connection involving properties signified by the terms mentioned in the rule as fixed for further inquiry. Here I am assuming that the terms do have signification, for the question of adequacy arises only for such terms. But the meaning rule does not guarantee that the connection holds. I propose, then, a necessary condition for saying that our language for talking about certain aspects of entities is "adequate": the meaning rules for terms in that part of the language must not conflict with the connections that properties signified by those terms have to other properties. It would be overly demanding to say our language for a given domain is inadequate unless there is a meaning rule corresponding to *each* connection between any two properties, each signified by a term in that part of the language. Still, unless there are meaning rules corresponding to some of these connections, the language is, at best, a cumbersome guide.

I set out to show that if there are neutrally analytic propositions it does not follow that there are ontically analytic ones. That is, I set out to show that, even if there are propositions expressed by sentences that cannot be denied without violating meaning rules, there need be no propositions that are true by virtue of the meaning rules for terms in the corresponding sentences. This fact is easily seen to be contained in the fact that there can be inadequate terminology. In view of the distinction between signification and intension, it is clear that a term may signify a property even though this property does not have all the connections with other properties that, according to its intension, it does have. This lack of fit between actual connections and connections according to intension typifies an inadequate terminology. Now it is obvious that, if an analytic proposition is actually true, the connection among components that makes it true will agree with the intensions of the corresponding terms. But since a lack of fit is possible, the connection needed for the analytic proposition to be true need not obtain. In short, an analytic proposition expressed by inadequate terminology may be false.

From the point of view of reference and extension, the same result emerges. When the proposition expressed by *all F are G* is analytic, the extension of *G* contains that of *F*. As we saw, this is compatible with the possibility that the reference of *F* could fall, partly or entirely, outside the reference of *G*. So the analytic proposition may be false. And of course if it may be false, analyticity does not imply necessity. Newman captured this idea when he declared that "an alleged fact is not therefore impossible because it is inconceivable, for the incompatible notions, in which consists its inconceivableness, need not each of them really belong to it in that fulness which would involve their being incompatible with each other."[9]

As an example, consider the term 'isotope'. At one time it was reasonable to suppose that chemical inseparability from a given element was a part of the intension of this term. "Elements which are chemically inseparable, but have different atomic weights, were named by Soddy *isotopes*."[10] Later Urey investigated hydrogen isotopes. There was no serious doubt that the signification of the term was a component of deuterium. Deuterium had the kind property of the kind isotope-of-the-same-element. But Urey found hydrogen and deuterium could be chemically separated; deuterium is set free from oxygen after ordinary hydrogen in the electrolysis of water. The extension of the term 'isotope' excluded deuterium; the reference did not. The proposition expressed by 'Isotopes of the same element are chemically inseparable' was analytic, but it was false and thus not necessary.

What are the consequences of the alternative to this view? Suppose that meaning rules of themselves determine which properties terms signify. First, this alternative gives no assurance of a common subject matter for an inquiry that undergoes changes of meaning rules. For an inquiry maintains a common subject matter so long as its key terms have the same reference. Yet for this alternative, a change of meaning rules would change the signification and thus make possible a change of reference.

With the enlightenment afforded by the theory of special relativity, one recognizes that nothing satisfies the intension for the temporal term 'duration' as it would be used by a Newtonian. For it seems reasonable to say, with some interpreters of classical physics, that part of this term's intension as it was used by a Newtonian is the invariance of a duration on change of reference frame.[11] One would have to conclude, on the alternative view, that Newton spoke about nothing when he spoke about duration. To avoid this absurdity, it suffices to recognize that the component *duration* is a common signification of the term 'duration' as used by Newton and by the relativist. Nonetheless, this common component is related by each through different meaning rules to quite different properties.

Second, the alternative view, if consistently carried through, destroys any connection between general terms and the world. If to signify a property is merely to have certain conventional relations to other terms of the language, then those other terms will themselves signify properties merely by conventional relations to other terms. But this only produces a web of intralinguistic relations. To break out, we require that some of these terms have a stable use. But then we are back to the point of needing common properties and experiences of the belonging of these properties to entities to account for those uses. And this means the acceptance of terms with significations that have not been determined by meaning rules.

§3. *Are Logical Concepts Adequate to Logical Properties?* If we apply the preceding views to logical propositions, we arrive at the conclusion that even analytic logical propositions need not be true, and hence need not be necessary. This comes about because the logical properties possessed by entities may have connections among themselves that are not adequately represented by meaning relations between the corresponding terms. But what are logical properties?

Suppose that $(Fa \rightarrow Gb)$, where, in this section, the → replaces the commonly used *if-then*. Among the properties of *a* is the property it has when it is *F* only if *b* is *G*. I wish to suggest that this property is one of the properties in the signification of the →. If $(Ga \rightarrow Ha)$, then another property in the signification of the → is the property *a* has when it is *G* only if it is *H*. This multiplicity corresponds to the multiplicity of rednesses in the signification of 'red'. All the properties so far mentioned here belong to entities referred to from the antecedent of a conditional. In addition, there is the property *b* has when it is *G* if *a* is *F*, and that *a* has when it is *H* if it is *G*. These belong to entities referred to from the consequents of the above conditionals. Thus we can distinguish the signification of "antecedent →" from that of "consequent →." As before, it is convenient to speak in a Platonic manner of each of these significations as though it were a single property; in fact, each is but a collection of similar properties. I shall call the signification of antecedent → the "antecedent conditionality" property. It, like the "consequent conditionality" property, is a "logical" property.

Likewise, suppose it is true that $\sim Fa$ and that $\sim Gb$; the properties of a and b that make these propositions true belong to the signification of $\sim$. That is, the property a has when it is not F and that b has when it is not G belong to the signification of $\sim$. Treated as a single property, this signification can be called the "negation" property. And the property a has when it is F and b is G will be in the signification of the conjunctive connective $\cdot$. Likewise, this signification is to be called the "conjunction" property. Each of these logical properties is also a "complex" property; in describing it a logical connective is used in addition to at least one predicate. But this descriptive mechanism need not imply an ontological complexity.

However, there is one simple logical property, the "component" property. The property a has when it is F and that b has when it is G belong to the signification of the juxtaposition between subject and predicate, that is, to the signification of predication. The properties in this signification are part of what will be called the component property. But how can F be in the signification of both 'F' and predication? This would be absurd only if it implied that F alone is signified by a predication involving the predicate 'G'. But the signification of a predication anywhere involves both properties.

Now if entities have conditionality properties, one may go far wide of the mark in attempting to lay down, by meaning rules, just how these properties are related to other logical properties. Specifically, conditionality properties may have relations to conjunction and negation properties quite different from those expressed by the meaning rules of truth-table logic. Truth-table logic tries to tie the $\rightarrow$ down by proposing as a rule that $(Fa \rightarrow Gb)$ is not to be denied if $\sim Fa$ is affirmed. Thus it becomes analytic that $(Fa \rightarrow Gb)$ if $\sim Fa$. This analytic proposition may, however, be false since the intensions given by the meaning rules for $\rightarrow$ and $\sim$ may conflict with the connections between the conditionality properties and the negation property.

It is certain to be objected that the meaning rules of truth-table logic are used to coin terms, not to govern the use of established terms with significations. Thus it is preposterous to hold that a logical claim such as the above, which is analytic by truth-table rules, may be false.

In response, I shall face the objector with a dilemma. If, on the one hand, the terms are merely coined, then there is no basis for the truth, or even the falsity, of the resulting analytic propositions. If, on the other hand, the terms have significations, then if the analytic propositions expressed with them are true, their truth is not due to meaning rules. In either case, analyticity does not imply truth, and hence it does not imply necessity. I need to establish only the first horn of the dilemma, the second having already been dealt with. Grant that it is a rule that $(Fa \rightarrow Gb)$ is not to be denied when $\sim Fa$ is affirmed. This does not make it true that $(Fa \rightarrow Gb)$ if $\sim Fa$. All one knows is that the rule would be violated by denying the conditional. Indeed, at the times the terms are coined, there is no basis for $(Fa \rightarrow Gb)$ itself being either true or false. One has agreed to say it is true under certain conditions and false under others. But agreeing to say it is true under those conditions does not mean it is true under those conditions.

Likewise, if I agree not to deny 'There is an earth goddess under us' whenever we experience an earth tremor, my utterances of the sentence are still no more than ritualistic until such a time as experiences of earth goddesses become current. For the sentence with $\rightarrow$ and for the sentence with 'earth goddess' to express a truth or a falsehood, what the assertion is must be clear. Merely to agree that it can be asserted or denied when other sentences are asserted or denied is to be given no clue as to what it asserts. Indeed no condition is being asserted by the sentence when key terms lack signification. As determined merely by meaning rules "concepts are empty; through them we have indeed thought, but in this thinking we have really known nothing; we have merely played with representations."[12]

Though laying it down that things are true does not make them so, a term with signification can be used to express a true proposition. A term has signification only through widespread consistent usage ultimately based on experience. Logical predicates that can be used to express true propositions will have significations and hence widespread consistent usage based on the experience of entities' having logical properties. Analytic propositions expressed with such logical predicates may, then, be false. By a logical predicate I mean one, like '$(F\_ \rightarrow Gb)$', that signifies a logical property. If the logical predicates lack signification, then analytic propositions expressed by sentences involving them will be neither true nor false. A so-called interpreted logical system will, in general, not involve terms whose consistent usage is based on experience; therefore, the system's terms will lack significance and its analytic propositions will have no truth value.

I have not yet discussed the "universality" property. How could an individual have the universality property, when the very notion suggests that the property transcends individuals? But notice that $(x)Fx$ is equivalent to the conjunction $((x)Fx \cdot Fa)$, where a is an arbitrary individual in the range of x.* The property a has, when both it is F and $(x)Fx$, is a property in the signification of the universal quantifier. The universality property is this signification. Again, it is not a tautology, but a synthetic claim, that the universality property of entities is accurately represented by an analytic connection laid down for the universal quantifier in a given logic-*cum*-semantics.

Consider $((x)Fx \rightarrow Fa)$. This proposition is a logical necessity if, by nature, the connection holds that it asserts between, on the one hand, having the universality property and, on the other hand, having the corresponding component property. The antecedent is equivalent to $((x)Fx \cdot Fb)$, where b is an arbitrary one of the x's. Thus the conditional proposition asserts a connection–not between the proposition that $(x)Fx$, in the antecedent, and the proposition that Fa, in the consequent–but between a condition that any arbitrary individual, b, has and a condition that a has. One need not, then, resort to intentions, such as propositions, to discover the source of the necessity, for logical necessities are natural necessities. The above proposition is a logical necessity provided that, by the nature of b or as well by the nature of a, b's being such that it is both F and $(x)Fx$ implies a's being F. That is, $((x)Fx \rightarrow Fa)$ is a logical necessity if, by the nature of b or as well by the nature of a, b's having a property in the signification of the universal

*If this range is empty, then both conjuncts can reasonably be taken to be truth valueless, and thus the equivalence is not upset.

quantifier implies *a*'s having the corresponding property in the signification of predication.*

The so-called universality property and the so-called component property are in reality only collections of properties. So, to say that an entity has the universality property is to say only that it has one of the properties in the signification of the universal quantifier. To say that it has the "corresponding" component property is, then, to say it has that property in the signification of the predication operation that is described using the same predicate. Even the logically true $\sim(Fa \cdot \sim Fa)$ will be said to assert a connection—in this case, one of exclusion—between logical properties of *a*. The component property excludes the corresponding negation property.

The fact that variables for propositions are employed in the propositional calculus should not lead us to think that the logical necessities of this calculus are intentional simply because propositions are themselves intentional. Rather, we should consider that the propositions for which variables are employed are ones with references to entities; it is ultimately the natures of these entities that ground logical necessities. These necessities of the propositional calculus are laws of the real and not of the intentional.

§4. *The Factual Content of Logical Truths.* If logical connectives signify logical properties, meaning rules may be misleading in regard to connections among these properties. Analytic logical propositions may be false. To be true, the logical properties would have to have the connections asserted. Since entities must manifest these connections if there are to be logical truths, logical truths have factual content. There is a condition of an individual corresponding to the logical truth that whatever holds universally holds in an instance. In this case its condition is one of having a connection of implication between having the universality and having the corresponding component property. By requiring this condition in any individual the logical truth is not vacuous.

Opposed to this logical realism is the view that logical truths are

*In this case, if this implication holds by the nature of *b*, it will also hold by the nature of *a*. This indifference is associated with the fact that the necessity is logical. But as was shown in Chapter III, §2, it does not hold generally where the necessity involves more than one individual.

vacuous in the sense that no *specific* conditions of entities need obtain when logical truths hold. They would have factual content if, for them to hold, entities had to have some specific conditions. Even so, vacuous logical truths are thought to be true in a correspondence sense. For, no matter what conditions obtain for entities, it is these conditions that are thought to be the actual basis for the truth of logical truths. If no specific condition is required, then logical properties are not required and they become otiose. But if there are no logical properties, then logical connectives have no significations and are completely characterizable by meaning rules. Logical terminology cannot then be inadequate since there is nothing for it to be adequate to. Analytic logical propositions could not be false.

How might one support the vacuity thesis? Not, certainly, by pointing out merely that logical truths remain true no matter how the truth values of atomic propositions are varied. This only shows that if logical truths do require that entities have certain special conditions, these conditions are not ones that make atomic propositions true. Similarly, it does not suffice to point out that, since logical truths hold in all possible worlds, they are true no matter what properties entities have. For this is true only of properties that it is logically possible to vary. But the properties corresponding to logical truths would be precisely those it would not be logically possible to vary. Of course, to assume there are no properties which it would be logically impossible to vary would be to beg the question of whether there is a specific property that entities must have—say, that *b* has when it satisfies $((x)Fx \cdot F\_) \rightarrow Fa$—if a logical truth is to be true.

To make these arguments for the vacuity thesis work, it is necessary to add to them a premiss indicating precisely when complex properties are to be treated as superfluous. The logical atomist has tried to show that there is a reasonable basis for holding that no specific conditions are needed if logical truths are to hold. Such conditions, and logical properties along with them, are superfluous since they are superfluous in respect to atomic conditions and properties. This view is far from dead[13] despite old and unanswered objections to it, which are therefore worth repeating.

First, a word about complex properties. In our ontology, the important distinction as regards properties is that in Chapter V between basic and derived properties. Some basic properties may be complex—the property signified by the complex predicate '$(F\_ \rightarrow Gb)$' may well be basic for *a*—and some simple properties may be derived—where '$(F\_ \rightarrow G\_)$' signifies a derivational connection the simple property *G* will be derived in, say, *a*. The notion of a complex property is inevitably relative to a particular system of concepts, perceptions, or terms. Unlike the notion of derived property it is a notion that has import for the intentional rather than the real order. The property signified by '$(F\_ \rightarrow Gb)$' may belong to something that has neither *F* nor *G*. So this property will not be made up of *F* and *G*, which is as it should be in the component ontology for which individuals but not properties have components. The atomist says that predicates formed with the primitive ones of a system by the use of connectives do not signify properties. Since the distinction between simple and the rejected complex properties is relative to a system, one might suspect that it cannot have the ontological consequence the atomist wants to derive from it.

The atomist's argument can be put in the following form:

(i) Let *A* be a true complex proposition.
(ii) There is then a set of true simple propositions, *S*, sufficient for the truth of *A*.
(iii) So no more is required for the truth of *A* than is required for the truth of all the simple propositions of *S*.
(iv) Hence, there is no complex property such that when one or more entities have it *A* is true.

In particular, since logical truths are complex propositions, there are no conditions of having complex properties making them true. But they are also true no matter what simple properties entities have. Since, then, their truth does not depend on specific conditions—complex or simple—of entities, they have no factual content.

It is sufficient to consider examples from the propositional logic to see how the argument is flawed. Russell himself was worried about eliminating negative facts, and as regards negation I shall give a modification of his argument.[14] Where *Fa* is a simple proposition, suppose $\sim Fa$ is true. What simple propositions are sufficient for the truth of the complex proposition ~*Fa*? Now let *G* be a simple property that *happens* to belong to all and only those things to which the property *F* does *not* belong. Then *Ga* is sufficient for ~*Fa*. (In place of *G* we could have had a set of simple properties jointly coextensive with the complement of *F*.) The crucial question is: In what sense sufficient? If we mean sufficiency in the sense of material implication, then an arbitrary true simple proposition is a sufficient condition for any other true proposition. And thus, by the reasoning of the atomist's argument, the assumption of any more than one property in the world becomes gratuitous. For an entity's having any one simple property is a sufficient condition, in this weak sense, for the truth of any true proposition whatsoever.

To avoid this absurdity, 'sufficient' in (ii) should be construed in a stronger sense. But for any stronger sense that is not *ad hoc, a*'s having the property *G* is not sufficient for ~*Fa,* since by hypothesis it just happens that the extensions of *F* and *G* are complementary. Even if we adopted the different hypothesis that *F* and *G* do not just happen to be complementary, disaster would await us. For then there would be a true proposition containing both *Fa* and *Ga* for whose truth no simple propositions are sufficient in the stronger sense. So the inference from (i) to (ii) fails unless we accept the absurdity that there is only one property.

Suppose then we admit, over and above simple properties, the negation property, which *a* has by not being *F*. Is there now any reason to go one more step and admit properties corresponding to molecular complex propositions? Suppose the truth of *Fa* and the truth of *Ga* are sufficient for the truth of (*Fa* · *Ga*). If they are sufficient only in the sense of being a conventional basis for saying (*Fa* · *Ga*) is true, then indeed there is no point to positing, over and above simple properties, a conjunction property. For as was noted in §3, insofar as we only agree to take (*Fa* · *Ga*) as true when *Fa* is true and *Ga* is true, (*Fa* · *Ga*) is not yet actually true or false. Even so, the sufficient condition itself—the truth of *Fa* and the truth of *Ga*—is conjunctive. When this sufficient condition is satisfied, is there not something with a complex property described by the sign for some logical connective? Not, of course, if it too has a conventional basis for satisfaction made up of non-molecular positive or negative facts. We can imagine still higher conventions, each positing conditions that are satisfied without recourse to the realization of complex properties in the world in view of still higher conventions. So to escape complex properties we must agree that any bit of molecular discourse is prepared for by an infinity of conventions.

But there is an alternative to all this. At some point the sufficiency may not be conventional. The truth of certain simple propositions may not be merely a conventional basis for saying something complex, but rather a sufficient condition for something complex being true. The inference from (ii) to (iii) is then blocked, for a non-conventional sufficient condition is often quite distinct from what it conditions. Striking a match might be sufficient for producing a flame, but the flaming and the striking are nonetheless quite different processes.

In view of this failure of the logical atomist's argument, there remains no serious obstacle to supposing that there are complex properties. But if there are complex properties, there is no objection to saying that the truth condition for a logical truth is that entities have a specific complex property. That is, if there are complex properties, one can hold that logical truths are not vacuous. They have factual content even though they are true under any variation of conditions involving simple properties. The condition that entities must have for a proposition to be a logical truth is one that involves some connection among logical properties. The connections logical properties actually have are not determined by meaning rules for the corresponding logical connectives. Thus a proposition that cannot be denied without violating a meaning rule for a logical connective is not, for that reason, a logical truth. The meaning rules may misrepresent the connections among logical properties.

However, if the atomist is right, there are no logical properties, and hence logical propositions do not assert connections among logical properties. If logical propositions are analytic, there is, then, no room for saying they might misrepresent the connections among logical properties. Since the atomist's argument has been shown to be a failure, the analyticity of a logical proposition is not a guarantee of its truth and is thus not the nature of its necessity.

In view of the thesis of the univocity of necessity, it follows that neither a logical nor a physical proposition must be necessary because it is analytic.

An obvious consequence of the atomist's view is that analytic logical propositions cannot be false for any reason. It might be thought that they could be false even without the conditions of having complex properties playing the role of their truth conditions. For, nonetheless, the possession of simple properties will, by the meaning rules, be their truth conditions. And these rules may give a misleading picture of what these truth conditions are. Such simple properties are not the significations of complex predicates—such as '$((x)Fx \rightarrow F\_)$'—obtained by abstraction from logical sentences. Rather, they are signified by simple predicates.

However, falsity cannot arise under these conditions. Since there are no complex properties, the complex predicates will, in general, have no significations. The link between simple predicates and such complex ones is, then, by meaning rules. The net effect of these rules will be to tell us to take as true of any entity a logical predicate like '$((x)Fx \rightarrow F\_)$', no matter what simple predicate is true of it. By our earlier reasoning, this means, however, that only simple propositions will actually be true or false. The rest, including logical ones, will be neither true nor false since the sentences expressing them fail to meet the requirement of signification. Atomism then leads to the view that, though logical propositions can be analytic, they cannot be false since they are neither true nor false.

Earlier I granted the possibility that logical truths could be true in a correspondence sense even if they were vacuous. This possibility seemed warranted in view of the semantic conception of truth. But since then I pointed out that truth or falsity requires that terms be significant in a quite demanding sense. Since logical truths are vacuous for the atomist, logical terms within them will not have signification. Thus, for the atomist, nothing in logic can be true in a correspondence sense.

§5. *Two Classical Arguments for the Apriority of Necessities.* Once having set aside the notion that necessity has its source in analyticity, we have set aside a major obstacle to viewing necessity as real, that is, as being grounded in components of entities rather than in propositions, concepts, or terms about entities. We have shown that being necessary does not follow from being analytic. It is equally clear that the converse is true, that being necessary does not imply being analytic. For there is nothing in the notion that a proposition follows from the fact that an entity has a certain component—a nature—that implies the proposition cannot be denied because of its form. Of course, some necessary propositions are analytic; at best, this is a happy coincidence between natures and rules. We are then led to the view that there can be—and very likely are—synthetic necessities.

Are we thereby committed to the view that there can be—and very likely are—*a priori* synthetic truths? By an *a priori* truth, I shall mean one that can be confirmed, up to any degree, by methods other than those that are considered empirical. This description is intentionally schematic; no indication is given of what a non-empirical method might be, and for our discussion none need be given. Intellectual intuition has often been spoken of as a non-empirical method. There is also the method of examining the presuppositions of empirical methods, which I employed in Chapters IV and V.

Now one argument that leads from synthetic necessity to the synthetic *a priori* is Kant's argument from confirmation. If a proposition is necessary then presumably one can have a warranted belief that it is necessary. But how can it be warranted? Not, it would seem, through experience. For "experience teaches us that a thing is so and so, but not that it cannot be otherwise."[15] Some other method must be looked for. Only if the proposition can be confirmed by a non-empirical method can we have a warrant for asserting its necessity. According to Kant, using the non-empirical method requires a "faculty of *a priori* knowledge."

The validity of Kant's argument—the strongest and most influential for the apriority of what is necessary—is unquestionable. But the premiss about the limits of what is taught by experience is false. Indeed, if experience confirms any propositions it confirms explicitly modal propositions. For an assumption of necessities is behind all learning from experience. The form of assumption argued for in Chapter V is that the ratio of favorable to over-all possibilities for two of an entity's properties being necessarily connected is finite. On the basis of this assumption, there is finite support for their being connected necessarily.

Let us say further entities are observed, and they all have the one property if they have the other. Now if additional instances can increase the initial support for a universal claim, then additional instances will increase the initial support for a modal claim. If experience teaches anything, it can teach us something modal. However, this procedure differs from the one Kant mistakenly identified as the only way to learn a modal truth from experience. He thought he had rejected the possibility of learning a modal truth from experience when he rightly rejected the possibility of getting a measure of support for a modal claim only on the basis of experience. Here we have presented another possibility. A modal content is injected from the start into all learning from experience, for there must be the assumption of necessities. It is not then surprising on this basis that experience adds support to modal claims and thus teaches us modal truths.

Modal claims could be unconfirmed by experience only because there is no initial support for them. But if there is no initial support, there could be no chance that there are necessities, and hence no confirmation of non-modal claims either. This is not an *ad hoc* rebuttal of Kant's perceptive argument since it is a direct consequence of my argument for necessity as a presupposition of learning from experience. Moreover, it is not to be objected that the modal claims are *a priori* because the assumption of initial support is not based on experience. For, by our argument, the confirmation of even the most contingent claim involves a non-empirical assumption of necessities. The conclusion would have to be the absurd one that all claims about the unobserved are *a priori*.

Another argument is Hume's argument from inconceivability. If a proposition is necessary, Hume wanted to contend, its denial is inconceivable. In the special case of temporal succession, a necessary connection implies "the absolute impossibility for the one object . . . to be conceived not to follow upon the other."[16] To determine whether it is conceivable that the connection should fail, we have but to "compare these ideas" of the two objects. This comparison of ideas is a non-empirical procedure, and thus were there necessary connections we would confirm them *a priori*.

I know of only two ways in which conceivability is important to inquiry. In one way it enters as "weak" conceivability, and then the first premiss of this Humean argument—that necessities have inconceivable denials—is false. The denials of many necessities are weakly conceivable. In the other, it enters as "strong" conceivability, and then the second premiss—that inconceivability is an *a priori* affair—is false. The denial of a claim is strongly conceivable only if as one conceives of it, *a posteriori* considerations enter in.

The philosopher is adept at counterexamples that are weakly conceivable. He tells a logically consistent tale containing a counterexample to a certain view and a context for it. Yet when a natural scientist arrives at a counterexample to a theory by a thought experiment, he supposes not only that the story is a logically consistent one but that what happens in it is consistent with the natures of the things making up the context of the counterexample. Such a counterexample is then strongly conceivable. The counterexample typical of the philosopher serves only to show that the logical possibilities have not been exhausted by the view in question.

When only weak conceivability is required, it is false that counterexamples to necessities are inconceivable. At least it is false if there are non-logical necessities, and so far we have no reason to doubt that there are some. The counterexample typical of the natural scientist's thought experiment serves to show that the possibilities afforded by the natures of things have been underestimated by the view in question. But a sense of what the natures of things are rests on information derived from empirical investigation. So when strong conceivability is required, it is false that the inconceivability of the counterexample is an *a priori* affair. These matters admit of illustration, but hardly of strict definition.

Strawson provides an illustration of the usual way a philosopher puts conceivability to work.[17] The illustration concerns vision. Normally, the character of a visual experience depends on the state of the eye, the position of the body, and the direction of the head. Moreover, the dependency is on the eye, the body, and the head of one and the same animal. Now Strawson wants to show that this dependency on a single body is contingent. For, he says, one can imagine that a given visual experience depends on the state of the eye of one body, the position of another, and the direction of the head of yet another. He does not bother to ask how, given what is known about light, the eye, and the brain, factors at such diverse locations manage to come together to form a single visual experience.

The only work done before he claims that it can be imagined is the work done in checking the account of what is imagined for logical consistency. That is, he has checked to see that he does not contradict himself in saying that some visual experience depends for its clarity on the state of the eyes of a body in one room; for its range on a body in another room—only objects in that room are possible objects of the experience; and for its actual object on the direction of the head of a body in a third room—the actual object seen in the second room being selected by the direction of the head in the third. As merely an abstract exercise in not contradicting oneself, the construction of the counterexample fails to indicate—apart from the question begging assumption that all necessities are logical—that visual dependence on a single body is contingent.

To conceive a counterexample in the strong sense, it is not sufficient to juxtapose imagined things arbitrarily; they must be related in a way thought to accord with what they themselves are. There is a notable case where Einstein and Bohr differed on whether this condition was satisfied. Against the claim that definite values of position and momentum cannot simultaneously characterize a physical system, the following situation was imagined.[18] Two systems are in interaction up to a certain time; afterwards, they exist separately.

Because of the prior interaction, they are subsequently correlated. For if, after the separation, a position measurement is made on one of the systems, the position of the other system can be inferred. Similarly, if a momentum measurement is made on one, the momentum of the other can be inferred. The measuring device does not interact with the system with inferred values. But if either a definite position or a definite momentum value can be inferred, depending only on the choice of measurement to be made on the other system, then, Einstein concluded, the unmeasured system must have both definite position and momentum values. For if a student can answer correctly either the question "What is

2 plus 3?" or the question "In what country is London?" then even though, after answering the question asked first, the student becomes so confused that he or she cannot answer the other, it would be natural to say that, just before receiving the first question, the student knew the answer to both.

Now Bohr denies that this is a genuine counterexample to the disputed claim.[19] The question is whether it conforms to the nature of physical states. This is not just an *a priori* question, for answering it involves appeal to experimentally based claims about the nature of physical states. Physical states are, for Bohr, relational in that they exist only in relation to the application of some measurement device. The system separated from the one directly measured has, then, no definite position (or momentum) apart from that distant position (or momentum) measurement. Only on the supposition that it does—a supposition Bohr sees as incompatible with the quantum nature of states—is there a counterexample. If necessity were a matter of inconceivability and if Bohr were right that it is strongly inconceivable that position and momentum can simultaneously characterize a system, then the necessity of this incompatibility would not thereby be *a priori*.

The question of whether there is a synthetic *a priori* is left unanswered by these criticisms. There may be a synthetic *a priori*, but there appears to be no basis for believing that the synthetic necessities called for by the principle of levels of limited variety are *a priori*. That there must be some necessities is a condition of the reasonableness of action on prior experience. Thus this condition is not first confirmed by inductive practice, since it is required for inductive practice. If whatever is presupposed by human practice is *a priori*, then the existence of some necessities is indeed *a priori*. However, the apriority of this general condition for reasonable practice in no way implies the apriority of any specific necessities. As we saw, experience can confirm the necessity and hence the truth of specific necessities. But from this it does not follow that *a priori* methods are excluded for the confirmation of these necessities.

CHAPTER VII

The Myth of Relations

§1. *Necessity and Relations.* Belief in relations has had the authority of so many distinguished minds of the twentieth century behind it that it has by now become dogma. If an argument is needed to support belief in relations, one feels secure in merely repeating old points.

Great weight, for example, is still attached to the fact that Aristotle did not develop a logic of relations. His ontological emphasis on things and their (monadic) properties is thought to have rendered his logic incomplete. Even the validity of so simple an argument as "All doves are birds; so all wings of doves are wings of birds" cannot be proved in his logic. Yet it is far from evident that this logical deficiency resulted from an insufficient ontology. In fact, the validity of the argument can be proved in a logic appropriate to an ontology without relations. One gets such a logic by strengthening monadic predicate logic with a scheme for eliminating relational predicates. Part of my task, then, will be to develop such a scheme.

Moreover, great weight is still given to the seeming impossibility of accounting for facts of serial order solely on the basis of the properties of the entities ordered. For, without relations, a series seems to reduce to a mere collection. But perhaps it is possible to have relatedness—that is, a condition an entity has of being related to another—without relations, and, in particular, to have seriality without relations. I shall attempt to show that this is indeed the case. Relations, thought to be so secure, are supported only by a handful of arguments that falter under scrutiny.

The case against relations is as strong as the one for them is weak. So far, our reason for excluding relations from any ontology that includes the required ontology has been the following. Natures require an ontology of components rather than an ontology of simples. Yet a relation cannot be a component of its relata, where its relata are distinct entities. For a relation is unitary, and if it were a component, it would be a component of each of its relata. If it were a component of only some of them, then not all of them would be brought into the relationship. So, as a component of each, it has to be multiple in contradiction to its being only one.[1] But relations and properties should, it would seem, be given the same ontological status. If properties depend on individuals for their sameness and are thus components of individuals, then relations would seem to be similarly dependent and thus have the status of components. Thus there are no relations, since they cannot be components, and since components are the only things they could be.

It is the analogy between relations and properties that is the weak step in this argument. Can we not recognize natures and properties as components and make an exception for relations? After all, the argument of Chapter III for an ontology of components establishes only that natures must be components. Other entities are given the status of components, not out of any necessity but for the general coherence of the view. So a stronger argument is now needed against treating relations as distinct entities.

The image suggested by the doctrine that relations are distinct from their relata is that of a network of wires. Individuals are like rings to which segments of wire have been anchored. Since individuals stand in many relations to other things, rings anchor numerous wires linking them to other rings. Even nominalistic thinkers who do not admit that properties are different or distinct from what has them succumb to the network model of relations. Hume denies that a cube's blackness is different from the cube itself, but the idea of time is for him derived from a "succession of objects." This succession must be different from, and thus for Hume distinct from, the distinct objects in the succession, for otherwise there would be as many successions as there are objects succeeding one another, which is absurd.[2]

The idea of the universe as a collection of entities kept from being worlds apart by a constraining network has, then, become an unquestioned part of many different strands of philosophical thought. But inevitably the network model discourages reflection on the question of why entities have the relationships they do have. As distinct entities, relations are simply there between their relata; the relata provide no basis for selecting which relations will be there. You can link any two rings by any wire, and any wire between two rings can be replaced with another. That this is inevitable on the network model must now be shown.

This calls for showing that relations that are distinct from their relata are external. A relation is "external" if possession of it is not *essential* for any one of its relata. Traditionally, a relation was called external, in a second sense, when it was not a *component* of any individual.[3] Correspondingly, a relation is internal in this second sense when it either is a component of its relata or is a component of an encompassing individual of which its relata are also components.

Now it was thought that these two senses of externality had the same implications. The reason for this was the mistaken Humean belief that what is not distinct is inseparable and what is inseparable is not distinct. Thus, when relations are components of their relata and hence not distinct from them, their relata are inseparable from these relations, and hence have them essentially. Conversely, when relations are essential to their relata, they are not distinct from their relata and are hence components of them. Moreover, when a relation is a component of a whole encompassing its relata, neither the relation nor the relata are distinct from the whole; therefore, they are not distinct from one another, and are thus inseparable. Conversely, if they are inseparable, the relation is not distinct from the relata, which are then not distinct from one another, and thus the relation and the relata are components of an encompassing whole.

Since I reject the Humean premisses here, I must insist on keeping the two senses of externality apart. In fact, I shall henceforth take 'externality' only in the first sense, the one implying contingency. If it can be shown that relations are external when they are entities distinct from their relata, then it turns out that certain necessary connections needed for the practice of action on prior experience are denied. But, first, to show they are external.

If relations are distinct from their relata, what is the nature of their relation to their relata? There seem to be only two answers. Either there is a distinct entity that must be inserted between the relation and each of its relata, or there is, instead, either a component entity or no entity at all. Each alternative leads to the conclusion that if relations are distinct entities, then nothing has a relation to anything else.

The first alternative raises a difficulty made familiar by Bradley.[4] To posit, in addition to the relata *a* and *b* and the relation *R,* a third entity to relate *R* to *a* is like requiring that the wires in a network of wires and rings be tied to rings with additional wires. The third entity between *a* and *R* will be an entity signified by the word 'has' when we say that *a* has *R* to *b*. Let us call it the having entity, or simply *having*. There is now the question as to how *a* and *having* are related. How is the wire that ties the main wire to the ring itself tied to the ring?

Since *a* must have *having* to *R,* the above logic calls for a second having entity. There is then a regress of havings of *having,* since a further having entity is called for at each stage. However far one traces the regress, one gets no closer to satisfying the conditions for the truth of *Rab*. As is customary, this regress is taken here as a *reductio ad absurdum* of the view that relations need a distinct entity, *having,* in order to be related to their relata. But is there a viable alternative?

As for the second alternative, the truth condition for *Rab* includes no more than the three distinct entities, *R,a,b*. Here it is as though the main wires were simply twisted around the rings they connect in the network. There are no wires between the main wires and the rings. One way of describing this is to say that relations relate simply of themselves. One might then suppose that the ontological gulf between relations and relata has been successfully bridged without any entity at all. But has it been bridged? If a relation relates, then something needs to be said about how this comes about. Otherwise, one is not sure that is a viable alternative to the view Bradley expressed. There are several possibilities for describing how relations relate. The relating that a relation does might be a further distinct entity. It might, however, be a component of the relation. Or, finally, it might be that the relation is just the relating it does and nothing more.

If the relating is a distinct entity, then we are back to the case Bradley dealt with. There will be a relating of *relating* to the relation, and this pattern will go on endlessly. Suppose, however, the relating that the relation does is a component of the relation. Can a regress then be avoided? *Relating,* the component, would insure that the entity with it, the relation, did relate. But *relating* itself would not relate, as the relation does. A regress would not then get started by there being a need for a second *relating* as a component of the first *relating*. However, a regress does get started in a quite different manner. *Relating,* as something the relation does, is like an action of the relation. The relationship of *a* to *b* is then a result of the relating *R* does. The relation *result of* must in turn relate the relationship to the relating. And so the regress starts. The relationship of the relationship of *a* to *b* to the relating *R* does is a result of the relating *result of* does. So the quasi-agent view of relations, which attributes relating to them as a component, leads to a regress of relating *result-of* relations.

We are down, then, to the alternative of collapsing the difference between the relation and *relating*. This involves a change in perspective whereby a relation is no longer viewed as a quasi-agent that relates individuals to one another but is viewed as a quasi-process in which they come together. Now it is odd to suppose that the quasi-process of relating in which *a* and *b* are involved is an entity distinct from them. Yet on the supposition that relations are distinct entities, we are forced to say this. Our original problem was to find out how three distinct entities could form a unitary condition of relatedness. And replacing the relation with *relating* does not begin to solve this problem. For how can a relating that is distinct from both *a* and *b* become a relating of *a* to *b?* This is the same as the problem of how a relation that is distinct from *a* and *b* becomes a relation of *a* to *b*. To solve this problem, there is no choice but to revert to our already rejected alternatives. That is, *relating,* to which the relation is now reduced, will itself have to have *relating* as a component or as an entity distinct from it in order to bridge the gap. But this just leads back to the preceding difficulties.

In short, if relations are entities distinct from their relata, then nothing has a relation to anything else. But if nothing has a relation and if relatedness requires relations, then nothing is related to anything else. But clearly entities are related. So either relations are not distinct entities or relatedness does not require relations. If relations are not distinct, they are components. Yet Leibniz's argument makes it impossible to view them as components. So relatedness must exist without relations. However, the reason for positing relations is to account for entities being related. So since relatedness is incompatible with relations, there are no relations.

It is worth noting that the argument of the last few pages can be varied to show that if properties are distinct from the entities they qualify, nothing can have a property. Suppose the assumption of a distinct entity relating an individual to a property leads to absurdity. One is then led to ask how a property can by itself qualify an individual. It can if it has *qualifying* as a component. But *qualifying* is an action, just as in the above argument *relating* was an action. We are thus faced with a regress of *result-of* relations. Likewise, to say that the property just is *qualifying* is to raise the original question again, for one still wants to know how *qualifying* and the individual are joined, despite their being two distinct entities, into a unitary condition. So if properties and relations are distinct from individuals, nothing is qualified or related. To avoid this conclusion, I say that properties are components. But since relations cannot be components, we are still left with the result that, if relatedness is based on relations, nothing is related.

It is now time to observe two facts about necessity. First, the network model, which treats relations as distinct entities and yet as the only possible basis of relatedness, has the consequence that nothing is related to anything else. It certainly follows then that, if relations are still allowed to exist at all, they are external to individuals. For there is no relation an individual *must* have to something else, since there is no relation at all that it has to anything. And since relations are assumed to be needed for relatedness, yet are not had by any individuals, there is no way an individual *must* be related to some other individual, since there is no way it is related.

Second, the practice of acting on the basis of prior experience requires that there be necessities. Certain individuals will have certain properties of necessity, and they will thus be of necessity in the conditions of having these properties. But if there are relations, *condition of* is a relation. So at least this relation could not be external. For if no condition was a condition of any individual of necessity, all properties would be contingent. (Recall that conditions are distinct from their individuals.)

But we have just shown that, since relations must be distinct entities, entities are not related by relations and hence are not necessarily related by relations. If relations are the only bases for relatedness, nothing can be necessarily related to anything, and hence, in view of *condition of,* there are no necessities of any kind. An ontology of relations and the practice of acting on prior experience are incoherent.

This conclusion was clearly stated by Whitehead when he argued that unless "the relationships of an event are . . . constitutive of what the event is in itself" induction fails "to find any justification within nature itself."[5] By a constitutive relationship he meant not a relation, but what in the next section I shall call a relational property. Since if there were relations, there would be no basis for relatedness other than relations, inductive practice is reasonable relative only to an ontology without relations. Strange as it sounds, a condition for there being entities that are necessarily related is that there be no relations. To make sense of this, we must now provide an interpretation of being related that does not appeal to relations.

§2. *Relational Properties and Their Foundations.* In my interpretation of how things are related, two kinds of entity will play a crucial role: relational properties and their foundations. If six is greater than five, then six has the relational property *greater than five,* which is to be distinguished from the relation *greater than.* Relational properties, unlike relations, can be components. But, as components, they are not composites of relations and their relata.[6] For if relations were parts of relational properties, then relations would be components of individuals, which they cannot be in view of Liebniz's argument. Moreover, since five is not a part of *greater than five,* one cannot say there is an *x* such that six has the relational property *greater than x.* Positions in relational property predicates are not open to quantification.

To each relational property there correspond several foundations.[7] To six's relational property *greater than five* there correspond the magnitudes of six and five. One foundation alone is insufficient for a relational property. It is six having its magnitude and five having its magnitude that is the basis for six having such a relational property. The same pair of foundations in the relata will also be the basis for a relational property in five, the property *smaller than six.*

Relational properties are correlated, though foundations need not be. That is, when Smith is taller than Jones, Smith's having the relational property *taller than Jones* will coimply Jones's having the relational property *shorter than Smith.* But where their respective heights are the foundations, Smith's having the height he has will not imply, or be implied by, Jones's having the height he has.

Still, taken together, the foundations coimply the relational properties. If Smith has one height and Jones has a dissimilar height, one of them will be taller than the other. The implication in the opposite direction seems at first sight more controversial. One wants to say that being taller than Jones is associated with many heights, and thus Smith's having this property cannot imply a particular height for Smith and one for Jones. But this is to overlook the difference between relational properties and relations. Indeed, Smith's being a relatum of the relation *taller than* does not imply a specific height for Smith and one for Jones. But here the property of Smith, *taller than Jones,* is in question. And observe that this property is correlated with *shorter than Smith,* and is thus not similar to Hayes' property *taller than Jones,* since this is correlated with the clearly dissimilar property *shorter than Hayes.* Of course, it would be appropriate to call them similar if the relation *shorter than* were a component of both the correlated properties, *shorter than Smith* and *shorter than Hayes.* But there are no relations. So Smith's property *taller than Jones* is quite specific enough to imply specific heights for both Smith and Jones.

On the one hand, it will not do to interpret relational claims just in terms of correlated properties. The reason for this is that the correlated properties involved must be of a special sort. They must be correlated because they have the same foundations. Correlated properties at the basis of a relationship—that is, properties that by their presence make a relational claim true—rest in their turn on foundational properties. The correlated properties might be correlated simply because the entity with one of them is in causal interaction with the entity with the other. And in this case no foundations would be required for the two properties. Neighboring warm bodies affect each other's temperature, and for this reason their temperatures are correlated. But it does not at all follow that their temperatures are relational properties.

On the other hand, it will not do to interpret relational claims merely in terms of pairs of properties that happen to be foundations. For it needs to be explicitly mentioned that the properties in these pairs are indeed the basis for correlated properties. Relatedness does not consist in the foundations just by themselves, but in the correlation of the relational properties based on the foundations. To interpret relational claims without making this explicit would be to give the misleading impression that the correlation of relational properties is an accidental by-product of relatedness. Nonetheless, relational properties are ontologically dependent on foundations and thus derivative ontologically from foundations. The asymmetry required for this dependence comes from the fact that, in general, one can have one foundation without the other and hence without either relational property, but never one relational property without one of the foundations.

We can, then, leave out neither the correlation of relational properties nor the basis for relational properties in foundations. Thus where *Rab* is a singular relational claim, the following equivalence will be true:

$$(1) \qquad Rab \leftrightarrow (fa \cdot (fa \leftrightarrow gb) \cdot (fa \leftrightarrow (Fa \cdot Gb))).$$

Here f and g are properties correlated between the relata a and b. And F and G are the foundations, in the distinct relata, of these correlated properties. Having foundations, the correlated properties are relational properties. Of course, one need not know which relational properties and which foundations will do the trick for the specific case of R holding from a to b. Nonetheless, when they are found, one knows what it is that makes a relational claim true. (In §3, which follows, I shall make clear that relevant coimplication provides a natural interpreation of at least the $\leftrightarrow$'s on the right-hand side of (1).)

Though (1) indicates how singular relational propositions can be true without relations, it is not adequate as a pattern for eliminating relational formulas in quantified propositions. I shall try to indicate why this is so. Consider the quantified proposition that every number is less than some other number. Working on the basis of (1), it might be thought that this is equivalent to the proposition that $(x)(\exists y)(fx \cdot (fx \leftrightarrow gy) \cdot (fx \leftrightarrow (Fx \cdot Gy)))$. But this would be a mistake. For f here is some fixed relational property such as *less than ten*, and as such it is correlated with—that is, it coimplies—another fixed relational property, say *greater than eight*.

Thus only the number eight has this particular relational property *less than ten*. The relational property *less than ten* that the number nine has is not similar to the one eight has since it is correlated with the dissimilar property *greater than nine*. Moreover, the foundation F here is some fixed foundation, say the magnitude of eight, and clearly not every number has this magnitude. In short, though it is true that every number is less than some other, our monadic counterpart is plainly false.

This can be taken to indicate that quantified relational claims are incompletely expressed. To say that every number is less than some other number is, in fact, to say that every number is less than some other for some pair of relational properties associated with *less than* and for some pair of foundations associated with *less than*. To make this clear, I must clarify what it is for an entity to be "associated with *less than*." The four features f,g,F,G are associated with *less than* when the following two conditions are satisfied. For some pair of individuals, say, a and b, (i) $(fa \cdot (fa \leftrightarrow gb) \cdot (fa \leftrightarrow (Fa \cdot Gb)))$ and (ii) $(a$ is less than $b \leftrightarrow (fa \cdot (fa \leftrightarrow gb) \cdot (fa \leftrightarrow (Fa \cdot Gb))))$. I shall symbolize the fact that f,g,F,G are associated with R by '$f,g,F,G \in \mathrm{R}^*$'.

I am saying, then, that $(Qx)(Qy)Rxy$ incompletely expresses what is completely expressed as $(Qx)(Qy)(\exists\phi,\psi,\theta,\zeta \in R^*)Rxy$. Here (Qx) is either the universal or the particular quantifier. Now the quantification over ϕ,ψ,θ,ζ is intended to capture variables concealed in Rxy. This makes it reasonable to see Rxy in this context as having the structure $(\phi x \cdot (\phi x \leftrightarrow \psi y) \cdot (\phi x \leftrightarrow (\theta x \cdot \zeta y)))$. Thus there is the equivalence:

(2) $(Qx)(Qy)(\exists\phi,\psi,\theta,\zeta, \in R^*)Rxy \leftrightarrow (Qx)(Qy)(\exists\phi,\psi,\theta,\zeta \in R^*)(\phi x \cdot (\phi x \leftrightarrow \psi y) \cdot (\phi x \leftrightarrow (\theta x \cdot \zeta y)))$.

Since R^* has been defined on the basis of the equivalence for singular relational claims, its presence does not imply that one must still contend with relations. The view of relational claims embodied in (1) and (2) is easily extended to ternary and other higher cases. Where there are three relata there will be three correlated relational properties and also three foundations that together are sufficient for each of the relational properties.

Philosophers who spoke of foundations for relational properties emphasized the role of quantity and action as foundations.[8] "Since relation [i.e. relational property] has the weakest existence, because it consists only in being related to another, it is necessary for a relation to be grounded upon some other accident. . . . Now relation is primarily founded upon two things which have an ordination to another, namely quantity and action. For quantity can be a measure of something external, and an agent pours out its action upon another."[9] Having already said something about a relational property based on quantity, let us turn to one based on action.

The relational property *parent of Otto* belongs to Hugo since Hugo has as one of his components a mating action and since one of Otto's components is his existence, which comes about as a result of the mating action.[10] The foundational components of Hugo's relational property are his act of mating and Otto's existence. Now it will be objected that the fact that Hugo mated and Otto exists does not logically imply that Otto was the offspring. Only if we add that Otto's existence came about as a result of the mating can this logically follow.

But it was not claimed that the implication from foundations to relational properties had to be of this logical character. All I have claimed is that the presence of certain components, by being the ontological base for relational properties, implies the presence of certain relational properties. In the special case of Hugo, his mating and Otto's existence are physically, though not logically, sufficient for his being a parent of Otto. If we had to rely on the existence of the relation *comes to be as a result of* between Otto's existence and Hugo's mating for it to be the case that Hugo did beget Otto, then Hugo would not only have to mate but he would also have to act to bring about this relation in order for him to acquire the relational property. To avoid the regress implied here, the action of mating and the component of existence (it can be a component without being a property) must be the foundations for the relational property *parent of Otto*.

It is important to keep in mind that relational properties in respect to distinct individuals—say, *parent of Otto* as compared with *parent of Felix*—are not similar. Hugo's mating and Otto's existence imply Hugo's being the parent of Otto. This does not mean that Hugo's mating and Felix's existence lead to Hugo's being the parent of Felix, for clearly Barnabas may be the male parent of Felix. Given the first implication, the second might well hold if the relation *parent of* were a component signified by a part of each of the consequents, which it is not. Since, however, the relational properties *parent of Otto* and *parent of Felix* are dissimilar, the second implication need not hold. Our principles do not lead to the absurdity that Hugo is everyone's parent.

Conversely, even though Hugo's mating and Otto's existence lead to Hugo's being a parent of Otto, it does not follow that Barnabas's mating and Otto's existence lead to Barnabas' being a parent of Otto. For, despite linguistic similarity, *parent of Otto* as had by Hugo is correlative with *child of Hugo* and would thus not be similar to *parent of Otto* as had by Barnabas, if contrary to fact Otto could have two male parents. For as had by Barnabas *parent of Otto* would be correlative with the clearly dissimilar property *child of Barnabas*. So our principles do not lead to the absurdity that Otto is the child of everyone who mates.

§3. *Asymmetry Without Relations.* Apart from objections to the details of my specific program to eliminate relations from relatedness, there are some familiar objections to the general program of doing without relations. Perhaps the best known is Russell's objection that asymmetry cannot be accounted for if there are properties but no relations, that is, if what he calls monadism is true.[11]

Russell's objection contains a misconception about relational properties. His objection can be formulated as follows. Suppose R is asymmetrical, so that if Rab then $\sim Rba$. Let (Rb) and (Ra) be the relational properties *R to b* and *R to a*. In view of the asymmetry, if $(Rb)a$ then $\sim(Ra)b$. Since R is irreflexive if it is asymmetrical, it will not be the case that $(Ra)a$. So (Ra) and (Rb) are not similar properties, for $(Ra)a$ cannot be true though $(Rb)a$ may be true. Since asymmetry involves both relational properties, one cannot account for asymmetry without accounting for their not being similar. But it would seem that only by saying that (Rb) is composed of b and that (Ra) is composed of a can one explain how the two properties are dissimilar. If this is the root of their dissimiliarity, then how can one escape the existence of relations? For if (Rb) is composed of b it is also composed of something that relates a to b. This something must be R itself. Likewise, (Ra) must be composed of R as well as of a.

In the monadistic view of §2, however, there is no need to account for the dissimilarity of the above relational properties by appeal to their composition. Of course, if one supposes they are composite, as Russell never doubts they are, then one will drag relations out of them. If, however, the connection between relational properties and foundations is kept in mind, there is no temptation to resort to the composition of relational properties to explain their dissimilarity. Russell's mistake[12] was to treat foundations and relational properties as belonging to two different analyses of relations. In fact, any adequate analysis must include both. If Rab is true there will be foundations F and G such that $(Rb)a$ coimplies $(Fa \cdot Gb)$. And if Rba were true, there would be foundations H and K such that $(Ra)b$ would coimply $(Hb \cdot Ka)$. This is the explanation of the dissimilarity between relational properties implied by asymmetry. It is their derivations from different foundations that account for their dissimilarity. Even where F is similar to H and G is similar to K, the derivations are from the two different bases, $(Fa \cdot Gb)$ for the relational property (Rb) and $(Fb \cdot Ga)$ for the relational property (Ra).

One will still want to know how asymmetry comes from dissimilarity, which is symmetrical. Suppose $(Rb)a$ has as its foundational base $(Fa \cdot Gb)$. If this is also the base for $(Ra)b$, then R is indeed symmetrical. The relatedness is asymmetrical not just when the relational properties are dissimilar. Rather, associated with this dissimilarity must be an incompatibility of foundational bases. If the base for $(Ra)b$—say $(Hb \cdot Ka)$—is incompatible with that for $(Rb)a$—$(Fa \cdot Gb)$—then R is asymmetrical.

Let me turn now to some other questions about monadism. Does the monadistic view, as expressed by (1) and (2) of §2, preserve the customary connections between properties of relations? Earlier formulations of the monadistic view were some version of the claim that Rxy is equivalent to $(Fx \cdot Gy)$. But this has the immediate consequence that symmetry implies reflexivity.[13] For if $((Fx \cdot Gy) \supset (Fy \cdot Gx))$ then $((Fx \cdot Gy) \supset ((Fx \cdot Gx) \cdot (Fy \cdot Gy)))$. Yet there are symmetrical irreflexive relations such as *spouse of*. But relatedness involves not just a conjunction of foundations but also the grounding of relational properties in foundations. When treated in this way, the connections among the properties of relatedness are precisely the customary ones. Thus asymmetry implies irreflexivity. For to say that R is asymmetrical is to say that $(x)(y)((\exists \phi,\psi,\theta,\zeta \in R^*)Rxy \supset \sim(\exists \phi,\psi,\theta,\zeta \in R^*)Ryx)$. Replacing '$Rxy$' here with '$\phi x \cdot (\phi x \leftrightarrow \psi y) \cdot (\phi x \leftrightarrow (\theta x \cdot \zeta y))$' and '$Ryx$' with a corresponding formula allows one to derive the proposition that $(x)\sim(\exists \phi,\psi,\theta,\zeta \in R^*)(\phi x \cdot (\phi x \leftrightarrow \psi x) \cdot (\phi x \leftrightarrow (\theta x \cdot \zeta x)))$.

Apparently, one of the most damaging objections to monadism has been that it allows the derivation of quantificational laws that are not valid. Thus it is claimed that, if monadism holds, then the doubly quantified claim that $(x)(\exists y)Rxy$ will imply that $(\exists y)(x)Rxy$.[14] Since this implication does not in general hold, monadism must be false. However, the objection is based on the assumption that monadism must treat Rxy as a truth function of monadic formulas. On this assumption, the illegitimate switching of quantifiers is indeed sanctioned. But should we grant the assumption?

A consideration of the correlation of relational properties and of the basing of relational properties on foundations reveals that it would be incorrect to treat the conditionals on the right-hand side of (1) and hence of (2), of §2, as truth functions. Relational properties are not correlated simply because of a similarity of truth values of corresponding atomic sentences. They are correlated since a relatum's having one of them depends (in a way that does not involve context) on the other relatum's having the other. To try to express what is involved in a relatedness claim without expressing such a connection between the relational properties would be to give an incomplete account of relatedness. Likewise, basing relational properties on foundations is a matter of (non-contextual) dependency and not of a similarity of truth values. Relational properties are properties that relata have because there are certain foundations in those relata.

Let us consider the exact point at which the kind of conditional involved becomes crucial. To show that (2) allows the illegitimate switching of quantifiers around Rxy, one must show that they can be switched around $((\phi x \leftrightarrow \psi y) \cdot (\phi x \leftrightarrow (\theta x \cdot \zeta y)))$. If this is possible, then it is possible to derive $(\exists y)(x)(\phi x \leftrightarrow \psi y)$ from $(x)(\exists y)((\phi x \leftrightarrow \psi y) \cdot (\phi x \leftrightarrow (\theta x \cdot \zeta y)))$. But for this to be possible it will have to be the case that $((y)\psi y \rightarrow (x)\phi x)$ implies $(\exists y)(\psi y \rightarrow (x)\phi x)$. Though this is notoriously the case for material implication, it is not the case for any implication that expresses the way relational properties are correlated. Intuitively, it does not follow from the premiss, that if everyone is comradely there will be peace, that there is someone such that if he or she is comradely there will be peace. Strict implication satisfies this intuitive requirement, but it suffers the limitations discussed in Chapter II, §2, that make it unsuitable as a device for understanding natural connections generally. This makes relevant implication an obvious candidate for the implication connecting correlative properties among themselves and to their foundations.

A final objection to the general program of monadism concerns the undecidability of first-order quantificational logic. If one eliminates all but monadic predicates by applying (1) and (2) and their counterparts for higher adicity, then what was first-order logic becomes first-order monadic logic, which is decidable.[15] But if (1) and (2) are genuine equivalences, how can they turn an undecidable into a decidable system? So it seems that monadism cannot be correct, whatever form it takes. Though (2) does introduce higher-order quantifiers, they can effectively be ignored in making inferences within first-order logic. So their presence will not introduce the needed undecidability. Moreover, if the → is a relevant implication, as I have taken it to be, then the first-order monadic logic will be undecidable,[16] as the standard first-order monadic logic with truth functions is not. But I do not choose to save the day in this way, since there is a more important mistake lurking behind the objection.

There is simply no reason to expect that the elimination of the polyadic predicates should leave us with an equivalent logical system. For these predicates will, in general, be non-logical expressions. Thus to state a connection between them and an expression for what must be the case for them to apply will not be to state a logical law. (1) is no more a logical law than is the claim that humans are rational animals. However, in order to state the correct connection between necessity and possibility or between disjunction and conjunction one will need to state a logical law. So a propositional calculus from which disjunction has been eliminated might well be equivalent to one with disjunction. The equivalence of the two logical systems will require that it be a law of the system with disjunction that the connection hold between disjunction and conjunction that was used for the elimination.[17]

But there is no question of (1) being a logical law. To assume (1) for purposes of eliminating polyadic predicates is not to assume something that can be proved as a logical law in a system with polyadic predicates which purports to be a logical system. To assume (1) and similar equivalences for other polyadic predicates and other relata is to assume a host of non-logical claims. Since the elimination is based on such claims, it is not at all surprising that these claims can be true even though the resulting logical system is not equivalent to first-order logic.

§4. *The Interconnection of the World.* A philosophy that denies relations as entities distinct from their relata would seem committed to separateness, whereas a philosophy of relations as distinct entities would seem committed to togetherness of entities. But we have seen that a philosophy of relations as distinct entities is committed to the view that there is such a gap between individuals and relations that what the individuals are cannot affect what relations they have. If relations make for togetherness, it is an imposed togetherness, and the relata have nothing to do with its maintainence. In short, it is not a togetherness at all.

On the other hand, the paradox is rounded out when it becomes clear that the denial of relations as distinct entities in the context of our required ontology excludes separateness and introduces togetherness. There are many ways in which individuals are together in the world, and any view that obscures this fact is in some way wanting. The togetherness must be understood in such a fashion that it is internalized by the entities involved. That is, their relatedness is not external to them but is both based in their components—the foundations—and reflected in their components—the correlative properties.

If *F* and *G* are foundations, there will be some relational property *f* such that when *a* has *F* and *b* has *G a* will have *f*. This is not just a contingent connection. Suppose *Fa* means that *a* is male and mates, and *Gb* means that *b* exists. Suppose further that *Fa* and *Gb* suffice for *fa,* where *fa* means *a* is the father of *b*. They suffice for *fa* not because of any special circumstances. Rather, they suffice simply because it is of the nature of each of the individuals involved—*a* and *b*—that when they have these foundations *a* has the relational property of being *b*'s father. Of course, if *father of b* and *father of c* are mistakenly treated as similar properties, then it will seem that the connection is at best contingent. For where *c* is not *a*'s son, (*Fa* · *Gc*) does not imply that *a* is *c*'s father.

Now the notion of togetherness, or relatedness, can be interpreted in the light of this necessary connection. Two individuals are "together" when their natures are such that each is determined to have a relational property by a pair of non-relational properties whose members do not belong to the same individual. Since it is the nature of the individuals that is behind such determination, no mere accident accounts for the way they internalize one another. Each "internalizes" the other when it has one of a pair of relational properties as a component. Put another way, it is the natures of the relata that give certain of their components the status of foundations. Those components are foundations when it is the natures of the individuals which have such components that they also have certain relational properties.

This is so far only one side of the story. Not only does (*Fa* · *Gb*) necessarily imply *fa,* but also, in some cases, *Fa,* under appropriate circumstances, necessarily implies *Gb*. When this is the case, I say that not only are the individuals together but that they are "necessarily together." If they have properties from which relational properties are derived, they are together; if, in addition, one of the foundations is necessarily connected with the other, they are necessarily togther. Necessary connections across time between foundations of relational properties are one form of necessary togetherness.

But are relations being reintroduced here in the guise of necessary connections? As always, such a connection is merely the necessity of a conditional. It is the necessity in certain circumstances of *a*'s having ($F\_ \rightarrow Gb$). So if relations are abandoned, there will be reliance on properties described by means of logical connectives. But independent reasons were already adduced for the existence of such properties in Chapter VI. These properties are then not an extravagant price to pay for relatedness without relations.

Togetherness does not, in this view, require a "pre-established harmony." Leibniz was forced to postulate such a harmony, not because of his rejection of relations, but because of the special way he conceived of natures. A Leibnizian nature accounts for every condition the individual has. This conception seems at first to conflict with Leibniz's view that every individual "mirrors" all the other individuals. There are what appear to be causal reflections, such as heat due to fire. And there are non-causal ones, such as Caesar's difference in make-up from the Rubicon. But the heat of an individual is not really due to the burning of another, and Caesar's being of a different stuff from the Rubicon is not really due, even in part, to the watery stuff of the Rubicon. Otherwise, the natures of the hot entity and of Caesar would not fully determine their conditions. So to account for the fact that there is a correspondence, Leibniz must go back to the source of the corresponding natures. God chooses individual natures that do in fact correspond. The correspondence of conditions between individuals cannot result from a mutual dependence of these conditions.

Otherwise, not all conditions would flow from the natures of the individuals with them.[18]

To avoid making the source of togetherness external, it suffices to modify Leibniz's notion of a nature. The notion of nature developed here grants that some conditions of an individual are not due to its nature. In particular, an individual might be in the condition of having a relational property contingently. Having that property could then depend on the features of another individual that, in fact, exists only contingently. The source of togetherness is then in the individuals related and not beyond the world of concrete individuals.

It is well to note that if *a* had the relational property *f* by its nature then it would be true that $\Box\, a(Fa \cdot Gb)$ and hence that $\Box\, a(Gb)$. There will then be a strict correspondence between *a* and *b*. This suggests a way Leibniz might have had of avoiding the pre-established harmony without giving up his conception of natures. For *b*'s burning might be held to be a consequence of *a*'s—the heated object's—nature. And the Rubicon's wateriness might be held to be a consequence of Caesar's nature. But such possibilities are too remote to be given serious treatment.

Still, it might seem objectionably mysterious that it is by nature that an individual should have a relational property when it has a certain foundation and another entity with which it need not be interacting has a certain foundation. For how can its nature "know" that the isolated individual has the appropriate foundation? A telepathic power seems to be required. Short of this, and without relations, a pre-established harmony seems needed.

This objection could be sustained if the relevant notion of nature were Locke's notion of a constitution of small particles. For then, indeed, a nature would not be the source of anything in respect to another entity unless it were directly interacting with that entity. If *a*'s nature were a constitution of parts, then it might be the basis for *a*'s being smaller than *b*, since *a* by this nature might act on *b* to make it grow. But the material composition would not be responsible for *a*'s being smaller than *b* if there is no causal action between the two and the two possess only a difference of magnitudes.

Clearly, then, the objection derives its bite from just such a scientific conception of natures. However, we were discussing natures of a quite different kind. We were discussing a nature that gave rise to the conditional property $((F\_ \cdot Gb) \rightarrow f\_)$. Having f as a result of having this property is merely a matter of having $(F\_ \cdot Gb)$. And this is no more problematic than *modus ponens* ever is. There is no need for the nature to "know" that b does have G in order for the entity with the nature to have f. In the Lockean view, however, a nature could not give rise to such a conditional property. For one of the conjuncts in the antecedent need have no conceivable causal connection with the entity that has the conditional property. Because we need to account for the fact that such an entity will have the above conditional property by its nature, the Lockean kind of nature is inadequate.

The notion of togetherness developed here differs not only from the Leibnizian notion of togetherness with an external source but also from the view associated with Whitehead of togetherness with no source at all. In the present view, togetherness requires foundations. Suppose though every individual has relational properties in respect to every other, but relational properties are the only kind of property. Whitehead expresses such a view when he says, "The aspects of all things enter into its [the enduring object's] very nature. It is only itself as drawing together into its own limitation the larger whole in which it finds itself."[19] There is, in this view, universal togetherness without a source, since there are no foundations for relational properties.

This is unacceptable because of the obvious need to account for the fact that one individual has a property correlated with that of another individual. Individuals are not correlative for no reason at all. What they are of themselves gives them the special kinds of correlativity they have. ". . . The properties of a thing are not the result of its relations to other things, but only manifest themselves in such relations."[20] In addition, there is an important systematic inadequacy in this view that basic individuals have as components only their reflections of the world. For one cannot coherently hold this view and also engage in the practice of action on prior experience.

To see the incoherence, recall the difficulty about relational properties raised in Chapter V, §3. Each individual has so many independent relational properties that, if they are all included, any sort of postulate of limited independent variety, even one for levels, would fail. Thus we excluded the relational properties of any individual and put their foundations in the individual in their place. A finite number of foundations in the individual could sustain an infinite number of its relational properties. This puts no limitation on the kinds of hypotheses to which induction could be applied, since hypotheses about relational properties would be consequent upon hypotheses about individuals with foundations. However, if, as Whitehead's ontology requires, there are no foundations but only relational properties, then one cannot replace relational properties by their foundations in considerations of limited independent variety. Thus there will be no limited independent variety, even of the weak, levels sort. Whitehead's ontology, which rejects non-relational properties in its eagerness to give importance to relational ones, is then incoherent with the practice of action on prior experience.

§5. *Sameness and Unity.* It might seem that so long as we still have a component ontology we have not done with relations. For components are components of individuals; components differ from one another; having a component is a condition of an individual; and components of distinct individuals are distinct from one another. Even if relations among distinct relata have been reduced to properties, we have left as a residue the relations of composition, difference, condition, and distinctness. The philosopher of relations has waited thus far to set his trap. For to do away with relations at this point is to do away with all composition, all difference, all conditions, and all distinctness. In short, it is to fall into Parmenidean monism.

But the relation of composition, for example, does not have distinct entities as relata. So our strictures against relations among distinct entities no longer apply. It would, then, be consistent with all the preceding to allow that the relation *component of* exists. If it exists, it can be a component of the individual that contains its relata. It was only relations among distinct entities that could in no way be components of individuals. But in this case, in which the relata are the same particulars, the relation can be a component without the risk of being multiplied by the number of its relata. However, there is no need to admit relations that are internal in our second sense. I shall now try to show this.

The task can be simplified by noting that composition can be defined in terms of the other relations. Suppose *F* is a component of *a*. Then (i) *a* is an individual or a condition, and (ii) *a* is the same particular as *F* but nonetheless is different from *F*. Thus components are components of individuals or conditions and of nothing else. In particular, properties, actions, and physical parts, though components of individuals, are not entities with components, since they are neither individuals nor conditions. This account of components introduces the relations of difference and sameness. So we are led to concentrate on these.

In Chapter III, distinctness of conditions was said to be a sign of the difference of corresponding entities. But to define the difference of entities by means of the distinctness of conditions would make conditions prior to components, which they are not. Yet, though difference cannot be defined by other relations, such as *condition of,* it is reducible to relational properties and foundations. Since difference holds, in many cases at least, among components, it seems natural to attempt this reduction by means of relational properties and foundations of the components themselves. I just said, however, that components have no components. Thus in the case of a putative relation among components, one must search for the corresponding relational property and foundations in the individual or condition with those components.

Thus, if the property *F* of *a* differs from the property *G* of *a,* then (i) *a* encompasses the difference of *F* from *G* in *a* itself, and (ii) *a* is both *F* and *G*. The encompassing of (i) is a relational property *a* has in respect to itself. The properties *F* and *G* of (ii) are the foundations associated with this self-relational property. These foundations do imply that relational property, for being *F* and *G* will imply that *a* encompasses the difference of *F* from *G* in *a*. The foundations of the difference of components are simply different components.

In case it is an individual that is different from a component, a slightly different approach is needed. The foundation cannot be the individual; it must be, rather, the individual's sameness with itself. Thus the foundations for *F*'s differing from *a* are *F* itself and *a*'s self-sameness. Now sameness also appears when we attempt to make *condition of* yield to our reductive machinery. If being yellow is a condition of *a,* then the foundations are the yellow in *a* and the sameness of the condition with itself. More will be said on the self-sameness of conditions in Chapter XI, §4. For the moment it is clear that all our relations point back to sameness.

But there seem to be no obvious foundations for sameness. Strangely enough, though, if sameness does not exist, we fall back into undifferentiated monism. Yet if sameness exists, it would seem that there are relations. This relation—one that is internal in our second sense—would then be the price to be paid for having composition, difference, and distinctness.

But perhaps sameness is not a genuine relation. Then abandonment of all relations, even the internal ones, leaves sameness intact and does not force monism on us. I think sameness claims are, in fact, attributions of unity and that unity is a non-relational component of individuals and conditions. Thus the foundations of the relation *condition of* are a component of the individual with the condition and the unity of the condition. To say Cicero is himself is to say Cicero is a unity. To say Cicero is Tully is to say the entity Cicero and Tully is a unity. To say Cicero is not Catiline is to say the entity Cicero and Catiline is not a unity. Moreover, to say Cicero is the same particular as his hunger is to say that the entity Cicero and his hunger is a unity. Without unity as a component, Cicero could not be unified with, could not be the same particular as, his hunger. Not only does the component unity account for the sameness of individuals with their other components, but it also accounts for the sameness of individuals with their unity.

It will be objected that this account of sameness merely introduces the part-whole relation and that we fall into the monist's trap if the part-whole relation does not exist. When we say the entity Cicero and Catiline is not a unity are we not saying that the whole whose parts are Cicero and Catiline is not a unity? Are we not saying that the whole is a multiplicity rather than a unity? In at least one important respect, a negative unity claim is like a negative existence claim. When one says Pegasus does not exist, one's claim is significant even though 'Pegasus' lacks a referent. Now in the ontology of components, only unities exist. Properties exist only because a property is the same particular as its individual, and is thus the same unity. So when one says the entity Cicero and Catiline is not a unity, what one says is true even though there is no entity, that is, even though there is no entity referred to by the phrase 'Cicero and Catiline'. If, contrary to fact, there were such an entity, one would call it a whole and say Cicero and Catiline are its parts. Then, indeed, one would be committed to mereological relations. But what about positive unity claims? If there is no entity that is a whole with many particulars as parts, one is not forced in the case of true positive unity claims to say one is referring to wholes with only a single particular as part. One is free to say that in claiming that the entity Cicero and Tully is a unity, or that the entity Cicero and his hunger is a unity, one is referring not to a whole that has one or more parts, but simply to an individual.

Philosophers of different times and different schools have also held that sameness was not a relation. But they have as often as not made something intentional out of it. For Aquinas it was a relation of reason;[21] for Wittgenstein a sameness claim signified the interchangeability of the terms set out in it.[22] Here, by contrast, I have treated sameness claims as ascribing the real component of unity to particulars. Suppose these claims were not true or false on the basis of what is real; suppose, that is, they were true or false on the basis of concepts of relations or on the basis of linguistic interchangeability. Then since distinctness, difference, condition, and composition all rest on sameness, the ontology of components would only describe the structure of particulars as conceived or talked about. It would not be an ontology of the real.

CHAPTER VIII

Action and Time

§1. *Necessities Across Time.* In this and the following chapter I shall develop the view that time is based on action. It turns out that the actions required are components of physical individuals rather than separately existing entities. The action view of time is, then, neither an absolutist nor a relativist view. The "absolutist" gives instants a reality that is independent of what occurs in them. The "relativist" views instants as derivative from relations among occurrences. So construed, relativism requires that relations exist, either temporal relations or other relations to which temporal relations might be reduced, such as causal relations. The advocate of the action view, like the relativist, rejects the independent existence of instants, but, unlike the relativist, rejects the existence of relations. The action view of time is a special case of the general view of relations described in the preceding chapter. In this view, there are only temporal relational properties, and they are grounded by actions.

Is it a consequence of the action view of time that actions belong to the required ontology? I contend that it is for the following reason: among the necessities required for the practice of action on prior experience will be necessities between conditions at distinct times. How else could the practice of action on prior experience be what I called in Chapter I a fundamental practice? The reason there would be no communication or no theorizing without such a practice is that communication and theorizing suppose that people have beliefs as to how speakers and hearers and simply bits of matter react *after* being submitted to certain stimuli. Forming these beliefs is a matter of action on prior experience.

But now suppose action on prior experience involved merely the projection of the *coexistence* of conditions on the basis of prior experience. The practice of action on prior experience could then no longer be called fundamental. Other human practices would be conceivable without it. Necessities between conditions at distinct times cannot be rejected without rendering the practice of action on prior experience in its role as a fundamental practice incoherent with our view of the world. This need for necessities across time, taken together with the action view of time, puts actions into the required ontology.

But how do necessities across time fit into the picture of limited variety (or of levels of limited variety) drawn in Chapter V? Suppose a's being F is not just followed by b's being G at a later time, but that *if* a is F *then* b is G later. Thus a has the conditional temporal property ($F\_ \rightarrow Gb$ later). Also suppose a has the property H. So, given the assumptions for limited variety, there will be a chance that $\Box\, a(Ha \rightarrow (Fa \rightarrow Gb$ later)). If induction is to allow us to assert this universally of individuals other than a that are also H, there must then be a chance that H is a kind property, and thus a chance that $\Box\, a(Ha)$. It follows immediately that there will be a chance that $\Box\, a(Fa \rightarrow Gb$ later), that is, a chance that there is a certain necessity across time.

However, there are two reasons why one might deny that the limited variety picture yields a chance for such a necessity across time. First, it might be held that a's conditional property ($F\_ \rightarrow Gb$ later) is a relational property. It would then fail to come under the properties considered by the limited variety principle. Recall that relational properties are not just correlative, as this one is, but also have foundations. Yet ($F\_ \rightarrow Gb$ later) can be a property of a even though no properties of a and b are foundations for it.

Second, it will be pointed out that there are possibly an infinite number of conditional temporal properties in any individual. How then can a requirement of limited independent variety be satisfied? This is a crucial question at this point. So far, I have ignored time in that I have not indicated whether the necessities needed were merely necessities among coexistent features or also necessities across time. Now, however, it is clear that the practice of action on the basis of prior experience requires necessities across time. We have just seen that, for there to be such necessities, conditional temporal properties should be among the properties that individuals have. Yet if such properties are to have a chance of being necessary, their presence should not lead to an unlimited variety.

It might seem, though, that any individual could have, as a result of all of its states, an infinite number of consequences, and that these consequences could be mutually independent. As a result, the principle of limited variety could not be invoked to say there is a chance any of these connections is necessary. For the principle to be usable at all, conditional temporal properties would have to be excluded from consideration, just as relational properties were—and for the same reason. The structure of individuals required by limited variety would become irrelevant to the practice of action on prior experience, because none of the necessities posited by such a structure would be necessities across time.

To meet this difficulty, two assumptions must be accepted. First, it is to be assumed that conditionals relating a single condition of a given individual to temporal consequences of the same kind for other individuals are not independent. If *a*'s condition of being *F* gives rise to *b*'s condition of being *G* sometime later, then it will also give rise to *c*'s being *G* sometime later. ($Fa \rightarrow Gb$ later) and ($Fa \rightarrow Gc$ later) are not then independent, and the thrust of the objection is partly deflected. For this assumption to be important, *G* will generally be unspecific in a number of ways. A match's flaming does not imply specific temperature increments for bodies warmed by it. Rather *G* would here be expressible by a formula relating variables for distance, intervening medium, size, and material to change of temperature. To repeat, our first assumption is that similar consequences of a given state do not arise independently.

This first assumption is not of itself sufficient. There could still be an unlimited number of independent temporal conditional properties for a given individual. This would be the case if the conditions of an individual had, jointly, an unlimited number of different kinds of consequences and if the connections between the conditions and the consequences were independent. So our second assumption is that the temporal conditional properties of an individual with different kinds of consequents are not of an unlimited independent variety. I am able to speak here about the number of kinds of consequents, rather than about the number of consequents, since, by the first assumption, conditional properties with the same antecedent and with consequents of the same kind for distinct individuals are not independent.

In sum, the practice of action on prior experience requires necessities across time. Specifically, the necessities across time that are needed are given by the requirements that (1) individuals have to have conditional temporal properties, that is, properties such as the property *a* has when ($Fa \rightarrow Gb$ later), and that (2) individuals have conditional temporal properties in such a way that the principle of limited independent variety (or the principle of levels of limited independent variety) is not upset. To insure that it is not upset, it must be assumed that (a) conditionals relating a single condition of an individual to temporal consequences that are of the same kind but are for distinct individuals are not independent conditionals, and that (b) the independent temporal conditional properties of a given individual with different kinds of consequents are not unlimited. But if action is taken among the foundations of temporal relational properties, then the existence of conditional temporal properties—that inevitably imply the existence of temporal relational properties—must rest, in part at least, on action.

§2. *Temporal Atomism and Temporal Holism.* The action view of time contrasts with two classical views of time, the atomistic and the holistic views. The atomistic view is simply the application to time of the doctrine that relations are entities distinct from their relata. In this view of time, there are, in addition to conditions such as being red and being green, temporal relations among these conditions. It was seen in the last chapter that relations among distinct entities are external. And, in particular, temporal relations are external to the conditions they stand between. Hence no condition can be necessarily followed by another, or necessarily preceded by another.

There will, however, be such connections if there are necessities across time. For, if it is a necessity of *a* that if *Fa* then *Gb* later, then, quite obviously, when the condition of *a*'s being *F* obtains, it is a necessity of *a* that *A*'s being *F* is followed by *b*'s being *G*. Thus the existence of temporal relations abolishes necessities across time. The conditions in a network of temporal relations must, then, be like isolated atoms.

The holistic view, on the other hand, does not regard temporal relations as fundamental. The fundamental factor in regard to time is, in this view, a kind of action that encompasses a multiplicity of different entities as a whole encompasses its parts. The conditions that we speak of as temporally separated are among the entities encompassed by the surge of action. The encompassed conditions are not then independent unities; they have the status of components of action. Temporal relations among conditions encompassed by an action will themselves be components of the action.

So the holistic view is a special case of the view that Russell called the "monistic" view of relations. A relation, on this view, is a component of an entity that also has the relata of this relation as its components. So the relation is internal in our second sense. Clearly then, in the holistic view, the conditions that are components of an enduring action are not distinct from one another or from the encompassing action. "In short," says Bergson, an advocate of the holistic view of time, "it is necessary to admit two types of multiplicity, two possible senses of the word 'distinguish', two conceptions, the one qualitative and the other quantitative, of the difference between *same* and *other*."[1] Bergson overcomes the atomistic isolation of conditions in time by dissolving their numerical distinctness in a whole where they are only qualitatively distinct, or, in our terms, where they are only different components.

It has often been supposed that temporal holism is the only alternative to temporal atomism. Holism is definitely on the side of an ontology of components; actions are not simple entities but entities with different, though not distinct, components. On the other hand, temporal atomism does not require that there be entities with components. It might then seem that we should side with holism against the ontology of external relations of the atomistic view of time. There is, though, a non-holistic alternative to temporal atomism.

But why not be satisfied with holism? Holism seems most plausible for actions that do not have effects outside their agents. But consider the case of Jones's sanding a block of wood. The conditions encompassed by the action are not only conditions of Jones, but also conditions of the block of wood. Both the condition of Jones's forearm as he begins a stroke and the condition of the wood's surface after Jones has completed the stroke are dissolved into the unity of the sanding.

It is a minimal requirement for the sameness of conditions that conditions of distinct physical individuals be distinct. But for the holist, the condition of Jones's forearm and the condition of the wood's surface are not distinct, but at best different. It then follows that Jones's forearm and the block's surface are not distinct, but at best only different. Yet at the same time, the holist would want to be able to claim that some things are genuinely distinct; for example, Jones's sanding and Jones's walking would be distinct actions. On the face of it, if anything is distinct from something else, then surely it is absurd to claim that Jones's forearm and the block's surface are the same particular. There is the additional objection that holism displaces individuals by actions as the ultimate determiners of sameness. But only in Chapter XI will the basis of this objection be established.

The non-holistic alternative to atomism—to be prepared for by the discussion of action in this chapter and to be presented in detail in the next chapter—is a special case of the theory of relational properties described in the preceding chapter. It can be described briefly as follows. Suppose an individual performs a certain action. There will be conditions that are the results of this action. These results are not swallowed up by the action; they remain distinct from it. The action and any component corresponding to one of these results are, together, the foundations for a temporal relational property. Since the foundations imply the temporal relational property, there is no isolation of entities at different times as there is in the atomistic view. There is a genuine togetherness supplied by the foundations, which may be components of distinct entities.

Atomists have typically seen their own position as a response to a holistic destruction of the distinctness of instants. Their commitment to a certain view on the nature of distinctness has prevented their consideration of the action view of time just outlined. Descartes, for example, seems to have thought that if moments of time are distinct, there can be no causal action between the occurrences that fill them: "The present time has no causal dependence on the time immediately preceding it."[2] It seems probable that his argument for this was as follows:

(1) If one moment can be clearly thought to be distinct from another, the former could exist without the latter.[3]

In other words, if one moment is necessarily connected to another, they cannot be thought to be distinct, and hence, for Descartes, it is not possible that they are distinct. But:

(2) A causal action between moments would be a necessary connection between them.

So if moments were joined by a causal action they could not be distinct. Hence, since distinct moments can be clearly thought to be distinct:

(3) If moments are distinct there is no causal action between them.

So in Descartes' view of distinctness, if there were causal action, it would have to be like the action of temporal holism. It would dissolve the distinctness of moments within it into a unity. Nonetheless, the distinctness of moments is for Descartes compatible with God's causal action in respect to them, provided that the content of each moment is produced by a distinct action of God's.[4]

The crux of Descartes' argument is premiss (1), that is, the implication from distinguishable to separable. All along I have insisted that this premiss cannot cohere with human practice. If then we deny this premiss, causal action need not be interpreted as a whole within which there can be no distinctness of moments. That is, if we deny (1), the acceptance of causal action between moments does not commit us to saying, with the holist, that those moments are not distinct. And so by denying (1), we get beyond the dichotomy of atomism and holism.

Hume adds little to Descartes' reasoning when he argues that the idea of a duration is not the idea of a whole encompassing successive objects, but is rather the succession of ideas of objects. Since the distinct is treated by him as separable, atomism is the only alternative he sees to the holistic view he rejects. Since five notes played on a flute are distinct, they are, for Hume as for Descartes, separable. But then if there is a whole—say, the act of playing the flute—that encompasses them all, one would be faced with an absurdity. For this playing is not separable from these notes being played, and hence this playing is not distinct from the notes. Yet since there are five distinct notes, the one playing must, contradictorily, be five playings. So there is no act of playing at all but only the succession of notes.[5] That is, the alternative to holism is the view that relations of succession stand between isolated events. However, if the distinct need not be separable, the notes might be distinct from the playing even though each of them is an intermediate result of the playing. Their temporal relations to one another need not be taken any longer as irreducible. Rather, the foundations of these relations are to be found in the stages of the action of playing (Chapter IX, §3, *ad fin*).

I shall tie this section to §1, by the following observations. First, the atomist's conflation of the distinct with the separable is incompatible with the requirement that necessities across time not be denied if one is to engage in the practice of action on prior experience. For necessities across time are necessities connecting distinct conditions. But the conflation of the distinct with the separable is the chief premiss for temporal atomism, which is the view that relations, not actions, are needed for temporal relatedness. So the direct argument for temporal atomism given by (1)-(3) has to be rejected as unsound.

Note, second, that this argument can be turned around. That is, starting with temporal atomism, one can attempt to show that there are no necessary connections across time, and hence that what is distinguishable in time is separable. In fact, this reverse argument has already been constructed. This was done in Chapter VII, §1, when it was shown that if there are relations between distinct entities they are external. So, in particular, if there are temporal relations, they are external, and hence there are no necessary connections across time. The argument is valid, and it is the backbone of Humean and post-Humean anti-necessitarianism. It relies on temporal atomism as a premiss, which in turn relies on the existence of relations between distinct entities. But we saw that such relations make relatedness impossible. Since, however, there is temporal relatedness, temporal relations and hence the premiss of temporal atomism must be rejected. Temporal atomism will be deprived of any residual appeal if we can establish below the action view of time as a positive alternative.

Third, let us note that the conflation of distinct with separable that is behind the temporal atomist's argument (1)–(3) is not the same as the conflation of distinct with different that characterizes the ontology of simples. Thus the temporal atomist's relata may be complex in the sense of having different components. However, the prime motivation for a component ontology is, as we saw in Chapter III, the need to integrate natures and things. If necessary connections across time are denied by conflating the distinct with the separable, then the role of natures is greatly limited. Once natures have in this way lost their importance, the problem of integrating them with things will be ignored. The step of conflating the distinct with the different then seems the obvious one to take, since there is no apparent need for entities with components.

§3. *Progressive and Complete Actions.* Whether it will be possible to establish an action view of time that avoids both atomism and holism will depend on whether we are forced to embrace what is apparently the most commonly accepted philosophical view of action. This is the view that what I shall call "complete" action is the only kind of action. Just as there is a contrast between a property and the having of it, so too there is a contrast between an action in what I call the "progressive" sense and the doing of the action. The doing of the action is the correlative complete action. In terms of our earlier distinction between components and conditions, a property and a progressive action are components of individuals, whereas the having of a property and the doing of an action are conditions of individuals. Conditions that are the doings of actions make up one of the various kinds of conditions that are generally called events. If we are forced to accept action only in the form of complete action then, indeed, as I shall presently show, the action view of time must fail.

Verbs in their gerundive form give us ambiguous referring terms for actions. They can be made to refer to progressive or to complete actions. But we also have some terms that unambiguously pick out complete actions. 'Race' is a complete-action term, but 'running' serves for both progressive and complete actions. If I say that the running took four minutes, I am referring to the complete action, to the performing of the running. If, however, I say that the running continues to be done or that the running is swift, I am referring to the progressive action.

It is important to notice that progressive action is not extensive and hence not extensively divisible. The running you are doing just does not have a first half and a second half. This is not because it is an extended whole that somehow cannot be divided. Rather it is because it is not an extended whole at all. Your doing the running, as opposed to the running you are doing, does have a first half and a second half. There are, then, various phases of your performance. The third lap is a phase in your doing the running, and it may have taken more time than either of the first two. But the progressive action of running does not have phases or stages; there is no earlier and later progressive action of running during the race.

Whitehead is perfectly right on this when he says that "in every act of becoming there is the becoming of something with temporal extension; but . . . the act itself is not extensive, in the sense that it is divisible into earlier and later acts of becoming."[6] The temporally extensive entity that comes to be is, in my analysis, the complete action. It is correlative to the progressive action. What Whitehead calls the act of becoming I am interpreting here as a generic expression for various progressive actions.

The condition of being red may last ten minutes. But the component red is not itself lasting or ephemeral. Likewise, the condition of doing cutting may be a condition I am in for a full hour. But the corresponding component, cutting, is, like red, neither lasting nor ephemeral. Not only does the condition of being red last ten minutes, but also I am in that condition at instants within that stretch. And so the condition of doing cutting that lasts a full hour is a condition of me at each instant in the hour. There is, of course, the peculiarity of speaking of conditions lasting through times, during parts of which the obtainings of the conditions were interrupted. My condition of doing cutting lasted a full hour, even though I rested several times during that hour. I shall ignore these peculiarities in identifying complete actions and treat what we speak of as unitary complete actions as though they were uninterrupted.

Why, then, must the action view of time fail if we admit only complete action? In the first place, since complete actions are, in general, extensive, they can hardly serve in an attempt to ground time. For a ground for time should give some account of how there can be entities, such as complete actions, that have temporally separate parts. And merely to say there are such entities is not to give an account of them. So if temporal relational properties have foundations, then the temporal structure of complete actions has the same foundations.

It will not be complete action but progressive action that can serve us here. Complete actions depend upon progressive actions in the same manner that any condition of an entity depends upon a corresponding component of that entity. But there is also a special dependence in the case of complete action, a dependence that has to do with time. In the absence of progressive actions, there are no foundations for temporal relational properties. Without temporal relational properties the conditions of entities would lack a temporal structure. So a complete action—an event, an actual occasion, an occurrence of action, a state of action, or a fact of doing something—exists through dependence on progressive action and has its extensiveness on the basis of progressive action.

In the second place, if we should try to ground time on complete actions without reliance on progressive actions, we would fail to ground it on components of individuals. But the action view of time puts forth precisely such a grounding on components. The difficulty is that by cutting ourselves off from progressive actions, there are no components of physical individuals that are correlative with those conditions that are complete actions. For what components are the correlatives of complete actions if not progressive actions?

When progressive actions are rejected, complete actions are cut off from their roots in physical individuals. Not only do we fail in this way to ground time in the components of physical individuals, but we erect a dualism of events and things, for an event that is associated with a thing is no longer dependent on there being an action that is a component of that thing. The things themselves are static; change comes into the picture by associating them with complete actions, which are numerically distinct from the things since they are conditions of those things.

Needless to say, this way of attempting to bring change into the picture is abortive. For, in effect, it is an attempt to have races without running, falls without falling, and dances without dancing. By excluding progressive actions, we have the absurdity of there being the complete performance without something performed. A parallel view would associate the condition of having red with individuals that lack the component red. There would be a condition of having a property without the property.

Inevitably, this view requires modification. It is absurd to have races without running (*cf.* Chapter XI, §4). For an ontology of simples, there may be a running that corresponds to the race even though this progressive action, the running, is not a component of the runner but, rather, a distinct entity with the character of a universal. In such an ontology, the distinction between progressive and complete action would be a special case of that between universals and exemplifications of universals. Still, complete actions without progressive actions would be impossible. The natural course for those who do not countenance progressive actions is to deny that even complete actions are genuine actions. Complete actions are reduced to sets of conditions that are the havings of properties, where these conditions are strung out in unbroken sequence. A multiplicity of property conditions in sequence replaces a unitary action condition. So not only is the running rejected, but the race is rejected as an action. Each of the conditions in the sequence is correlative with a property that is a component of a physical entity. The dualism of things and events, resulting from breaking this correlativity between conditions and components in the case of conditions that are complete actions, is overcome at a level that does not involve action at all.

Ockham, who believed that everything is either a substance or a quality, claimed that words like 'action' and 'motion' do not stand for anything.[7] Rather, for a body to be in motion "it suffices that . . . [it] . . . continuously—without any interruption of time, or rest—acquire or lose something, part by part, one after another."[8] But such a reduction of complete action to property conditions in sequence posits the atomistic view of time. The property conditions are in sequence, and any attempt to fasten on the sequential relations and discover the grounds of these relations will lead straight back to the actions that Ockham wished to eliminate. Relations must then be taken as irreducible. The property conditions in the sequence are separated by distinct in-between entities.[9] Since there are no relations, however, the reduction of complete actions cannot be carried out. Nonetheless, this reduction was called for, once progressive actions were pulled out from under complete actions. We are not put into a position of needing to carry out this impossible reduction if we allow for progressive actions in the first place.

§4. *Components and Conditions.* The distinction between progressive and complete action has been drawn in terms of that between components and conditions. Further elaboration of this latter distinction, as it applies to actions, is desirable. This shall be done by illustrating some further consequences of the component-condition distinction.

Components, but not conditions, are distinguished numerically on the basis of the entities with them. The summer green and the autumn yellow of this leaf share the unity of the leaf, though they are different components. But "a changing thing changes from one definite condition to another (*ek tinos eis ti*)."[10] The leaf changes from the condition of being green to that of being yellow. Now if this is, in turn, only a matter of difference within the unity of the changing being, we are faced with the consequence that the multiplicity in time of the conditions of a changing being is not a multiplicity of distinct moments and that the life of a single changing being is, in fact, only a single moment. Change does not then involve sameness through distinctness of states, but sameness with difference. Of itself, this consequence is not an impossible one to have to live with.

But if the condition of having green is, like green itself, not distinct from the green entity, then it, like green itself, will be a component of the green entity. Now each component has a corresponding condition. So the condition of having green will correspond to the condition of having the condition of having green, and so on endlessly. The sequence of requirements for green to be a component of any entity is then never complete. There will always be a further condition of having a condition. To avoid this objectionable regress, it suffices to regard conditions as entities distinct from the entities with the corresponding components. Since a condition is a distinct entity there is no condition of having a condition, and thus no regress. Granted, then, that conditions are distinct from their parent entities, are they distinct from one another when they have the same parent entity? Perhaps the cube's conditions of being made of stone and of being grey are only different from one another. But this cannot be, for then—since neither condition would be a component of the other—they would have to be components of some entity different from each condition. And again there would be a regress of conditions of having conditions.

But what justification is there for putting performances, doings, events, and the like under the heading of conditions? The justification comes from treating progressive actions as components. For entities with components can be said, quite literally, to be in the condition of having those components. Now if progressive actions are components, then entities with these components are in the conditions of having them. But what is it to have a progressive action if not to do a progressive action? For an agent to have pulling as a component it is necessary for that agent to be doing pulling. So if having pulling is a condition, doing pulling is a condition. This accords with the idea that doing pulling is not two actions, a doing and a pulling, by interpreting the doing the pulling as merely the condition of having pulling as a component. But this all supposes that sense can be made of the notion that a progressive action is a component.

What else might be the pulling, cutting, teaching, or exploding that an entity does? Perhaps the progressive action is a universal. Its being exemplified would then be a complete action. One would be tempted by this interpretation only if one were antecedently committed to viewing properties as universals rather than as components. One would be strongly motivated to do this on one of only two assumptions. First, one would treat properties as universals if the individuals that have properties are simples. Properties would then be distinct from individuals and could be had by several individuals. Second, one would treat properties as universals if, in one's ontology, there were no individuals but were instead conditions of having properties, actions, and parts. What is had when there is a condition of having a property is not the same particular as this having itself. Either it is the same particular as some individual, which is impossible here, or it is an entity with its own unity that could then be had in several conditions.

Neither the first nor the second assumption can be accepted by the ontology of components, since it is incompatible with an ontology of simples and since for it conditions are dependent on individuals. It is reasonable for us, then, to consider the doing of cutting as having the component cutting rather than as participating in the universal cutting. (Even so, resorting to universals allows one to treat doings as conditions. For participating in the universal cutting is just being in the condition of having cutting, though not of having cutting as a component.)

Discussions of action are often vitiated by failing to distinguish progressive from complete action. Consider, for example, the problem raised by the fact that actions recur. Jones runs after breakfast and then again after lunch. The recurrence could be explained if the running were a universal. But it might be objected that this explains too much. Smith's running and Jones's running would be one running, not two. Yet there is an obvious reply. Is it the progressive or the complete actions of Smith and Jones that must be distinct? Even if their progressive actions are the same universal, their complete actions are distinct instantiations of that universal. This is sufficient to account for the obvious fact that Smith and Jones are engaged in two performances.

Suppose actions are said to be propositions in the realistic, not the intentional sense. Thus, *proposition* here means what *fact-of* or *condition* means. Jones's running after breakfast is one proposition, but his running after lunch is another, for otherwise it would be impossible to say Jones ran twice. But this seems to make it impossible to explain the fact that the second running is a recurrence of the first.[11] Since the propositions are distinct entities, we are left with no basis for saying it was a repetition.

Again the answer to the conundrum lies in the distinction between progressive and complete action. As distinct, the propositions serve well in the role of complete actions. For, indeed, there were two performances. But to say that the running recurred is to make a claim about progressive action. The progressive actions of an individual are not entities distinct from that individual. This fits with the fact that recurrence does not seem to imply distinctness. To go on to say that we should call actions that recur "quasi-propositions" is to make the mistake of supposing that, since complete actions are propositions, progressive actions are sufficiently like them to be similar to propositions. Far from being similar to propositions, progressive actions are the components that by being had give rise to propositions in the present realistic sense.

Still one wonders how, in fact, the component view of progressive action handles recurrence. The problem is like that of how redness of the skin recurs with a new exposure to the sun. In the conceptualist theory of difference—that if *a* is different from *b* their concepts are not the same—the redness in June and that in August are not different, though the corresponding conditions are distinct. But we have correlated difference with distinctness of conditions. Since I lived through two sunburns, the color component I had in June is different from that I had in August. Analogously, Jones's two runs involve different, though not distinct, components of running. In this view, there is no universal entity instantiated by Jones during each run that makes the second a recurrence of the first. But can we explain the recurrence if the two components are different? The key to the matter is similarity. The June redness and the August redness are different entities, but they are similar entities. There is recurrence of a component when it is followed by a different but similar component of the same particular. Jones's running recurs since his different components of running are similar. Jones's running does not recur in Smith since Smith's running, though similar, is not a component of the same particular.

Whether actions are treated as progressive or complete, there is a problem associated with the use of adverbial and prepositional modifiers in statements reporting actions.[12] If I say that Jones ran to the door, am I saying that Jones has the component running-to-the-door? If so, is this component different from running *simpliciter*? (Or, in terms of conditions rather than components, am I claiming that Jones is in the condition of having running-to-the-door? If so, is this condition distinct from that of having running?) And is there, over and above the component running and the component running-to-the-door, also the component running-to-the-door-in-a-bathrobe?

There seem to be three options here. If we take the first, all components but the running *simpliciter* are rejected. In the second, all components are admitted. That is, we admit running *simpliciter,* running-to-the-door, running-to-the-door-in-a-bathrobe, and so on until we arrive at a component that contains the full complexity of the situation. In the third option, all components short of the one that reflects the full complexity of the situation are rejected. They are rejected as unreal abstractions from the component with full complexity. Taking the second option involves unnecesary multiplication of actions if either the first or the third is defensible. The third prohibits our saying anything true about actions, since a true statement would doubtless have to have an endless number of modifiers as constituents. Is then the first defensible? It is only if one can explain how a modifier makes a difference in a statement to which it is added without requiring a more complex action in the world.

How this is indeed the case may be explained as follows. In general, a modifier in an action statement serves to indicate the role of the component action in regard to the individual with it. Thus, to say Jones ran to the door is to say (i) that running is a component of Jones and (ii) that this running puts Jones in the direction of the door. The putting of Jones in that direction is not a component of the running, for components do not have components. Rather, to say the component puts Jones in that direction is to say the component is the basis in Jones for his direction.

Conversely, to say Jones necessarily runs is to imply that running is a component of Jones and that this component is due to his nature. Here the role of the progressive action is that of being dependent on something about Jones, his nature, whereas in the previous case the action was the basis of something about Jones, his direction. When Jones runs fast, his running enables him to be at a greater distance from a given point in a given time than the typical member of his kind would be. (Depending on the context, 'Jones runs fast' can mean other things as well.) Again, the speed is not a property of the progressive action. Rather, the modifier 'fast' indicates what the progressive action does for the individual with it. Similarly, a bright blue vase has a component that gives the vase a bright appearance. So in the case of properties as well as actions, modifiers serve to indicate the roles these components play for the individuals with them.

Is a new entity—a role—being added in order to understand modifiers? Not at all, for roles can be treated as conditional properties, which are already familiar enough in the required ontology. To say the component puts Jones in a certain direction, enables him to be in a certain place, or gives the vase a certain appearance is to say—beyond implying that the individual has the component —that *if* the individual has the component *then* it will be in that direction, be enabled to be at that place, or be given that appearance. (For the modifier 'necessarily', reference to the component will occur in the consequent, not the antecedent, of such a conditional.) The same pattern can be used for modifiers in relation to conditions, rather than components. When Jones runs to the door, having running is a condition that puts him in the direction of the door. That is, he has this condition only if the door is the direction he is headed in.

Of course, only if these components and conditions are conceived in the manner of our present ontology can they have such implications. If running were a universal, then its being instanced in a certain individual would not imply any particular direction for that individual. But in our ontology, running is not distinct from the runner, and two different runnings of the same runner may well be dissimilar. Dissimilar components, or conditions, will have different implications.

Not all modifiers serve to indicate the role of a component. Some, in fact, serve to deny that a certain component is present.[13] For example, nearly running is not running at all. My concern, however, is solely with cases in which the truth of the statement with the modifier requires the presence of the corresponding component. Moreover, adjectival modifiers of kind nouns do indeed signify components rather than simply indicate the roles for components. Thus 'red' in 'red ball' signifies a component of a ball and not just the role of the kind-property signified by 'ball' in relation to the individual ball.

Though the distinction of component from condition is not crucial for understanding modifiers, it is of greatest importance as regards causation. If *a* causes *b*, then it seems reasonable to say that *a* causes any particular that is the same as *b*. However, acting beings and their progressive actions are the same particulars. So if *a* causes the running that Jones has, then, by this principle, *a* would also cause Jones, which, of course, *a* need not do. However, if *a* causes the corresponding condition—the complete action of doing running—then, since conditions are not the same particulars as the individuals with them, it does not follow that *a* causes Jones as well. A similar line of reasoning would support the view that it is the having of properties and not properties that are caused. "In making the bronze round one makes neither the round nor the spherical, but something else; one puts this form into something other than itself."[14] What is caused has a unity of its own, whereas components have their unity from individuals with them.

But if *a* causes Jones to be doing running without causing the running itself, one seems forced to conclude that the running existed prior to Jones's doing it. The cause, *a,* merely brings Jones and a pre-existent running together.[15] Running could no longer be viewed as a component. Both actions and properties would have to be entities distinct from the individuals they come to be associated with. This retreat can be halted only by appealing to a variation on the Aristotelian notion of "potential forms."[16] If *a* succeeds in causing Jones to run, then it was true of Jones that, if he were subject to a certain influence, he would run. The cause, *a,* provides this influence, and then it is only a matter of logic that Jones will run.

It is not, then, necessary to appeal to a running that existed apart from any individual. It is only necessary to appeal to a conditional property, the property an individual has when it will run provided there is a certain influence. As was observed earlier, to have a conditional property it is not necessary to have the components associated with either the antecedent or the consequent. So, given conditional properties, causes can cause conditions without causing components even though the components do not preexist. Notice that if *a* causes the condition of Jones's existing, then clearly the relevant conditional property is not Jones's but rather it is *a*'s property of being such that, if it is in certain circumstances, Jones will exist.

§5. *Action as Required by Temporal Separation.* So far we have seen that atomistic and holistic views of time are inadmissible. The atomistic view eliminates the possibility of necessities across time; the holistic view destroys the distinctness of the agent and what is acted upon. We have also seen that if an action view of time is feasible, it must be progressive action that grounds time rather than complete action, since the latter is already temporally extended. Now it is time to ask if there are any reasonable alternatives left to the view that actions are among the foundations of temporal relational properties.

Perhaps the temporally separate property conditions of entities are such that their corresponding properties are the grounds of their temporal separation. The two different sizes of a balloon are the ground of the temporal separation of its conditions of being of the two sizes. This view has all the advantages of temporal atomism without the disadvantages. For it avoids introducing actions as components additional to properties without having to resort, as temporal atomism must, to temporal relations. Let us call this the property view of time in order to contrast it with the action view, where here and henceforth I shall mean by action progressive action unless a qualification is added.

The property view of time conflicts with a fundamental fact relating change and difference. It is this fact that vindicates the inclusion of actions along with properties and parts among the components of individuals. In the property view, an individual's being in conditions of having properties that we would normally think of as incompatible properties implies the temporal separateness of these conditions. But will these conditions be temporally separate if the individual does not lose one of the properties and gain the other? Of course not. Saying that it has both properties implies just such changes. Otherwise, one would be making an impossible claim by saying that it has both properties. The obvious fact is that not only do the incompatible conditions exist, but also the changes involving the losing of one property and the gaining of another exist. The property view of time supposes erroneously that time can be accounted for by ignoring these changes and considering only the properties. It is clear, though, that without these changes a given individual would not even have the incompatible properties.

There are two ways of combating this argument against the property view. The first accepts the general framework of this discussion, whereas the second poses a radically different ontological framework. Neither way is entirely successful.

The first way is to treat losing or gaining a property in the same way the property view of time treats any supposed change. In this view, a change is a multiplicity of havings of different properties. In particular, losing a property, *F,* would be a pair of conditions, the condition of having *F* and the condition of having a property, *G,* incompatible with it. But this response fails to take into account the generality of the above argument. For, according to that argument, even this pair of conditions requires a losing and a gaining of properties. Since temporal relations are not to be assumed, any pair of incompatible properties can be had by the same individual only if there is a losing and a gaining. The losing of *F* cannot be reduced to the pair of conditions, for losing *F* and gaining *G* keep the obtaining of the pair of conditions from being impossible. Since the objection leaves this principle untouched, it is groundless.

The second and more radical way is to adopt an ontology that does away with individuals and retains conditions in their place. The effect of this is to eliminate the entity that could lose one property and gain another. The changes appealed to in order to refute the property view are eliminated. I shall show in Chapter

XI that such an ontology of conditions, events, or states of affairs is incompatible with the requirements of necessities for induction.

But now I wish to show only the more limited fact that, in the present context, such an ontology does not eliminate change. It only shifts the substratum of change from individuals with properties to what were formerly conditions of these individuals. Instead of the individual losing a property, we now have the condition ceasing to obtain. If there are individuals, then their ceasing to have a property might be said to be the only genuine change involved when we say truly that a corresponding condition ceases to obtain. But without individuals, the condition itself becomes the bearer of this change. With temporal relations assumed, there is, of course, no need to appeal to the condition's ceasing to obtain, since incompatible conditions can then be separated by a temporal relation. But the property view assumes no temporal relations. So it would be impossible for there to be a pair of incompatible conditions unless one of them ceases to obtain.

Granted that changes are needed for time. How is this relevant to the action view of time? It is relevant only if changes are actions. So a broad conception of action is required. A component is an action of an individual if the individual "does" or "undergoes" that component, as it might do exercises or undergo modifications. Hence, an individual with an action need not be a genuine agent, for when it does or undergoes something it need not bring anything about. Losing a property is an action even when the entity that loses it does not bring about this loss. In this broad sense, action signifies what Aristotle called *praxis*.[17] Walking and building are types of *praxis,* and their subjects bring about the doing of them and are thus agents. But coming to be and being moved are also types of *praxis,* even though their subjects need not bring about the undergoing of them.

Finally, action in our broad sense need not be directed toward a result, even though there will be, as in other cases, a result of its having been done. Seeing, for example, is not seeing toward a result of seeing in the way that a linear motion is motion toward a certain place. Nonetheless, there is a result of seeing in that the brain is in a different state after it is done. But seeing qualifies as *praxis* simply because to see is to do something. Anything that qualifies as action in this broad sense can be a foundation of temporal relational properties.

If it is true that there is no transit from one time to another without action, then we reach an important conclusion about how natures function. To reach this conclusion let us begin by comparing non-temporal with temporal necessities. First, suppose *a* has *F* and *G* all at once and that its having *F* necessarily implies its having *G*. In this case, the nature of *a* makes its having *F* sufficient for its having *G* by being such that an individual with that nature has *G* given that it has *F*. Second, suppose *a* has *G* after it has *F* and that the connection is necessary. The nature does not make *a*'s having *F* sufficient for its having *G* just by being such that an individual with it has *G* given that it has *F*. For then the nature would only provide that *a* has *G* if it has *F*, but it would not provide that *a* has *G* after it has *F*.

What is needed is that the nature should guarantee that *a* changes to a *G* once it is *F*. Thus the nature must be manifested in changes. There are necessities across time only if there are changes that occur by nature under certain conditions. The growing, falling, and corroding that are components of individuals are not mere intermissions between an antecedent and a consequent that follows necessarily. They are as much by nature as it is by nature that the antecedent implies the consequent.[18] If *G* is a property *a* has by nature once *a* is *F*, then the process of arriving at this result, which result is by nature, is itself a consequence of the nature of *a*.

CHAPTER IX

Temporal Asymmetry

§1. *Actions Versus Sequences of Conditions.* Armed with the principle that temporal separation requires action and with the distinction between action as a component of entities—progressive action—and action as a condition of entities—complete action—we can now show just how action enters into the foundations of temporal relational properties.

I shall try to show, in the next section, that action is asymmetrical. This means that if any condition is the result of an action, then this action is not a result of that condition. So if time can be founded by action, then both relational properties corresponding to symmetrical temporal relations and relational properties corresponding to asymmetrical temporal relations can be founded by action. Not only will relational properties corresponding to *at a different time from* and *between* be founded, but also those corresponding to the asymmetrical relation *prior to*. Accomplishing the task for *prior to* automatically accomplishes it for the symmetrical relations. To complete the program of the action view of time, it suffices to carry it out for *prior to*.

Over and above these temporal relations, there are of course the time modes, past, present, and future. It is a mistake, though, to suppose that these have foundations in entities. An entity is said to have a time mode not because of any special property it has of itself or because of any property it has in view of there being minds. Rather, the claim that an entity is past is made true merely by its occurring before a given time, the time of the claim. Sentences contain various devices that help us interpret what propositions they express in certain circumstances. Tenses are one such device. A tense in a sentence indicates that the proposition expressed by that sentence is about a time to be fixed relative to the time of utterance of the sentence. To treat time modes as realities is to project the tensed character of sentences that express propositions true of an untensed reality onto that reality.[1] Since the action view of time is intended to be applicable only to temporal relational properties, time modes, not being properties at all, fall outside its scope.

Suppose action does account for temporal asymmetry. It turns out then that it is an *a priori* matter, not a matter of empirical confirmation, that there are events that have asymmetrical temporal relatedness. This can be seen as follows. First, there must be events that are temporally related. Otherwise, there would not be the necessities across time required by the practice of action on prior experience. Second, if there is temporal relatedness, there must be actions. For without a ground in action for temporal relatedness, the relatedness would have to be seen as derivative from relations themselves. But this would be incompatible with necessities across time. Adding to these two premisses the supposition that an action and its result are the basis for temporal asymmetry, we arrive at the conclusion that there must be events that have asymmetrical temporal relatedness. In short, there are events that are separate in time, and, since action is the basis for time, these events will be asymmetrically related. In saying that this is *a priori,* I mean that there is no human practice, judgment included, whose presuppositions are compatible with denying that there are events that have asymmetrical temporal relatedness.

This view fails to accord with those accounts of temporal asymmetry that ground it on factors less basic than action. A physical basis for temporal asymmetry has been sought in (1) the expansion of the universe and (2) the tendency of systems branching from the main body of a larger system to increase their entropy. Doubtless, if these possibilities prove to contain difficulties, reference will be made to (3) the fact that a neutral meson in an antisymmetric state may decay in such a way as to violate charge-parity symmetry. To right the balance required by special relativity of a charge-parity-time symmetry, the temporal converse of such a decay cannot be realized in nature. Meson decay thus becomes a basis for temporal asymmetry in nature.[2] There is the additional possibility that temporal asymmetry might stem from (4) the irreversible way in which a measuring apparatus affects the quantum mechanical *psi*-function characterizing a physical system.

None of these factors of scientific interest needs to be present, however, in a universe in which action is the basis of temporal asymmetry. Such a universe need not expand; it may lack the kind of micro-structure that would permit the application of a statistical entropy concept; there may be no mesons in it; and, finally, it may obey classical rather than quantum physics. Since action is part of the required ontology, temporal asymmetry will characterize time in any universe coherent with human practice. But the proposed scientific factors are not part of the required ontology. So if one of them were the genuine basis for temporal asymmetry, it would be an *a posteriori* matter whether temporal relatedness is characterized by asymmetry.

If the basis for temporal asymmetry is right under our noses, why have so many powerful minds looked for it so far afield? It surely cannot have escaped their notice that action is at least a *prima facie* candidate. Why did it seem a bad choice? The answer lies in a metaphysical preconception that has rarely been questioned by scientifically minded philosophers. This preconception is the Ockhamite view that action is merely a temporal sequence of property conditions, that is, of the havings of properties. Let us call such a sequence, with the addition of a result of the action, an "action-result" sequence. Of course, temporal relations between conditions in the sequence are required until a ground for them has been proposed. But these relations cannot be grounded in action since they are part of what action is reduced to in the Ockhamite view.

What will be the basis for an asymmetrical temporal relation in the sequence to which the action is reduced? There are two approaches to this question. According to the first, the basis must be found in the property conditions of the sequence. If we do not consider the contents of these conditions, but consider instead the conditions just as conditions in a sequence, there is no basis for saying that conditions at one end of the action-result sequence are before or after those at the other end. Indeed, there is no basis for saying which end of the sequence contains the result. To establish a basis for these distinctions one must look to the contents of the conditions. In some sequences, a condition at one end is such that conditions like it—those with similar content—can only occur before, never after, conditions like the one at the other end of the sequence. This irreversibility of the seqeunce can be appealed to as the basis for the asymmetrical temporal relations in it and as the basis for calling certain conditions results. A low entropy state, for example, is prior to a higher entropy state if it is the case that the increase of entropy is irreversible.

In the Ockhamite view of action, we are to say that, in a world of exclusively reversible processes, "the assertion that a given motion of a ball was *'from A to D'* rather than *'from D to A'* expresses not an objective physical relation between the two terminal events of the motion, but only the convention that we have assigned a lower time-number to the event of the ball's being at *A* than to its being at *D*."[3] This cannot be disputed if the motion—an action in the sense of *praxis*—is nothing but the sequence of events terminated at the ends by the ball's being at *A* and its being at *D*. If the motion is but a sequence, there would be an objective basis for the distinction between the beginning and the end of the motion only if some difference between members of the sequence were irreversible.

However, the appeal to irreversibility is unnecessary if the action is not reducible to a sequence of property conditions. It is solely the Ockhamite prejudice that entails a search for facts like (1)–(4) in order to find a basis for temporal asymmetry. Irreversibility is used here in a reduction of time to certain differences between conditions in sequence. The differences might be those between successive entropy states. But since the differences are in sequence, they will be associated with the actions of coming to and ceasing to obtain, as we saw in Chapter VIII, §5. So action is available even here to ground temporal asymmetry. It is only the mistaken Ockhamite view of action that motivates the appeal to irreversibility.

According to the second approach, the basis for the temporal relation in the sequence to which an action is reduced is a causal relation. On the atomistic view, there are temporal relations, and hence no necessary connections across time. Those who try to replace temporal relations by causal relations agree with us in rejecting temporal atomism. One causal theorist expresses his dissatisfaction with temporal atomism by noting that "Hume begins his definition of cause by saying, 'The cause is an object precedent . . . to another', without appearing to care to know what the expression 'precedent' signifies."[4] But digging behind the temporal relation leads the causal theorist only to another relation: ". . . for us on the other hand those facts that are conditions of others in a group are said to precede them, and the others are said to follow the first, where these expressions signify no more than the relation of *occasional causality*."[5] But behind the problem of time is the question of how events can have relational properties, whether temporal or causal. This problem is not advanced by introducing a causal relation "as a *primitive* relation for the purpose of then defining temporal betweenness."[6] In my view, events have both temporal and causal relational properties on the basis of action. To hold for anything less is to accept the network view that posits property conditions set in isolation by external relations. Ontologically, matters are as hopeless if the relations are causal as they are if the relations are temporal.

Granted that the Ockhamite view is unacceptable, do actions provide what is needed for temporal asymmetry? It will be seen that they do only if they have what I shall call a vectoral character.

§2. *The Vectoral Character of Action.* To say that action has a vectoral character is to say two things about action. First, it is an objective fact and not a matter of convention that certain conditions are the result of a given action. If being at *B* is a result of motion from *A*, then no mere switch of conventions or of perspectives will make being at *A* the result of this motion. Second, no action is the result of any condition that is itself a result of that action. This does not preclude interaction between systems,[7] for it allows the action to be influenced by some condition, other than its result, that is nonetheless a condition of the system that ultimately has this result. So, in all, an action is vectoral since its pointing toward any of its results is an objective fact, and since none of its results point toward it as their result. The first vectoral aspect can be called the "objectivity of results" and the second the "asymmetry of action."

Why are both objectivity and asymmetry needed? Suppose, on the one hand, results are objective but actions are not asymmetrical. It is an objective fact that condition *b* is a result of action *a*. But it is possible that *a* is also a result of *b*. Action and result can, then, no longer ground the asymmetry of time. Suppose, on the other hand, actions are asymmetrical but results are not objective. The asymmetry of action is then like that of the relation *left of*. This relation is not grounded in its relata but depends on a point of view. Under one convention or under one point of view, *b* is a result of *a,* whereas, under another, *a* is a result of *b,* which is no longer a result of *a*. Under each convention or perspective taken by itself, the action-result structure is asymmetrical in exactly the way *left of* is asymmetrical under any given perspective. But since there are several conventions or perspectives, it is not an objective feature of any given event to be a result. Consequently, the temporal asymmetry based on the asymmetry of action would not be objectively grounded. Yet our hope is to give *prior to* an objective grounding. To realize this hope, I must show that actions are indeed asymmetrical and results are indeed objective.

To show that actions are not asymmetrical, one attempts to show that a closed chain of action is possible. If such a chain is not possible then closed time—time represented in the form of a circle—is not possible. The priority relation is symmetrical for closed time. If, along one part of the circle, *a* is prior to *b,* then there is another part of the circle along which *b* is prior to *a*. The failure of previous attempts to deny the possibility of closed time has been observed by Grünbaum.[8] But he does not note that such attempts fail because they do not ground time in action. The impossibility of closed time must be viewed as a consequence of the impossibility of a closed action chain.

Suppose *a* is a complete action whose result is *b*. Suppose also that *b* itself is a complete action that, through various intermediate results, has the original action *a* as a result. Now the general feature of a result is that it involves dependence on an action. Since *b* is a result, it depends on the complete action *a*. Of course, this is not to say that *a* is a sufficient condition for *b*. It is obvious that, in a closed action chain such as this, any action depends on itself. For every action is, indirectly at least, a result of itself. Since *b* has *a* as a result and since *b* was in the first place a result of *a*, *a* is self-dependent. How, though, can a result depend on itself? Even a necessary being would not depend on itself, but would instead depend on no being. An individual could depend on itself in the sense that one of its components depends on another of its components. But it is strict self-dependence that is in question here, a state of affairs that is as absurd as owing yourself money in one and the same account. One condition owes nothing to itself. Otherwise, it would be (inconsistently) both itself and a condition other than itself.

Let us now turn to the objectivity of results. Does it not fail in an obvious way in certain cases? When an action-result sequence—a sequence of property conditions associated with an action where the sequence includes the result—is a reversible sequence, there seems to be no objectivity of results. For if this sequence of property conditions is reversible, there is no objective basis for the condition we happen to call a result being a result rather than an initial condition. Only when the action-result sequence is irreversible is there an objective basis for the condition called the result being a result. There is, then, no general objectivity of results, and hence not all actions are vectoral.

This objection holds only when actions are reduced to sequences of property conditions. To show this, let me begin by saying something about the reversibility of sequences.[9] Suppose a sequence of conditions can be described by saying that condition *a* is before condition *b* and condition *b* is before condition *c*. In respect to this description, the "converse" description is the proposition that *a* is after *b* and *b* is after *c*. One simply replaces temporal relational terms by their converses to obtain the sentence expressing the converse description. In Ockham's view, a given description and its converse purport to describe distinct actions since actions are sequences of conditions, and one gets a distinct sequence when the relation *before* is replaced by *after*. Nonetheless, the two sequences, and hence for Ockham the two actions, are not in all cases equally possible, for some sequences are irreversible:

(1) A sequence of conditions is "irreversible" if, though this sequence is possible, the converse description in respect to a description of this sequence is not a description of a possible sequence.

However, a sequence is reversible if it is possible and if a sequence fitting the converse description in respect to a description of it is also possible.

If a sequence is reversible, there is no objective basis in the conditions making up the sequence for saying one of them is before another rather than after it. There is no basis since both arrangements are in themselves possible. Consequently, there is no objective basis for saying that one condition is a result rather than an initial condition. In the sequence view of actions, results do not have objectivity when the sequences are reversible.

Suppose that, as I have argued, actions are not sequences of property conditions. Must, then, actions that have associated reversible sequences lack a vectoral character? I think not. A converse description of a sequence of property conditions associated with throwing a ball is still a description of a sequence associated with the same action, the throwing. The description does not become one of catching, for it was not a description of anything more than a sequence. Of course, the throwing cannot be associated with a sequence in which the initial condition involves the ball being in the air and the final one involves its being in the hand of the pitcher. But that is no more remarkable than that converse descriptions of some sequences of properties cannot be true.

Here we have a new kind of irreversibility, irreversibility not simply for sequences but for sequences with actions. A sequence with an action is irreversible if, though the sequence with this action is possible, this action with a sequence fitting the converse description of the original sequence is not possible. Clearly, every sequence *cum* action, whether the sequence by itself is reversible or not, is irreversible.

Why not talk about the converse description of the sequence

cum action, rather than merely about the converse description of the sequence alone? After all, it would seem that irreversibility for a sequence *cum* action should be defined relative to the wider description. This will change the description by including in its scope not just the property-condition sequence but also the stages of the complete action. The converse description of the sequence *cum* action will, for some division of the complete action into stages, have 'before' in place of 'after,' not just between references to property conditions but also between references to stages of the complete action.

This does nothing to change the preceding conclusion that every sequence *cum* action is irreversible. The reason is that the converse description only concerns the temporal relations between stages of a complete action. It dos not refer to stages distinct from the ones originally referred to. Hence it does not refer to a complete action, or even a progressive action, other than the one associated with the sequences originally described.

For example, suppose I report that Jones's wind-up was prior to his delivery of the ball. Here the wind-up and the delivery can be considered stages in a pitch. The converse description of this division into stages of the complete action—the pitch—is that Jones's wind-up was subsequent to his delivery. The stages referred to, on any division, remain the same under the converse description, since, by hypothesis, only the temporal relational terms have been replaced by their converses.[10] Of course, if the pitch is only a sequence of property conditions, the converse description will not refer to the same stages, since the stages will be different when the temporal relations between their associated property conditions are inverted. But it is not open to us to accept this Ockhamite view of action.

It follows, then, that every sequence *cum* action is irreversible relative to any division of the corresponding complete action into stages. For:

(2) A sequence *cum* action is "irreversible" relative to a division of the corresponding complete action into stages if, though the action with this action-result sequence is possible, either the action-result sequence that fits the converse description or the

sequence of stages of the complete action together with a result (relative to the given division) that fits the converse description is not possible.

How can this be applied to the question of the objectivity of results? In the sequence view of actions, the irreversibility of an action-result sequence is a basis for the objectivity of results. For, since the converse description of an irreversible sequence cannot be satisfied, a condition that is a result could not trade roles with the condition that is the initial one in the sequence. Similarly, when actions are treated as irreducible, the irreversibility of a sequence *cum* action is the basis for the objectivity of results.

Sequence *cum* action irreversibility implies that either the converse description of the action-result sequence or the converse description of a sequence of stages of the complete action taken together with the result cannot be realized. Either, then, the sequence of property conditions is irreversible. Hence a result in the sequence could not be an initial condition. Or the sequence of action stages followed by a result cannot occur in reverse order. Otherwise, in a pitch the delivery might be before the wind-up. So a result of such an action could not be an initial condition of it; that would require that the stages could also occur between inverted time relations.

This means that even the motions of classical mechanics are, together with their sequences, irreversible. Of course, the sequences by themselves are reversible. The sequence of conditions associated with a ball's rolling from *m* over a smooth surface to *n* is reversible. But it is an objectively based fact that the result is the condition the ball has of being at *n*. For the converse description—that the moving from *m* is after the moving to *n*—is unrealizable. Action even in the uneventful universe of mechanics is vectoral; it involves the surge toward results that has time as a product. Attempts to ground the temporal relation *prior to* on entropy increase, cosmological expansion, meson decay, or the collapse of the wave packet to an eigenstate under measurement are based on the assumption that, if sequences of property conditions were reversible, there would be no objective difference associated with that between *before* and *after*. This assumption is false since actions are not sequences of property conditions and since the objective difference between action and result can be associated with that between *before* and *after*.

Still, *before* would not be asymmetrical if a closed action chain were possible. The irreversibility of action, and hence the objectivity of results, would establish only that there is a difference between *before* and *after* along a given path in a closed time. It would be an objective fact that *a* is before *b* along the path in the circle. It would not, without assuming the asymmetry of action, show that there is no other path along which *a* might be after *b* instead of before *b*. Thus, the need for both objectivity of results and asymmetry of action.

§3. *Results of Actions.* Before appealing to results in order to ground time, the relation *result of* must itself be grounded.

It is not a mere tautology that actions have results in the sense of terminal results. For initially, at least, the suggestion that there might be actions that never end is plausible. Closer consideration is needed to show that such actions are not possible. For the doing of an action is not a multiplicity of entities. It is a single condition corresponding to a single progressive action. However, if it were a multiplicity, it could even be an infinite multiplicity. There is no reason why such a multiplicity, when ordered in a sequence, should ever end. But, in fact, there is a unitary doing of an action corresponding to each progressive action. This will entail that the doing of an action needs to be bounded. If the action went on without end, there would never be the unitary entity that is the doing of it. The doing of it would, as it were, be on the way but would never arrive. A result is then essential to an action, for only if there is a result is there one of the boundaries needed for there to be the doing of an action. Without a limit, an action would be incomplete and would lack the unity essential to any entity. Doing an action is then called a complete action in recognition of the fact that it is an entity only because there is a result.

Disagreement over this point arises immediately upon taking the Ockhamite view of action. For if doing an action is a multiplicity of property conditions in sequence, doing an action is not a single entity. There is no objection to an unending multiplicity, since a multiplicity is not a genuine entity. Thus the Ockhamite will insist on the possibility of actions that never end. This criticism is misplaced if, as I have claimed, doing an action is not a multiplicity.

The unitary character of actions has the further consequence that Zeno's paradox of the dichotomy[11] does not arise for uninterrupted motion. The problem is how one can walk to the end of a certain distance since doing so requires doing an infinity of actions. One must go half the way, then half of what remains, and so on without end. But if walking is an action, there is only one doing of walking corresponding to the one progressive action of walking. There is not an infinity of walks to be done in order to get to the end. The stages of the walk defined by the dichotomy are only components of the complete action and are thus not distinct from the single complete action. But saying there are unitary actions does not imply there is a temporally shortest action. An action can be of any finite duration.

Of course, if the walker were what Grünbaum calls a staccato walker—one who rests, but for progressively shorter times, at each division defined by the dichotomy—the walker would reach the end only by doing an infinity of walkings.[12] Zeno's problem clearly arises here, even though in my view it did not arise for the uninterrupted walker. The durations of the walks and of the rests between the walks become shorter and shorter, so that the sum of the times of the walks and the rests is finite. If the staccato walker can complete the infinity of walks, then the unitary theory of action was not needed in the case of the uninterrupted walker. But can the walker complete the infinity of walks?

The problem is not the mathematical one of showing that the sum of the durations is finite. It is, rather, the physical one of showing how the walker can perform an action in all of those durations with the result that he or she is at the end. The dichotomization yields no last duration. But can a last action be dispensed with if we assume that the walker gets to the end? The walker's being at a point beyond that where he or she is after any one of the walks in the infinite sequence is, in this case, not happenstance but is, rather, a result of walking. The only alternative to saying that it is a result of walking is saying that the staccato walker got to this point not by walking or any other action, even though he or she was not at that point earlier. This possibility is clearly not available to us since a walker who makes it through the infinity of walks will not be just anywhere—as would be possible if where the walker is does not result from an action of walking along the specified distance—but will be at the end of the distance walked.[13]

Yet there seems to be no action in the sequence that has being at the end as a result. Indeed, since there is no last walking, there is no action which results in being at the end. So, for a walker who arrives at the end of the specified distance, an infinity of acts of walking in traversing that distance in a finite time is impossible. Otherwise, there would be a result that is the result of no action. If the walker simply vanished upon completing the infinity of acts there would be no problem, but we assumed the walker made it through to the first moment after the walks.

What this shows is that the view of actions as single entities rather than multiplicities is indispensable if Zeno's problem is to be avoided or even solved for the uninterrupted walker. To suppose that actions are multiplicities of actions is to allow that the uninterrupted walker completes an infinity of walks. Consideration of the staccato walker makes clear that this is impossible. For being at the end is a result of some walk, yet it can be the result of no walk if there is no last walk.

I have argued that since doing an action is a single entity it is complete and that it is complete by having a result. A result serves to limit a corresponding action. Suppose x has progressive action A and that a is x's condition of having A. Then let b be a result of a, where b is y's having component B. There are two aspects to the *result of* relation, and we should consider each in getting foundations for this relation.

First, there is the limit aspect. A complete action has a result that plays the role of a limit. Second, there is the dependency aspect. A result depends on a complete action; it comes about because of this action. As for the limit aspect, a result, in a given context that will include other limiting factors, is a sufficient basis for the unity of the complete action. This suggests taking as one of the foundations y's component ($B_{-} > a$ is a unity), where the $>$

is the factive conditional connective introduced in Chapter IV, §3. In effect, where b is a result in a given context, that By makes it true that the complete action a has unity. I use the factive rather than the relevant conditional connective since the connection depends on the specific context. In another context, a similar result might limit a quite dissimilar action.

As for the dependency aspect, the appropriate connection seems again to be the factive conditional connective. If b is a result of a, then b depends on a in the sense that $(Ax > By)$. In the given context, that x does A makes it true that y has B. Since the factive conditional need not be causal, this dependency need not be causal, and hence not all actions need be causal. Pushing is causal though seeing is not. As a second foundation, we then have y's component $(Ax > B\_)$. (We could just as well have made this foundation x's component $(A\_ > By)$.) It remains only to bring in the action itself. The progressive action A of x is, then, the third and final foundation for *result of*.

There are two other types of entity that are often called results, but neither has the role of a limit. First, there are "intermediate results," such as being at the half-way point before the walk is over. Though the intermediate result satisfies the criterion of dependency, it limits only a stage of and not the entire action. It can limit a stage only if there is a complete action that has stages. As a limit and hence as a result, it depends on there being a limit and hence a result of a complete action. Second, there are "*pari passu* results," such as the motion of the surface of a cushion as a hard ball is pressed into it. Such a result is a complete action that must itself have a limit. Moreover, its limit will also be the limit of the action on which it depends. Of itself, it does not play the role of the limit of the pressing. When I speak of results, I shall not intend to include either intermediate or *pari passu* results. This is a significant restriction in respect to temporal asymmetry since neither type of result is posterior to action.

§4. *The Foundations of Temporal Asymmetry.* To provide adequate foundations for temporal asymmetry, it suffices to provide foundations for four different cases.

(I) In all those instances of temporal priority in which the priority stands between a complete action—the doing of *A*, say—and a result—the having of *B*, say—the progressive action *A* and the component *B* of the entity with the result are the foundations of the priority. Priority in such cases is to be called "action-result" priority. As we shall see, these are the basic cases of priority. The foundations here are components of individuals, even though the temporal relational properties for which they are the foundations are properties of conditions of individuals, that is, of complete actions and results. The dependency of conditions on things with them is merely emphasized by the fact that the foundations of the relational properties of the conditions are components of those things.

(II) Suppose an individual must lose one component, *B*, in order to gain another, *C*. If it changes from being *B* to being *C*, that is, from the condition *b* to the condition *c*, then *b* is prior to *c*. But *b* need not be a complete action at all. So the priority need not be action-result priority. It may, nonetheless, depend in an indirect way on action-result priority. For suppose there is a complete action *a* that not only has *c* as a result but also has being not-*B* as a result. Clearly, these action-result pairs provide a basis for the priority of *b* in respect to *c*. Since, by hypothesis, *B* and *C* are incompatible, the action must counteract the presence of *B* in order to have *c* as a result. Let us then call *b* a "counter condition" in respect to *c* whenever, for *c* to be a result of some action, being not-*B* must be a result of that action. Thus *b* being prior to *c* is a case of "counter-result" priority. The foundations of *b*'s counter-result priority to *c* are very simply the foundations of *a*'s action-result priority to being not-*B* and of its action-result priority to *c*.

Suppose an individual did not have *B* before having *C*. Even so, *a* might have *c* as a result, and *B* might be incompatible with *C*. In this case, one would not have to say that being not-*B* is a result of *a*. Why not? Simply because *B* was not present and thus did not have to be countered by *a*. Counter-result priority comes in when, since not-*B* is a result, *B* had to be countered. Discussion of a negative condition is feasible here in view of our earlier admission of negative properties.

(III) What is to be done with the temporal priority between two conditions separated by a chain of many actions? This calls for linking together many priorities, each of which is either an action-result or a counter-result priority. Suppose m_1 is a complete action or a counter condition and m_2 is the associated result condition. Likewise, suppose m_2 is a complete action or a counter condition and m_3 is the associated result condition, and so on down to m_n. Then we say that the sequence $m_1, m_2, m_3, \ldots, m_n$ is an "action chain" and that the members are "links."

Now suppose conditions *a* and *b* are such that there is an action chain terminating in *a* and *b* in which chain *a* is not a result of any link; no link is a counter condition in respect to *a;* no link is a result of *b;* and *b* is not a counter condition of any link. Under these suppositions, *a* is prior to *b*. We can call this "chain" priority, of which action-result and counter-result priority are special cases. The foundations of *a*'s chain priority to *b* are the foundations of the action-result priorities that are ultimately involved in the chain. I say "ultimately" since there may be counter-result priorities immediately involved. Moreover, action chains cannot be closed. This is a direct consequence of the asymmetry of action when action-result priority is the only priority in the chain (§2). By a more complicated reasoning, a closed action chain is excluded by the asymmetry of action even when there is also counter-result priority in the chain. But I shall omit this reasoning here.

An action chain need not be a chain of conditions of a single individual. A result in the chain may belong to an individual different from the one the action belongs to. This distinguishes my view from that of Leibniz, for whom temporal priority was grounded in the activity of a monad, which does not act on other monads. By its activity a monad develops itself into an ordered sequence of states; ". . . a body is not only at the actual moment of its motion in a place commensurate to it, but it has also a tendency or effort to change its place so that the succeeding state follows of itself from the present by the force of nature."[14] Without action between monads, temporal priority between states of distinct monads could not be grounded in action. Either there is no such relation or it is based on something other than the action of created monads. However, in my view, distinct individuals are linked in time only through their actions on one another. Asymmetrical temporal relatedness between conditions of distinct individuals is on an equal footing with that between conditions of the same entity. There is no fundamental importance in the distinction between "external" time grounded in action on the world and "internal" time grounded in self-development.

What about individuals that are not related at all by action? On the one hand, there is no reason to suppose that if there were such isolated individuals their conditions would be temporally related. On the other hand, it is doubtful that there are individuals unconnected, directly or indirectly, by action. The smallest mote, we are told, exerts a gravitational pull on the most distant star. Nonetheless, if one were to consider non-interacting worlds, separate time systems would be appropriate to them.

There is, though, a more subtle objection. Suppose Jones and Smith pass through childhood without acting on one another. Then, when both are adults, Jones does something that affects Smith. This action sets up a link between their histories that allows certain conditions of one of them to be prior to certain conditions of the other. Jones's action that provides the link is, say, chain posterior to his first hammering a nail. The effect in Smith is, we suppose, chain prior to Smith's wedding. So Jones's hammering is chain prior to Smith's wedding, as is plain in Figure 1. There are some interesting consequences of the fact that neither acted on the other during childhood and of the fact that it was Jones who acted on Smith and not Smith on Jones.

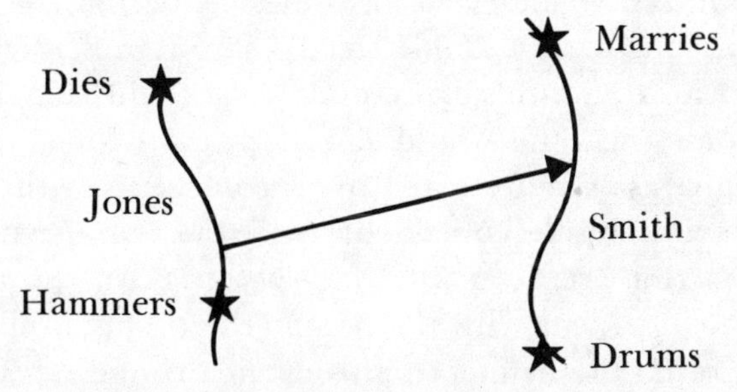

Figure 1: A one-way connection leads to gaps in temporal relatedness.

First, Smith's beating on a drum when he was a child has no temporal relation to Jones's early hammering. There is simply no chain of action from the one to the other. Second, Smith's drumming is not even prior to Jones's dying, since Smith never acts back on Jones. Thus in our uncompromising action view of time, there is no basis for temporal relations in such cases. It will not do to appeal to temporal measurement to put these events in a temporal order with one another. For if a clock is attached to Smith and another is synchronized with it and sent on a voyage to Jones, the two individuals are connected by acts of synchronizing and moving clocks.

Our example is unrealistic, for if Jones acts on Smith, then in all likelihood Smith would act on Jones. Only if one overlooks the unrealistic nature of the example will one find it objectionable that our view, as applied to the example, yields so many temporal gaps. But if it is still felt that there is a difficulty, it is tempting to try to overcome it by appealing to possibilities.[15] At the time Smith beat his drum he *could* instead have done some different action that *would* have had a result in Jones, a result that would be chain prior to Jones's hammering. If there is this possibility, then surely we can say that the drumming is prior to the hammering. But what is needed to have such a possibility?

What difference would there be between a case in which the connecting action is possible and a case in which it is not? Smith's drumming and Jones's early life up to the hammering might be indistinguishable in the two cases. The difference could only be that, when the action from Smith to Jones is possible though not actual, there must be an actual action-result priority from an event of Smith's to an event of Jones's. Specifically, either an *actual* "slow" action—a sound signal, say, represented by 1 in Figure 2—prior to Smith's drumming has a result coincident with Jones's hammering. This would make it *possible* for a "fast" action —a light signal, say, represented by 3—coincident with the drumming to have a result coincident with the hammering. Or an *actual* fast action—represented by 5—posterior to the drumming has a result coincident with the hammering. This would make it *possible* to reach the hammering from the drumming with a slow action—represented by 3. In either case, a possible action that is not actual presupposes an actual one because it presupposes an actual action-result priority. So the appeal to possibilities is of only limited usefulness in filling the gaps in temporal relatedness.

Otherwise, to say that an action is possible along one route, even when there is no other route with the same end points along

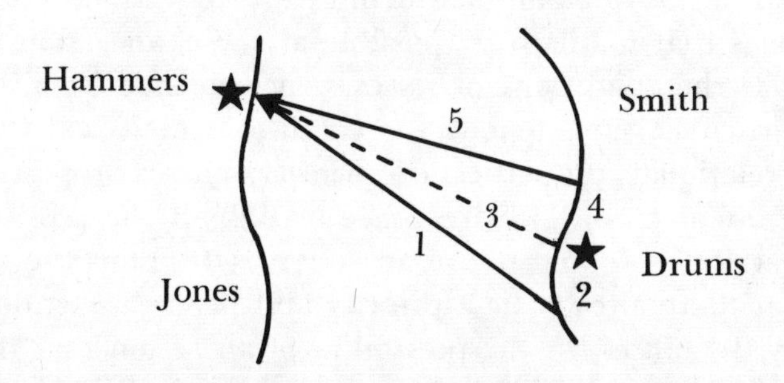

Figure 2: 3 is a possible action only if it is a side of a "triangle"—1 2 3 or 3 4 5—whose other sides are actual actions.

which action actually occurs is to hypostatize possibility. That is, it treats possibilities as independent of factors they depend on. It is possible for a poker to burn a hole in wood only because wood fibers oxidize. It is not because the poker has this possibility that there is this fact about the nature of wood. Similarly, it is not possibilities for action that are the basis for time. Instead, such possibilities depend on temporal relatedness. An action that does not occur, but that could occur, could occur precisely because some other action did occur that provided the temporal basis needed for a possible action.

(IV) We thus have a fourth case of priority. If an action chain from *a* to *b* is possible, then *a* is prior to *b*. This can be called "possible chain" priority. It exists only when it can be represented as the third side of a "triangle" whose other sides represent actual chain priorities. There are many foundations for the possible chain priority of *a* to *b*. First, there are the foundations of any two such actual chain priorities. Second, there is the conditional property of the agent that, if there are action chains corresponding to these actual chain priorities, there is a kind of action such that an action of that kind could connect *a* with *b*.

Does it follow that before an individual performs an action it has no possibility for any action? It would seem so since the possibility for action depends on temporal relatedness which, in turn, depends on actual actions. Yet if actions are impossible, as they seem to be for any individual that has yet to act, nothing will ever be done. In short, there will be no time.

There is an obvious mistake behind this objection. The objector assumes that for it to be possible at t_1 for an action to take place at t_2 the conditions of its existence must exist already at t_1. In particular, since among the conditions of its existence are certain relational properties of priority, these properties, too should exist at t_1. But we are concerned about the possibility at t_1 of an action at t_2, and not of an action at t_1. Thus the requirement that there already be a priority and hence an action is unnecessary. It suffices for the possibility of an action that there be priority when the action is done. And this condition is satisfied whenever the action is done.

Everything would be easy if events were located in a network of temporal relations. Possibilities for action could then be based on actualities by being based on the temporal relations in the network. They would not depend on actions being done in any part of the network. But since belief in such a network is incoherent with human practice, we cannot appeal to it to support possible actions. So the possibility of any action must depend either upon the doing of that action or upon the doing of other actions that provide the two actual sides of an associated temporal triangle. Two individuals belong to the same universe, not because they are in a spatio-temporal network but because one acts on the other.

§5. *The Impossibility of Counterdirected Action.* Even though action has a vectoral character, might it not be the case that some actions point in one direction whereas others point in another? Nothing we said in arguing for the vectoral character of action implies that all actions cohere in pointing in one direction. But if the direction from one action to its result is opposite to the direction from another action to its result, the attempt to found temporal asymmetry on action seems to face a serious obstacle. For such an attempt would then lead us to say, in some cases, that though a given event is before another, an event simultaneous with the first is after, not before, an event simultaneous with the second. This is an intolerable consequence for any theory of time. Can it be avoided on the action theory of time?

The possibility of counterdirected action has been conjectured in various areas of physics. First, the sequences of conditions associated with processes governed by classical electromagnetic theory are reversible. This means that an oscillating electrical charge could have *either* a "retarded" *or* an "advanced" potential associated with it. But it has been conjectured more recently that a charge might have *both* a retarded *and* an advanced potential. A charge would then act to have posterior results by the retarded potential, and prior results by the advanced potential.[16] It would not only set off oscillations in other charges at later times but also set off oscillations in other charges at earlier times. It would then have counterdirected actions.

Second, it has been conjectured that there are particles—tachyons—moving faster than the speed of light. Since they move faster than light, they move in space-time between points whose time order can be reversed simply by changing the frame of reference.[17] This reversal is a direct consequence of the relativity of simultaneity. It then follows that since they never move slower than a speed greater than that of light, their emission and absorption by atoms can be reversed merely by changing the frame of reference in which they are considered. An emission of a tachyon in one frame of reference would be an absorption in another. The result of an action in one framework would be before that action in another framework. An atom that might be a source of a tachyon would then act with posterior results in one framework and with prior results in another. Again counterdirected actions seem possible.

The following objection has been raised to such conjectures. It would follow from these conjectures that a result could exist without the action from which it results. Suppose there is an antecedent effect of the acceleration of a charge. This effect could be taken as a signal to trigger a series of events resulting in the charge's failure to accelerate at all. So the effect occurs without its cause. The same paradox confronts the tachyon. One could intervene to prevent what in one framework is the causal action. So in that framework there would be a prior result of an action that does not occur.

However, there are limits to intervention intended to prevent actions posterior to their results. Hesse notes that when a result occurs prior to its associated action, there may be no possibility of detecting the result in time to intervene and prevent the posterior action.[18] This will be true if the dimensions are small enough to make quantum uncertainties an important factor. Quantum uncertainties can then restrict somewhat the threat of paradox resulting from counterdirected action. In a micro-process, the amount of energy absorbed as a prior result of a posterior action will be small. The time of absorption will, by the uncertainty principle, be correspondingly large. But this absorption was to be the signal for intervening. There will not then be time to intervene and prevent the causal action. Since all counterdirected actions might be limited to the quantum domain, a different attack on the possibility of counterdirected action is needed if we are to be able to accept the action theory of time.

One can conceive of two types of counterdirected action. There are the counterdirected actions on different halves of a closed action chain. Counterdirected actions of this type are possible only if there can be self-dependent actions. Since, as we saw in §2, there can be no self-dependent actions, there are no counterdirected actions of this type. There are also counterdirected actions that run simultaneously. In a closed action chain, by contrast, counterdirected actions are not running concurrently; they are in distinct parts of time. I shall try to show that the second type of counterdirectedness implies the possibility of self-dependent action also. Thus there can be no counterdirectedness of the second type either. To show this it will be necessary to discuss simultaneity, which, like other temporal relations, has its basis in action. This discussion divides into two parts, one of simultaneity among conditions of one individual, and the other of simultaneity among conditions of distinct individuals. No special treatment is given here of spatial relations, but through priority and simultaneity, an action theory of space can be constructed.[19]

(I) As regards simultaneity among conditions of one individual, it is important to observe that an individual is the same particular as any component of it. Some of its components will, however, be had before others. So it in no way follows from the fact that an individual is not distinct from each of two components that the having of one is simultaneous with the having of the other. If not, though, what is the basis for simultaneity within an individual?

The actions, properties, and parts of an individual are alike in being components, but there is an important difference between actions and other components. An action will be what it is on the basis of at least some of the properties and parts of the individual with that action. The walking of a one-legged person is not similar, in the previous sense of exact similarity, to the walking of a two-legged person. The actions of reflecting white light from square and triangular surfaces are not similar either. By saying that a component is a "basis" for what an associated action is, I mean that if the component were not present, the action would not be similar to the actions that it was originally similar to. Such a basis is clearly not a causal one, for a dissimilar cause could still have an exactly similar action as effect.

This notion of a basis is directly related to that of simultaneity. The components that shape what an action, however caused, is to be are ones that an individual has *while* it is acting. So if a component of an individual is a basis for what an action of the individual will be similar to, then having the component and doing the action are, at least in part, simultaneous.* Two conditions that are partially simultaneous to a given complete action need not, by this account, be partially simultaneous to one another. But since they could be partially simultaneous, our task is unfinished since as yet there is no account of how they could.

Among actions are the actions of losing and gaining components. Associated components will determine what such actions are similar to. Losing weight by disease and by loss of a limb are dissimilar actions of losing weight. Magnetizing a paramagnetic substance, in which the presence of atoms acting as magnetic dipoles is the important factor, is not similar to the action of magnetizing a diamagnetic substance. Thus where *A* and *B* are components of an individual *j,* if *A* (or *B*) is a basis for what *j*'s losing or gaining *B* (or *A*) is similar to, then being *A* is partially simultaneous with being *B*.

One might wonder whether, beyond these two cases, there are

*Conditions are partially simultaneous when a stage of one is simultaneous with a stage of the other. But here there is no need for the notion of simultaneity, since the problem of counterdirectedness can be handled by that of partial simultaneity.

yet others of partial simultaneity for a single individual. One will so wonder if one is convinced that any two conditions of an individual must be either concurrent or successive. Yet this conviction stems from the view that over and above individuals there is a network of temporal relations that requires either concurrence or successiveness. I am content to say that strictly isolated components of a single individual are not involved in definite temporal relations with other components of this individual. The most one can say is that the individual has these components along with the others while it exists. If being *A* is neither a basis for what being *B* is nor a basis for what gaining or losing *B* is and, conversely, if being *B* is neither a basis for what being *A* is nor a basis for what gaining or losing *A* is, then if being *A* is neither prior nor posterior to being *B*, the temporal relation of being *A* to being *B* is indeed indefinite.

(II) Now consider simultaneity among conditions of distinct individuals. The motivating idea here is that, since actions are prior to results, simultaneous conditions are not connected by an action chain. If we give up this requirement of unconnectedness, we are faced with the prospect of treating simultaneity as an ungrounded relation. If we conform to it, we shall suppose that conditions of two entities are simultaneous only when they lie between an action of the one entity on the other and an action of the second back on the first. There is then no simultaneity between entities that do not interact. There is sufficient interaction in the world to make simultaneity a common sort of relatedness.

Suppose an individual *i* acts to produce a result in *j* and that, after the coming into being of the result in *j*, *j* itself acts back on *i*. Any condition of *j* after the coming into being of the result in *j* of the action by *i* and before the action by *j* itself is simultaneous with some part of any condition that *i* has that lasts from the time of its action on *j* until the change due to the action from *j*. Hence, the one condition is partially simultaneous with the other. The relations of priority employed here depend on both the relation of chain priority and on the relation of partial simultaneity within individuals. Thus the condition of *j* that is after the coming into being of the result in *j* brought about by *i* need not have chain posteriority to this coming into being of the result. It need only have chain posteriority to some condition of j that is partially simultaneous with coming into being of the result.

It is now time to apply this notion of partial simultaneity in order to show that actions cohere by pointing in the same direction. Consider the two individuals i and j. The complete action a_i of i is, we suppose, counterdirected to the complete action c_j of j, as in Figure 3. To suppose this is to suppose, since closed

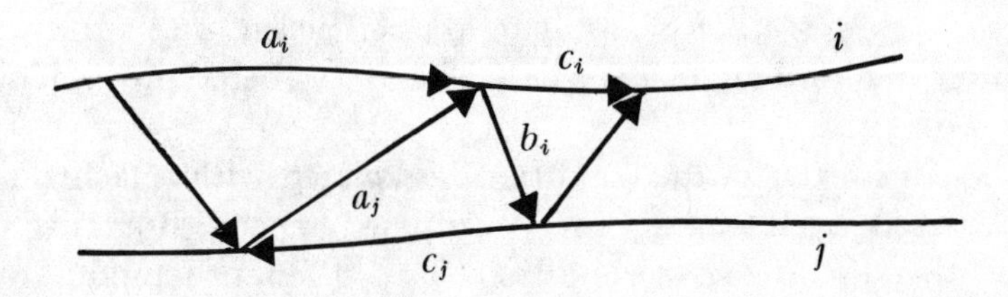

Figure 3: Counterdirectedness with simultaneity leads to self-dependence.

time was excluded, that i and j belong to a common time in which the directions of their actions can be compared. Thus there will be actions of each of these individuals with results in the other. Otherwise, there would be no simultaneity, partial or complete, between the conditions of the two, and thus no basis for comparison of the directions of their actions. But partial simultaneity and counterdirectedness generate a difficulty when taken together. To see this, notice that the following situation, described in Figure 3, is always possible.

The complete action a_j of j has a result b_i in i. Let a_j be a basis, along with at least one other action, for partial simultaneity between the beginning of a_j itself and a_i. Also, b_i is to have c_j as a result and b_i is to be a basis, along with at least one other action, for partial simultaneity between c_i, which is to be a result of a_i, and the beginning of c_j. Thus a_i and c_j are counterdirected since a_i is partially simultaneous with the beginning of a result of c_j—that is, with the beginning of a_j—and the beginning of c_j is partially simultaneous with a result of a_i—that is, with c_i—but not with a_i. There is then counterdirectedness since, though a_i is before c_i and the end of c_j is after the beginning of c_j, a_i and the end of c_j are partially simultaneous as are c_i and the beginning of c_j but not a_i and the beginning of c_j. But what has been allowed by all this is for a_j to be self-dependent, and as we saw, no entity can be self-dependent. Complete action a_j depends by counterdirected action on c_j, and c_j depends, indirectly, by forward action on a_j. Since such a situation can always arise under the above supposition, the possibility of counterdirected action must be rejected.

This criticism can be seen to apply to the case of a tachyon only after we have asked what it is that the transformation of coordinates reverses. But before applying that criticism, we shall propose an interpretation of tachyons that renders them unproblematic as regards time.

The time order of the conditions associated with a tachyon can be reversed by changing the coordinate system. But this only means that a sequence of conditions has a different temporal order in different coordinate systems. Recall that a converse description of a sequence is not a converse description of an associated action. Correspondingly, transforming the coordinates to obtain a reverse time order will not yield a counterdirected action. One will merely obtain an emission of a particle that is after its absorption. It was then incorrect of us to say that an emission in one system would be an absorption in another. The threat of counterdirected action is thus set aside. What remains is the absurdity of an emission occurring *after* the particle is already distant from the emitter.

This situation will not be absurd for the Ockhamite view of action. In this view there is no emission over and above the sequence of states of the atom and the tachyon. In particular, in the reverse time order obtained by transforming the coordinates there is no emission that occurs after the tachyon is distant from the emitter. There is only the sequence of positions of the tachyon.

However, in the view adopted here that actions exist along with sequences of property conditions, it is indeed impossible to have the reverse sequence associated with the original action. Precisely what an action contributes that a sequence need not contribute, because it may be a reversible sequence, is direction.[20]

Still it is undeniable that the existence of tachyons would imply the possibility of a reverse sequence. Since this sequence does not imply a reverse action, we must conclude, to avoid absurdity, that the emission and the absorption of tachyons are not genuine actions at all. They and tachyons with them are to be interpreted as mere sequences of property conditions. We thereby avoid having either an action in one coordinate system that is counter in direction to that in another or a single action that can be both before and after its result.

This reductionist approach of ours to actions associated with tachyons is mandatory if even more awkward consequences are to be avoided. First, since a tachyon is a "space-like" entity, the emission and the absorption of a tachyon can, by an appropriate choice of coordinate system, be simultaneous. This conflicts with the principle that an action and its result are grounds for priority. However, if, as I am claiming, the life of a tachyon does not involve the actions of emission and absorption, then tachyons are no exception to this principle that action implies priority.

Second, with the aid of a tachyon one can close an action chain, if its emission and absorption are genuine actions. In an appropriate coordinate system, the absorption of a tachyon will antedate its emission, and its absorption can then trigger its emission, on which the absorption depends. We again get the specter of self-dependency found in the general case of counterdirectedness. If, however, the life of a tachyon involves only a sequence of conditions and neither an action of emission nor an action of absorption, that part of the chain described as an emission is no longer an action; the objectionable self-dependency of closed action chains is thereby avoided.

§6. *The Branch Hypothesis as Superfluous.* The action view of time rests on two principles. The first is that action is *vectoral,* which was justified in §2. This principle implies that there is a distinction between an action and one of its results that is not eliminated simply by a change in the order of the sequence of associated conditions, and that the action is not a result of any of its results. The second principle is that actions are *coherent,* which was justified in §5. This principle states that all actions point in one direction; that is, given a certain action and one of its results, there is no other action in a relation of partial simultaneity with this result of the first action but not with the first action itself whose result is in a relation of partial simultaneity with the first action. I wish now to show that these two principles are relied on in using the so-called branch hypothesis of statistical physical theory to give a foundation to temporal asymmetry. Since they alone are sufficient for the action view of time, the branch hypothesis must then be superfluous in giving a foundation to temporal asymmetry.

Suppose you are blindfolded, and a cup of coffee is placed before you. The blindfold is removed, and you look at the cup. A cloud of milk is rolling over somewhere in the middle of the cup with a layer of black coffee still on top. You are now faced with the question of the origin of this state of affairs. You reply immediately that someone has just poured milk into the coffee. Naturally you would *not* reply that the state of imperfect mixture had been preceded by one in which milk and coffee had been thoroughly mixed together. However, if the cup and its contents are treated as an isolated system, then the response should be different. The response should be that it was more probable that the state of imperfect mixture was preceded by a state of more perfect mixture than by a state of less perfect mixture.[21] It is clear then that the rationale for your response is to be constructed by appealing to the assumption that the cup is very likely a system that was recently distinguished from its surroundings because it was affected by a special action. Thus we say the cup of coffee "branched off" from a system that included it through the action of pouring milk. Associated with this is the further assumption that a branching that leads to imperfect mixture began as an even less perfect mixture. In other words, since less homogeneity corresponds to lower entropy, the imperfect mixture, which is a low entropy state, is assumed to be a state of a system that has recently branched off in an even lower entropy state from a larger system.

Taking our cue from this reconstruction of the natural response to how coffee and milk came to be half-mixed, a general hypothesis can now be proposed that applies to any system in the universe. The hypothesis is that (a) there are many systems branching off from larger systems, and (b) the initial micro-states of similar branch systems with the same initial entropy are a random sample of all the micro-states associated with that entropy.[22] To this hypothesis, which does not follow from the laws of statistical physical theory, we add a consequence of that theory. Consider a permanently closed system over a long time span. Such a system will (c) have near maximum entropy most of the time, and (d) at other times it is overwhelmingly more likely that the system will be in a local minimum for entropy than on an upgrade, downgrade, or local maximum.[23]

Suppose, on the one hand, that a system branches off in a state of less than its maximum entropy. Now if (d) holds true for the less-than-maximum entropy states of a single closed system, then, by the principle (b) of randomness, (d) will also hold true for the less-than-maximum entropy states of a multiplicity of branch systems.[24] That is, a low entropy state of a system that has just branched off from a larger system is most likely a local minimum in that system. Hence, it will be followed by a higher entropy state, in all likelihood. But unlike the case of the permanently closed system, it will not be preceded by a higher entropy state. Being a branch system, it simply has no antecedent existence. If, however, (b) does not hold, our transferring (d) from application to closed systems to ensembles of branch systems would not be legitimate. For if the branch systems of a given less-than-maximum entropy were *not* random samples of the micro-states associated with that entropy, there need not be a general trend among them to higher entropy.

If, though, the micro-states are random samples, what holds for such states in permanently closed systems will hold true in an ensemble of branch systems. But given both (b) and (d), it follows that branch systems in less-than-maximum entropy states have a greater probability of increasing than decreasing their entropy. In view of (a), it can be concluded that among systems in less-than-maximum entropy states in the universe the majority are branch systems. So from (a), (b), and (d) it follows that the majority of systems in less-than-maximum entropy states increase their entropy.

It remains to consider, on the other hand, systems branching off in near equilibrium state, that is, in a state of near-maximum entropy. This time our problem is to transfer (c) from application to permanently closed systems to branch systems, making use again of the randomness principle (b). According to (c), if a permanently closed system is near equilibrium it is likely to stay there, for it is there most of the time anyway. Suppose a system branches off in a near equilibrium state. By (b), its micro-state is a random one of the micro-states that can constitute such an equilibrium. An ensemble of such branching systems will, since they are a random selection from the micro-states, tend to do what permanently closed systems tend to do in equilibrium, which is to remain in equilibrium. So from (a), (b), and (c), it follows that a majority of near-maximum entropy systems tend to remain in that state.

By (a)–(d) the majority of systems are such that, if they change their entropy, they increase it. This is then a basis of a physical sort for temporal asymmetry. For *earlier* and *later* can now be distinguished on the basis of lesser and greater entropy for the majority of systems that change their entropy.

This provides a magnificent demonstration of the probabilistic irreversibility of sequences of entropy conditions of non-equilibrium systems. That is, it shows that if (a)–(d) are true, then a converse description of the entropy sequences probably associated with such systems is not likely to describe actual sequences. But as we pointed out, temporal asymmetry need not be based on the irreversibility—and we now add the probabilistic irreversibility—of sequences of property conditions. It is certainly well to know that there are sequences that are most likely irreversible. But the character of action suffices to found the asymmetry of time.

(I) The vectoral character of action is relied on in this statistical account. That is, the branching and the blending back into a main system are not supposed to change into one another just by a redescription in converse temporal relational terms. The branching involves an action with the blending back containing its ultimate result. The pouring of the milk is the branching, and the result is the perfect mixture that exists when drinking the coffee blends it back into the main system. If the blending back could itself be the point of branching—if the result could cease to be a result—then by applying (b) to it this branching would most likely result in a maintenance of the equilibrium of the perfectly mixed coffee.[25] This contradicts the result of treating the pouring as the point of branching. For when the pouring is the branch point, tracing backward from the drinking would most likely lead to a decrease of entropy. Because of this conflict of results, the whole attempt to establish an entropic asymmetry would have to be scuttled. To avoid the conflict is merely to recognize the objectivity of results.

This is all on the supposition of the randomness principle (b). What now if (b) does not apply when the merger point is treated as a branch point? If it does not apply here, how can it apply in the above demonstration? And if it does not apply there, the whole attempt fails.

Clearly, then, (a) itself must introduce a vectoral notion of action by introducing the notion of branching off. However, if actions lacked a vectoral character, as they would if they were mere sequences of conditions, then a branching could be at either end of a branch system that an arbitrary time ordering happens to put first. Entropy increase would not then be an objective consequence of branching, but a consequence of describing the system in one time order rather than its converse. In one time order there would be the likelihood of an increase; in the other, though, there would be the likelihood of maintaining equilibrium.

(II) The coherence of action is also relied on. Let it be granted that the majority of branches are such that, at a remove from the branch point, the branch system is in a higher entropy state if it branched in a non-equilibrium state. If there is counterdirected action, then branching can lead to systems developing in opposite directions. Looking at time in either direction may then reveal an equal distribution of branches in which entropy falls to the branch point and of branches in which entropy rises from the branch point.

So in laying down (a) it is presupposed that the majority of branchings cohere. That is, if t_1 and t_2 are the distinct times of two branch points and if $\underline{t}_1'$ and $\underline{t}_2'$ are the times of conditions along the respective branch systems, then it is not the case both that the interval t_1t_2 is totally included in the interval $\underline{t}_1'\underline{t}_2'$ and that the latter is totally included in the former. But unless one can show that the majority of branchings cohere without also showing that all actions must cohere, as we have shown, the statistical account of temporal asymmetry presupposes that all actions cohere. I am concerned here not merely with the possibility of counterdirected actions that are as far apart as different galaxies,[26] but also with the possibility of counterdirected action in small localities as well.

It is clear, then, that the statistical account of temporal asymmetry must assume at least statistical variants of the two principles behind the action view of time. It must assume the vectoral character of the majority of actions and the coherence of the majority of actions as applied to the special action of branching. But even these statistical variants would suffice to ground temporal asymmetry. For the direction of the temporally later would be the direction of most results as judged from corresponding actions.

Thus the addition of special postulates of branching and randomness and the reliance on statistical physical theory for (c) and (d) are unnecesary for temporal asymmetry, however helpful they might be in establishing the quite different matter of the temporal irreversibility of sequences of conditions. Under the sway of the Ockhamite view of action, advocates of the statistical approach to temporal asymmetry will be reluctant to recognize the cogency of the action view of time. But it must be brought home to them that the hypothesis of branching harbors the very notion of action that Ockham rejected.

CHAPTER X

Capacities and Natures

§1. *The Stimulus-Response and Fine-Structure Models for Capacities.* It might seem that capacities should be part of the required ontology. If the existence of entities of a given sort follows from the existence of physical necessities, then entities of that sort are part of the required ontology. And it would seem that there are capacities if there are physical necessities, for an entity has a capacity to be whatever it *must* become in certain possible circumstances.

After admitting—over and above individuals—natures, properties, actions, and conditions, it looks as though there are no restrictions at all on admittance to the required ontology. Nonetheless, the entities thus far admitted are perfectly sufficient, when taken in combination, to play the role played by capacities. Our policy of admission is then restrictive enough to eliminate capacities, since they are not in fact required by physical necessities. The conclusion to the above argument must then be changed. It is, in fact, merely an argument from necessities to *either* capacities *or* whatever entities that in combination have the role of capacities.

Not only do necessities require either capacities or combinations with their role, but, conversely, unless there are necessities, the observational datum that individuals change will not be sufficient to warrant the conclusion that there are either capacities or combinations with their role. As I shall show, liquid water lacks the capacity to change into ice, even though it does change into ice, if there are no necessities. This result is incompatible with the

Aristotelian view that any action, such as the change from liquid to solid, is to be identified with an exercise of a capacity.[1] For, in this view, there could not be actions unless there were necessities, since to have a capacity involves the necessity of an action in certain circumstances. Though I introduced actions to allow for necessities across time, it does not follow that actions would be impossible in a world without necessities. Thus, in my view, it need not be the case that to act is to exercise a capacity. In a world without necessities there might still be actions, but they would not be exercises of capacities.

Return now to the question of the superfluousness of capacities. There are many arguments for denying capacities entitative status, but as they stand they are insufficient. On the one hand, there is the "stimulus-response" model for capacities.[2] The logical form of a capacity proposition is, on this model, a modal conditional proposition; its antecedent expresses an operation in certain circumstances and its consequent expresses a realization of the putative capacity. Unless the conditional is explicitly modal, it cannot be relied upon to support a counterfactual conditional. But a capacity proposition does support some associated counterfactual conditional. The modality must be that of necessity.

That is, associated with the capacity proposition that a is ϕable is the counterfactual that if a were ψed it would ϕ. To support this conditional, the modal stimulus-response conditional $\Box\, a(\psi a \rightarrow \phi a)$ is not required. For the counterfactual does not say that the consequent holds in all possible circumstances in which the antecedent holds, but only that it holds in certain of the possible circumstances in which the antecedent holds. Thus when a is ϕable, there will be circumstances K such that $\Box\, a(\psi a \text{ in } K \rightarrow \phi a)$. On the other hand, the non-modal conditional (ψa in $K \rightarrow \phi a$) does not suffice to imply the counterfactual, for the latter explicitly requires that a ϕ's in possible situations in which a ψ's and implicitly restricts these possible situations to those in which K holds. So the stimulus-response model requires a restricted modal conditional.

A further refinement is still needed. If capacity claims were equivalent to restricted modal conditionals, then, as a simple exercise in modal logic would make clear, an entity would have each of its capacities necessarily. But surely capacities are often contingent; this poker is not always able to sear wood but can do so only when it is hot. This suggests treating the logical form of capacity claims as conjunctive. One conjunct will be a modal conditional, whereas the other will not be modal and may be contingent. A full elaboration of the non-modal conjunct introduces considerations of the structure of entities, and these do not properly belong to the stimulus-response model.

On the other hand, there is the "fine-structure" model for capacities.[3] To have a capacity is to have components that are the causal basis for what is spoken of as the realization of the capacity in a certain stimulus situation. These components may be properties, parts, or actions of the entity with the capacity. They need not be components introduced by theoretical science; they may be quite familiar components. In this model, the entity with a capacity is not a black box of which a certain conditional is mysteriously true. Rather, the entity has a fine structure of components that are the ontological roots of the capacity.

The motivation for the fine-structure model was undoubtedly the conviction that there ought to be something about the entity with a capacity that implies the stimulus-response conditional. In the very concept of a capacity is the notion that an entity with it shapes that entity's conditional properties. But to be satisfactory, the fine-structure model has to account not just for a conditional, but also for the modality of the conditional. We just saw that, in view of the connection with counterfactuals, the stimulus-response conditional must be a necessary one. The stimulus-response model is incomplete, not just because it does not explain why a certain stimulus is followed by a certain response, but also because it does not explain why its being so followed is a necessity.[4] To take account of this additional requirement, it is natural to suggest that fine structure is also the basis for necessity. In other words, an entity will obey a given stimulus-response conditional of necessity provided the entity has a certain fine structure and having this fine structure implies that conditional.

It soon becomes evident that the difficulties in respect to modality remain for the fine-structure model. First, if a modal conditional of the above kind is equivalent to the existential claim that there is some component of fine structure the entity has the having of which implies the corresponding non-modal conditional, then this existential claim will itself be necessary. There is thus the problem of accounting for the necessity of there being some such component. Notice that it is not necessary that the entity have a specific component. The same entity in different circumstances may have the same stimulus-response conditional hold true of it because of quite different fine structures.

Second, if a given component of fine structure does account for a conditional, then there is not a mere contingent relation between the fine structure and the conditional. If it only happened that the fine structure implied the conditional, then the fine structure could not be the basis for the conditional. This will be argued in more detail in §5. The upshot of this second difficulty is that, independently of the attempt to account for the modality of the conditional by fine structure, modality appears in the fine-structure account of the unmodalized stimulus-response conditional.

The fine-structure model seems, then, to raise more problems of modality than it resolves. Is it possible, within that model, to make a frontal assault on the *general* problem of the basis for necessity? The prospect seems encouraging, for below any given level of fine structure there are always more basic levels. Necessities at the operational level are based on first-level fine structure; necessities of the kind we have just discovered about first-level fine structure are to be based on second-level fine structure; and so on. The general account of necessities in Chapter II in terms of natures then becomes gratuitous.

I shall argue that fine structure does not provide a solution to the problem of necessity that is raised by both the stimulus-response and the fine-structure approaches to capacities. But first I should like to refine the picture given so far of the fine-structure model to the point where it is not objected to beyond its failure to deal with the problem of modality. When the account of necessity by natures is integrated with this version of the fine-structure model, the result is what I shall call the "nature" model of capacities. The nature model will be crucial in the final chapter in the argument that there must be things as well as conditions.

§2. *A Regress Problem for the Fine-Structure Model.* Locke outlined one kind of fine-structure model. He made the common-sense observation that our idea of a substance of a given kind contains numerous ideas of powers of that substance. But he asserted a view of considerable metaphysical interest when he went on to say that the real essence of a substance of a given kind is not made up of those powers.[5] Rather, the real essence is that "constitution of the parts of matter" on which the powers of the substance depend.[6] It is such a constitution of material parts, "texture of parts," "internal structure," or "fine contrivance" that makes gold soluble in aqua regia, that makes antimony fusible, and that makes lead malleable. Even though he believed powers had a foundation in parts, Locke believed it would be impossible for us to know these parts in view of the limits of our senses. But his epistemological reservations in no way qualified his ontological conviction that capacities depend on unobserved parts.

Notice that in Locke's view only material parts are the components included in fine structure; properties, actions, and natures are not included. Now since material parts could be separated from the individuals with them and exist by themselves, as properties could not, it is plausible to ascribe capacities to them in the same way we ascribe capacities to individuals of which they are the parts. Atoms of lead, for example, are capable of combining, one by one, with atoms of sulfur to form the substance known as galena. The fine-structure view must then be applied to the atoms of lead and sulfur as well as to quantities of the stuff, the galena, they compose.

So, by Locke's logic, the atoms must—because of their having capacities—have material parts. These again will move and interact with other parts in such a way that we will wish to attribute capacities to them. Indeed, it is hard to imagine any point in an analysis by material parts at which the parts do not have some rudimentary capacities. But if there were to be parts without parts, then Locke's version of the fine-structure model of capacities would have reached a dead end. There would then be capacities without a basis in parts. So if any individual has a capacity, it has no simple material parts, that is, no material parts not composed of other material parts.

Such a strong conclusion must make one suspicious of the path by which it is arrived at. It seems clear that individuals ought to be able to have capacities whether or not there are simple material parts.

Our suspicions lead us to ask why Locke excluded components other than material parts from the foundations of capacities. The reason is that for him an individual simply has no components other than its powers and its parts. That is, the components of an individual are: (1) powers for affecting minds—its secondary qualities; (2) powers for affecting matter; and (3) parts in configuration—its primary qualities—which are the foundations of all these powers.[7] Solidity and extension are both a cohesion of parts; figure is a relation of parts; motion is presumably a multiplicity of parts of extension; and the fifth primary quality, number, is the unity of a part.

Since for Locke, "relation is not contained in the real existence of things,"[8] primary qualities are not both parts and the various configurational relations, but are simply parts. My expression 'parts in configuration' is designed to indicate that it is parts, not both parts and configurational relations, that Locke sees as sufficient. If the parts of a thing are themselves ascribed primary qualities, this can only mean that these parts are composed of parts.[9]

Certainly there are times when such a mereological ontology pays handsome dividends. Newton defined inertia as "a power of resisting" change of state, whether motion or rest, and attributed this power to all material bodies.[10] What is the basis of the power in question? Should we say simply that it is based on the property of mass? If we were thinking in Lockean terms, this alternative would not appeal to us. We would hold out for an account of the power of resisting in terms of parts. In view of the relation between mass and energy in the theory of special relativity, "we now recognize that the potential energy contained in material bodies is the cause of inertia."[11] But if potential energy is that capacity to do work that "depends on the configuration" of a system—be it a watch spring, a charge of gunpowder, or a system consisting of the earth and a stone lifted above its surface—then Newton's power of resisting is founded on parts.[12] We would then withdraw the suggestion that inertia as a capacity depends on a property, mass.

There is, however, a difficulty with Locke's ontology of parts that has never been satisfactorily resolved. As we have seen, since parts themselves will have capacities, there must be parts of parts. There is no escaping the fact that if there are no components of individuals other than capacities and parts, then there are no simple material parts. Now we must ask whether, first, what is composed of parts is ever a genuine entity or whether, second, the parts composing anything are entities though the thing is never itself a genuine entity.

For Locke, the second alternative—that composites are heaps and hence not unities or entities—leads to what might be called an ontological vacuum. For, since by Locke's logic parts are themselves composed of parts, no part is an entity. No matter how far the analysis into parts is pushed, one fails to reach entities, since the parts one reaches are all composites, and by hypothesis composites are not entities.

This forces us to consider the first alternative—that there are entities composed merely of material parts, even though those parts are divisible. So some composites are unities or entities and not just heaps or multiplicities. There are two difficulties with this alternative.

First, if the only components are material parts, there is the problem of how an entity with material parts can differ at all from a mere multiplicity of these parts. Surely there is a difference between a genuine entity with parts *a* and *b* and a non-entitative composite of *a* and *b*. But this difference cannot be in the entity, since in it there is only *a* and *b*. And any difference not in the entity will not serve to differentiate it from the non-entitative composite. Second, if the only components are material parts, there is the problem of how an entity can be the same as itself. An entity's sameness with itself is a component of it—its unity—as was noted in Chapter VII, §5. This is a component any entity must have, yet it is not a material part. In view of these two difficulties, one is thrown back to the alternative leading to an ontological vacuum. It is then clear that an ontology of parts is untenable.

But Locke allowed for capacities as well as the parts they depended on. A capacity might then be the element needed, over and above parts, if there are to be genuine entities. But if a capacity provides what is needed, then the parts would provide what is needed. For to have the capacity, it suffices, on the Lockean view, to have the parts. We have, however, just seen that parts by themselves are insufficient for an ontology. Hence capacities based solely on parts will not provide what is needed for there to be genuine entities.

Looking back, we find that the Lockean version of the fine-structure account of capacities—one that limits fine structure to material parts—is warranted only if an ontology is warranted in which entities have parts and powers but no other components. We have just found that such an ontology is unwarranted in that it leads straight to the result that there is nothing. In formulating a fine-structure model for capacities, we might then wish to allow for the possibility that properties and actions, in addition to parts, might be elements of a fine structure. Once having made this allowance, it is no longer the case that the fine-structure model commits us to the view that there are no simple material parts.

It might seem that, even with properties and actions, there is still a regress. For suppose the entity a has the capacity to ϕ since it has the component ψ. Will it not then be true that ψ itself has the capacity to make a to ϕ?[13] If so, this capacity of ψ will itself be based either on parts or other components of a, and whatever it is based on will have the capacity to make ψ to make a to ϕ, and so on. For example, the kinetic energy of a point mass is the capacity it has to do work "in virtue of being in motion." The motion will itself have the capacity to make what has it do work. And we must then look still further for the grounding of this capacity.*

However, I do not think the fine-structure model is committed to such a regress. Suppose the property or action on which a capacity of an individual depends is not a component of that individual but is a distinct entity. Then, indeed, it would be appropriate to ascribe capacities to such properties or actions. Whitehead, who treats eternal objects as distinct entities from events or actual entities, is then able to say that "an eternal object can be described only in terms of its potentiality for 'ingression' into the becoming of actual entities."[14] But properties and actions are merely compo-

*For the purpose of the example, I assume local motion is a component. However, genuine components are not relative to coordinate systems in the way local motions are. Since space and time are grounded in actions, and since mere local motion as between individuals is defined by space and time, local motion between individuals must be based on actions that are not simply locomotive. Two simples in relative motion is ontologically impossible.

nents of individuals. They are hence not distinct from the individuals of which they are components. So to ascribe a capacity to a property or action can be viewed only as a way of ascribing a capacity to the individual with that property or action. When I say ψ has the capacity to make a ϕ, I am saying exactly the same thing as when I say that a, since it is ψ, has the capacity to ϕ.

However, a's condition of being ψ is, unlike the property ψ that a has, distinct from a. It may be implausible to say that the component ψ has a capacity to make a to ϕ since components do not have the status of causes at all, as I shall try to show in Chapter XI, §3. But a condition can be a cause. It seems then that conditions do genuinely have capacities. It is easy enough, though, to account for their grounding without a regress. The condition of being a ψ has the capacity to make a to ϕ precisely because it is a condition of an entity, of which one component is ψ itself. The capacity of a condition is grounded in a corresponding component that has no capacity. Thus the regress is stopped. This is not quite the same as saying that properties ground their own capacities.[15] It is rather to say that properties, which do not have capacities, ground the capacities of the conditions that are the havings of these properties.

Parts of entities were treated as components in our discussion of Locke. From what I have just said it appears that capacities cannot be attributed to parts. But can Locke still be faced with the consequence that there are no simple material parts if parts as components do not themselves have capacities? At this point, a difference between parts and other components is crucial. A part may be separated from the entity of which it is the part and made an independent entity. It then becomes distinct from the entity of which it was the part. Though a property or an action might become a component of a new individual, neither thereby becomes an independent entity. Strictly speaking, the part has capacities only when it becomes a distinct entity. When the part is a component, its supposed capacities are, in actuality, capacities of the whole. Still, the capacities it has once it is distinct are, in the Lockean view, based on its parts. These parts of the separated part did not come from nothing. They were themselves parts of the whole from which the original part was separated. (They were not strictly parts of the unseparated part, for a component has no components.) It does not matter, then, that parts as components do not have capacities. For all that is important is that the capacities a part has, once it has been separated from the whole, require that this part have parts and hence require that the whole have a yet deeper internal structure of parts. So if capacities are based solely on material parts, there will be, in the entity with the capacity, no parts that, when separated from this entity, are material simples.

§3. *Conditional Causality.* The proposition that lead is malleable is undoubtedly true. But I am contending that its truth does not require that there be a component called malleability. In fact, my ontology is Megaric[16] in that it excludes such a "dispositional" property as a component of any entity.[17] If it is argued that lead must have the dispositional property of malleability for the proposition to be truc, it should be pointed out that the proposition admits of reformulation as the modal proposition that any chunk of lead is capable of having its shape changed. The problem, then, is one of describing the truth conditions for a modal proposition. The general form of this problem is that of finding in what contexts the truth conditions for the constituent non-modal proposition are to be found satisfied.

Some thinkers find it hard to draw a line between "dispositional" and other predicates. For the proposition expressed by almost any atomic sentence implies a capacity proposition. So, they reason, the predicate in such a sentence must be dispositional.[18] That is, if $(\psi a \rightarrow C\phi a)$, where '$C\phi a$' is an abbreviation for 'a is capable of ϕing', then 'ψ' is to be deemed a dispositional predicate.

On the one hand, if being a dispositional predicate means only that there is such an implication, then the designation is merely misleading. Analogously, we would not say that 'ϕ' is a modal predicate just because ϕa implies that a possibly ϕ's. Moreover, even one of the positivist's "occurrent" predicates, say 'looks orange', is generally taken to imply, when it is true of some individual, that something has the capacity to appear orange. But it would be misleading to call this a dispositional predicate when looking orange is so clearly not a capacity.

On the other hand, if 'ψ's being a dispositional predicate means that there is some θ such that the truth condition for ψa is identical to that for $C\theta a$, then it is patently false that the above implication—or even a corresponding coimplication—is a sufficient condition for 'ψ's being a dispositional predicate. This wheel's being round implies, under normal suppositions, its having the capacity to roll. But the truth condition for its being round is its having the "actualized" as opposed to the dispositional property roundness. The mere fact that having the condition of being round implies, or is also implied by, having the capacity to roll does not show that these conditions are identical.

In fact, there is a general difference between having an actualized property, an action, or a part and having a capacity. It is that having one of the former is often a cause, whereas having a capacity causes nothing, even though having it may be essential if a certain effect is to be realized. The wheel's having circularity may be the cause of my having a visual impression of it as circular, though its having the capacity for so impressing me is not the cause of the impression.

The reason for this is plain if the view of capacities presented in this chapter is accepted. If having a capacity were having a specific fine structure, then indeed having a capacity could be a cause. But, in fact, for *a* to have a capacity is for *a* to be such that there is some unspecified fine structure that *a* has. Such an existential condition is not itself causal. So the individual's condition of having one or more capacities is not the truth condition for the proposition that it has a certain actualized property.[19]

The moral of all this for our Megaric program is that when we treat certain unspecified components as bases for capacities it does not follow that these components are themselves capacities. Indeed, insofar as such a component is an actualized property, an action, or a part, it is not a capacity.

In giving an account of capacities, it is unavoidable that we shall have to emphasize two seemingly opposed factors. On the one hand, the components on which a capacity is founded are such that the conditions of having these components are causally responsible for the behavior envisaged by the capacity. Having the components of fine structure causes, in appropriate circumstances, what one calls the actualization of the capacity. On the other hand, capacities are often such that they can be exercised freely. While providing for causation, we must insert restrictions that do not preclude freedom.

If the causation is what I shall call "conditional," then one can allow for freedom without eliminating causation. Now condition *a* unconditionally causes condition *b* only if the occurrence of *a* in the given circumstances is sufficient for the occurrence of *b*. However, *a* conditionally causes *b* only if there is not this unconditional sufficiency. Rather, *a* conditionally causes *b* only if, *given that b occurs,* the occurrence of *a* in the circumstances involved implies that of *b*. The lack of unconditional sufficiency allows for autonomy in the exercise of capacities. Nonetheless, where there is conditional causality, the individual's having exercised the capacity implies that the fine structure together with the circumstances are sufficient for the exercise. The fine structure's sufficiency for the exercise is conditional upon the exercise itself.

A productive skill often requires special training. The training modifies the human organism; it changes the fine structure. The conditions brought about through training are involved when the skill is exercised.[20] Yet in free-enterprise capitalism, as opposed to an economy involving slavery, the trained laborer contracts freely with the entrepreneur for the use of his or her special skill. The contract is free in at least the respect that the laborer might have contracted for the use of some aspect of his or her labor power that did not involve special training. (There are other ways in which the contract is free that are not specific to the specially trained laborer.)

The point is that the exercise of the power of specially trained labor in the context of a labor market is not, for the individual laborer in the given circumstances, unconditionally caused by the modification of the laborer's organism due to training. Still, it is conditionally caused by this modification. If the labor power is exercised after its use is contracted for, then the components of fine structure induced by the training are—upon this condition—sufficient for this exercise in the given circumstances.

The following schema reflects the considerations adduced to this point:

(1) $C\phi a$ if and only if $(\exists\,\theta,K)(\theta a\cdot$ (in circumstances of type K, a's having θ conditionally causes the condition that is a's having ϕ)).

The θ's are components of a—components of a's fine structure—that are the basis for the causal conditions for realizing the capacity.* Note that dissimilar θ's may be involved when a θ's in circumstances of dissimilar K's. No specific components of the fine structure are selected for the role of basing the capacity; making a capacity claim amounts only to claiming that there be some components in that role. Of course, to say that $(\exists\,\theta)\theta a$ can only mean that some component θ of some individual is such that a has a component exactly similar to this θ. A related remark applies to quantification over K.

This schema tells us that the modal claim $C\phi a$ is true provided that in at least some cases when ϕa would become true it would do so by virtue of the causality of a condition of having some component of a. There is no question of its being true on the basis of a's having a dispositional property. So the existence of necessities does not require that there be capacities—dispositional properties—but requires that entities have components of fine structure, the having of which accounts causally for some of their behavior.

§4. *Causality and Necessity.* The notion of causality has not been an important one in the development of the required ontology. It is the more general notion of action that has been important. Actions are paired with results, which as such are not effects (Chapter IX, §3). To be an effect, a result must not only depend on an action but also be necessary in view of what has preceded it. Recall that dependence of results was explained by the factive conditional, which does not imply a necessary conditional even when the context for which the factive conditional holds is built into its antecedent (Chapter IV, §3). It may well be that all results are effects, but this will not be a consequence of our concept of result. In a world that includes action without causation there

*By emphasizing the causality of fine structure, our analysis temporarily loses sight of the stimulus-response relation. Here the stimulus is submerged in the circumstances of type K.

would be only mere togetherness, whereas in a world with causation there is also necessary togetherness (Chapter VII, §4). The reason, then, that the notion of causation has thus far not been examined directly is that the notions of action and of necessity are sufficient to account for it.

When a condition causes another we need to consider two factors. First, there is an *action*. It need not be an action of the entity with the causal condition; it may be an action of some entity in the circumstances. But, of course, the having of the action may be the causal condition itself. The knife's condition of being sharp caused the cut when someone pressed it against the skin. Here the action of pressing belongs to an entity other than the entity with the causal condition of sharpness. But one can also say that the pressing caused the cut and thereby relegate the sharpness to the circumstances. Second, there is a *necessary connection*. It stands between the causal condition in its circumstances and the result of the action. Putting these together we have:

(2) a's having θ causes b to have ϕ if and only if there is a type K of circumstances such that: (i) a's having θ in circumstances of type K and b's having ϕ both obtain; (ii) either circumstances of type K contain an action, or θ is itself an action, that has b's having ϕ as a result; and (iii) $\Box\, a(\theta a$ in circumstances of type $K \rightarrow \phi b)$.

When θ is a causal basis for a response ϕ and K resolves into stimulus S on a in K', then (iii) can be written as $\Box\, a(\theta a \rightarrow (Sa$ in circumstances of type $K' \rightarrow \phi b))$. Thus by emphasizing the causal role of fine structure in (1), we have not completely lost sight of the role of fine structure in explaining stimulus-response conditionals. However, the stimulus-response conditional here need not be necessary unless a has θ of necessity. In the case of many important capacities, the fine structure is indeed a necessary feature of the individual. But what of cases where this condition is not satisfied? Clearly, in many such cases the modal conditional needed for the stimulus-response model must have concealed in its expression for circumstances a reference to fine structure. The poker must sear the wood when pressed against it provided circumstances obtain in which the poker is hot. A stimulus-response model unmixed with elements from a fine-structure model is, then, utterly implausible.

Schema (2) is for singular causal claims, but the causal component in (1) is generalized for various circumstances of the same unspecified type. A causal claim that is general in respect to the occasions on which the circumstances occur can be dealt with as follows, where (ii) and (iii) are clauses of (2):

(3) In circumstances of type K, a's having θ causes b to have ϕ if and only if (ii) and (iii).

Finally, with a modification of (iii), an equivalent can be expressed for the notion of conditional causality:

(4) In circumstances of type K, a's having θ conditionally causes b to have ϕ if and only if (ii) and (iii′) $\Box\, a(\phi b \rightarrow (\theta a \text{ in circumstances of type } K \rightarrow \phi b))$.

So the conditionality of causality affects not the factor of action, expressed here in (ii), but it has to do exclusively with the necessary-connection factor.

If the conditional under the sign of necessity in (iii′) were a "material" conditional throughout, then it would be logically valid. For anything of the form $A \supset (B \supset A)$ is logically valid. The material conditional cannot be adequate in interpreting (iii′) since it is not to be merely a logical addition to the other clause in (4). But neither is a "strict" conditional adequate, for it is a necessary conditional. If the $\rightarrow$'s in (iii′) signified necessity, then what would most likely be a contingent fact—the actualization of the effect—would imply a necessary connection between the causal condition and the effect. Yet this seems implausible. In addition, since the first $\rightarrow$ in (iii′) is under a modal operator, this operator would be redundant if the $\rightarrow$ were itself modal.

But at least if the conditionals were modal, permutation would be blocked. We could not then infer $(\theta a \text{ in } K \rightarrow (\phi b \rightarrow \phi b))$ from (iii′). And this might at first seem an advantage, for does not the causal factor θ do more in K than lay the basis for an implication to a tautology? This might not seem much for θ to do if we are thinking in terms of material or strict implication, for any proposition materially or strictly implies a tautology. But we have moved beyond these forms of implication. We can then view the permuted form as the significant claim that the self-implication property is something b has as a result of a having θ in K. It might have it for other reasons as well, but it is informative to have this source of the self-implication property pointed out. Similarly, inertia is perhaps a necessary property of an atom, but this does not mean that an atom's having it is not due to anything. It may well be due to its configuration of physical parts. Thus, allowing permutation does not change (iii′) into a mere logical truth. Since "relevant" implication allows permutation and hence lacks the difficulties of a modal implication, it is again a plausible choice for interpreting *if-then* in the context of the required ontology.

In light of (4), (1) can now be rewritten to emphasize the factors of action and necessity. In doing so, let 'B' abbreviate 'the condition that is a's having ϕ':

(5) $C\phi a$ if and only if $(\exists\,\theta, K)(\theta a \cdot$ (either circumstances of type K contain an action or θ is itself an action that has B as a result) $\cdot \Box\, a(\phi a \rightarrow (\theta a$ in circumstances of type $K \rightarrow B$ obtains))).

Only the third conjunct here is modal. So capacity claims may well depend, as was noted in §1, on merely contingent features of entities and thus themselves may be contingent.

To see why 'B obtains' has been introduced in the last clause where we would expect simply 'ϕa', let us first look back at (1). There the causal condition was said to cause conditionally the condition that is a's having ϕ, not to cause conditionally a's having ϕ. In rewriting (1) as (5) I want to allow for this distinction. But why is the distinction made at all? Everyone would agree that a die has a capacity to turn up a six, even though it is assumed that there is no feature of the die that causes it, or even conditionally causes it, to turn up a six. But everyone would agree to this only if, when the die turns up a six, there is some feature of it that at least makes it turn up a face. And when it turns up a six, the event of turning up a face is the same as the event of turning up a six. So since there is a feature that causes it to turn up a face, there is, in this case, a feature that causes an event that is the turning up of a six. There can then be a capacity to turn up a six since there is causation of an event that is the same as that envisaged by the capacity. In order to indicate that such an event must be caused and that there need be no cause of six's being the side that turned up, (1) was written to say that the condition that happened to be a's having ϕ is caused.

This way of viewing the matter requires that there be two interpretations of a simple causal claim like:

(a) *x* causes the condition of *b*'s having ϕ.

It can be interpreted as an "opaque" context for the description of the condition. This means that substituting another description of the same condition need not preserve the truth value of (a). Under this interpretation, we agree that (a) is equivalent to:

(b) *x* causes *b* to have ϕ.

However, interpreting (a) as a "transparent" context does allow, without a change of truth value, the substitution of another description of the condition of *b*'s having ϕ. Under this interpretation, we agree that (a) is equivalent to:

(c) *x* causes the condition that is *b*'s having ϕ.

If getting a six is a matter of chance, then 'Jones causes the condition of the die's having six up' is true—when a six is actually thrown—under interpretation (c), but not under interpretation (b). In logical terms, (b) interprets the scope of the description for the effect in (a) narrowly, whereas (c) interprets it broadly to include the entire sentence.

It is of utmost importance that we recognize this distinction if microscopic systems are to have capacities for features that are subject to quantum indeterminacies.[21] It seems reasonable to say that an electron has a capacity to arrive at a certain spot on a screen at which it is shot. Yet when it hits that spot, it was not, according to present conceptions, determined to do so. Still it may well be that it must hit the screen. And when it hits a specific spot on the screen, its hitting this spot is the same condition as hitting the screen. So one can still use the causal interpretation of capacities in the midst of indeterminacy. This interpretation requires only that the event that is a hitting of the screen at a certain spot be caused. It does not require that the given spot's being where the screen is hit be caused.

The justification for the sameness-of-condition claims made here is as follows. Where '*F*' and '*G*' are related as generic to specific, '*Fb*' and '*Gb*' are not made true by different components of *b* (Chapter

III, §1). So '*b*'s having *F*' and '*b's* having *G*' refer to the same condition. But if the same component of *b* is signified by both '*F*' and '*G*', how can anything that causes *b* to have *F* then fail to cause *b* to have *G*? To answer this one must consider the necessary-connection factor in the analyses of causation—(iii) and (iii′) in (3) and (4). The conditionals (θa in $K \rightarrow Fb$) and (θa in $K \rightarrow Gb$)—to consider (iii) alone—need not both be true. Such conditionals are true or false whether or not it is true that *Fb* or that *Gb,* and hence whether or not '*F*' or '*G*' signifies any component of *b*. To decide the truth values of such conditionals, one must, then, consider what components the terms '*F*' and '*G*' might signify in *b*. Since the one is generic and the other specific, '*F*' might well signify a component in *b* that '*G*' does not signify. That is, *b* might belong to a species other than *G* in genus *F*. So what causes *F* to be a component of *b* need not cause *G* to be a component of *b*. But how then can what causes *F* to be a component of *b* cause the condition that is *b*'s having *G* to obtain? In this case, we are concerned with the causation of a previously fixed-on particular—the condition that is *b*'s having *G*. If '*F*' signified a property in *b* such that *b* could not be *G,* then there would be no such particular. But since the causal claim here concerns just this particular, such a possibility for '*F*' is irrelevant for this causal claim.

Similarly, if *a* is necessarily shaped and if *a*'s shapedness is identical with its circularity, it need not follow that *a* is necessarily circular. For otherwise both (*N* is the nature of $a \rightarrow a$ is shaped) and (*N* is the nature of $a \rightarrow a$ is circular) would be true. But since these conditionals could be true when their antecedents are false, *a* does not even have to be shaped for them to be true. To decide their truth values, one must consider what 'shaped' and 'circular' might signify in *a*. Since 'shaped' might signify squareness in *a,* the first conditional could be true and the second false.

Though the above refinement is needed in order to apply our view of capacities to indeterministic domains, it does not follow that quantum states are to be interpreted as capacities, in the manner of the Copenhagen school.[22] Indeed, since for us capacities are not entities, the two views are fundamentally opposed. The rationale for the interpretation of quantum states as capacities is that the interference phenomena of micro-entities require treating their states as superpositions of incompatible states. Being incompatible, the superposed states cannot all be actual. There is even difficulty with saying that one of them is actual. For how could an actual state interfere with non-actual ones? The conclusion that seems to be the most plausible is that the superposed states are capacities for certain values, such as those of position and momentum, under appropriate measurements. But to insist, as I have been insisting, that there are no entities that are capacities seems, from the Copenhagen perspective, tantamount to insisting that quantum theory could do without quantum states. This would seem to involve abandoning quantum theory.

But is it really plausible to interpret quantum states as capacities? If they are capacities, they are quite different from the ones we have been talking about, for they must have the strange property of interference. One quantum potentiality "may involve or overlap other potentialities."[23] But there is no reasonable extension of the idea of capacity, which has been seen to function as a modality, that involves the idea of interference. The interpretation of quantum states in a superposition as capacities is, then, hampered by the fact that the idea of interference coming from the theory of quantum states must be grafted onto the idea of capacity. Yet the latter idea positively excludes any aspect of interference. So it need not be thought that a Megaric ontology deprives quantum theory of quantum states.

It is, nonetheless, undeniable that a distinctive capacity is associated with each state in a superposition. The coefficient of each state in the superposition gives the probability of actualizing that capacity under a certain kind of measurement. Are these capacities based on fine structure? Does (5) apply to them as it does to other capacities? It applies to them through the use of the transparent causal context which, as we have seen, is needed to deal with indeterminacy. To see that it applies, note that the state function of the system describes the superposition of states that together make up the state of the system. So the capacities associated with the states in the superposition are based on just those features of the system that are referred to in calculating the state function. These features are actual, and hence quantum capacities are grounded in actual components.

Whether an alpha particle in a nucleus has the capacity to penetrate the energy barrier provided by the nucleus when it strikes that barrier depends on the width of the nucleus, the Coulomb repulsion between the alpha particle and the protons, and the short-range nuclear forces. Precisely these features of fine structure are referred to in computing the state function of the particle. This function describes a superposition of the two relevant states—one associated with the particle's capacity to be turned back at the nuclear wall and the other associated with its capacity to penetrate it. But to avoid the hopeless confusion resulting from holding that capacities interfere, one must distinguish these capacities from the corresponding states in the superposition.

§5. *Fine Structures and Natures.* Our job is not finished until an account is given of the necessity that appears in our fine-structure analysis. The appearance of this necessity is not a peculiarity of the analysis of capacities. For the problem of necessity arises not just when we consider the scientific realist's fine-structure analysis of capacities, but also when we consider his account of the explanation of regularities.

The scientific realist explains how it is that entities obey regularities relating operations to responses by reference to their properties, parts, and actions, that is, to their fine structure.[24] Entities that obey operational regularities are not, then, empty black boxes. Whether the scientific realist recognizes it or not, there is a consideration of modality involved here. If one explains how entities obey a given regularity by reference to their fine structure, then one must be prepared to hold that entities with such a fine structure *must* obey the given regularity, at least in the circumstances in which the regularity holds. It cannot be a mere happenstance that entities with this fine structure obey the regularity. Otherwise, one would have to say that the basis for the regularity might well be compatible with the regularity's being broken in the absence of extenuating circumstances. In short, if one thinks that having the fine structure is only contingently related to the behavior described in the regularity, then one would not explain the regularity by the fine structure. What one would do would be merely to deduce the operational regularity from the propositions that entities satisfying the conditions of the operation have the stated fine structure and that entities with this fine structure manifest the given response. But this purely intentional notion of explanation through propositions, rather than through fine structure, is characteristic of the instrumentalist rather than the scientific realist.

So in accounting for regularities by fine structure, it is supposed that entities with the fine structure *must* obey these regularities in the given circumstances.[25] These regularities are characteristic of entities with such fine structures. Granting that the problem of how entities obey operational regularities is solved by fine structure, the problem arises as to how entities with a certain fine structure *must* behave in a certain way.

The scientific realist will be forced to reflect that unless one forges beyond fine structure—beyond properties, parts, and actions—one's advantage over the instrumentalist is negligible. As regards capacities, the instrumentalist is, in the manner of §1, forced to recognize that he cannot account for the modality of the stimulus-response conditional needed by him to analyze capacities. The scientific realist might appear able to account for this modality by appeal to fine structure. But now he is faced with the unaccounted-for modality of the conditional relating fine structure to behavior. He is faced with this problem both with regard to explaining regularities and to grounding capacities. This time the problem of modality arises at the level of fine structure itself.[26]

Originally, scientific realism appeared more attractive to us precisely because it showed promise of solving the problem of the necessity of conditionals. But, in view of the seeming epistemological advantages of instrumentalism, it is inevitable that a certain disillusionment should set in over scientific realism once it is realized that it merely creates the same problem over again at the level of fine structure. Scientific realism and the fine-structure model for capacities—(5)—are only half-way houses.

Within the framework of scientific realism, one can at least approach the problem of modal connections in an ontological way. To say an entity has a necessity because of some component of it is not foreign to the framework of the scientific realist as it would have been to his positivist forebearers, who could not think beyond the notion that a necessity is based on intentions rather than on entities the necessity is about.[27] The question I am pressing is whether the components of fine structure—properties, parts, and actions—are the right ones for accounting for modality. Is the ontology of scientific realism rich enough? I have suggested that it is not. But I wish to give it one more try before going beyond it.

Perhaps a necessity like the one in the account we have given of capacities can be accounted for by going to a deeper level of fine structure. Of course, at the deeper level there will be further necessities; having the deeper level fine structure will necessarily imply that the surface level fine structure implies the observable behavior. This means going to a still deeper level. There is no one necessity left unaccounted for, even though not all necessities are accounted for at once. The regress appears then to be benign. The problem of modality is solved by not admitting that any level is ultimate in the analysis of fine structure.[28]

It is surely an inconvenience that, to account for modal connections, we must commit ourselves to the view that there is no end to the complexity of entities. I tried earlier to show that the fine-structure model for capacities is not committed to the view that there is no end to the complexity of entities by expanding the notion of fine structure to cover properties as well as parts (see §2). But that was before we discovered the problem of necessity lurking behind the notion of causality in the fine-structure model. Yet the scientific realist might simply reconcile himself to the infinite complexity of fine structure as the inevitable price for a universe with temporal necessities and hence capacities.

There is, though, another weakness, one to which we cannot reconcile ourselves short of abandoning all standards for explanation. The regress is simply not benign. Suppose we are set the task of explaining the *F*ness any entity might have. We are then to provide a general account of *F*ness. Imagine that all entities are ordered in a series without beginning. Each entity, we suppose, is both *F* and *G*. There will be two cases regarding the explanation of the component *F* of any entity in the series.

(i) The *F* of any given entity in the series can be explained by the fact that the preceding member in the series is *G* *only if* it is also the case that this member is itself *F*. That is, the *G* in the preceding member explains the *F* in the original one, not of itself but only if the *G* is accompanied by *F*. Thus the *F* of the preceding member is essential to the account of the *F* of the original member.

(ii) The *F* of any given member of the series can be explained by the fact that the preceding member is *G*. Even if the preceding member's having *G* depends on its having *F*, the explanation is, this time, possible without reliance on this fact. The *F* that the preceding member will, by hypothesis, have is accidental to the account of the *F* of the original member.

I shall, then, call explanations of type (i) "essentially repetitive," and those of type (ii) "accidentally repetitive." Both are repetitive since the account of the *F* of any member brings in the preceding member that, by hypothesis, is itself *F*. Whether its *F* is essential or accidental to the explanation, the attempt to explain *F* generally commits one to explaining *F* in an infinity of entities.

In earlier jargon, the explanations proceed to infinity *per se* in the type (i) case, and they proceed to infinity *per accidens* in the type (ii) case.[29] Consider a series, with no beginning, of objects, each of which is heated by a preceding one. The task is to explain the condition of heat in these objects. The explanation would proceed to infinity *per se* if a preceding object's condition of having heat were an essential part of the explanation of the succeeding object's having heat. In fact, there is no reason why an object that heats must itself have heat. So the explanation goes to infinity only *per accidens.**

An essentially repetitive explanation leads to a vicious regress, though an accidentally repetitive one does not. Suppose that *a* is *F*, that the *F* of *b* is essential to an account of the *F* of *a*, and that the *F* of *c* is essential to an account of the *F* of *b*, and so on. Can one argue that eventually each *F* gets accounted for and hence that the regress is benign? One could claim both of these things if the repetition of *F* were accidental to the explanations. All we would then need be concerned about is that, taken one by one, each *F* comes to be accounted for.

*In this example, the explanation was of a condition, not of a component. The explanation of heat, the component, would be quite another matter. Though having heat is, in many cases, caused by another object's having heat, the component had—the heat—is explained by fine structure—the motions of parts.

But with the essentially repetitive explanation there is another factor. This is the dependence of the explanations on one another. There is no explanation of the *F* of *a* unless, as part of this explanation, there is an explanation of some component of *b*—the *F* of *b*. For if an explanation of this component were not part of the original explanation, the original explanation would explain one *F* by another *F*. It would not then be an instance of a general explanation of *F*, which we have supposed it must be. So an explanation of the *F* of *b* must include an explanation of some component of *c*—the *F* of *c*. And so on. An explanation of the *F* of *a* must contain explanations of the infinity of *F*'s in the series.

Here is where the rub comes in. We could easily say that each *F* in the infinite series had an explanation if the explanations were not essentially repetitive. In each case, the explanation would be complete even though each entity referred to had *F*, independently of the explanation. Yet in the case of an essentially repetitive explanation, there is no assurance that there is an explanation until it contains an explanation of the *F* of the entity referred to. Until it contains this, the explanation is merely putative. By going back in the series one fails to get more assurance that the *F* of *a* is explained. Rather, by going back, one merely gathers up more putative explanations.

By pursuing the matter through the entire series—assuming this were possible—one would not have come closer to satisfaction. The reason is that a completed infinity of putative explanations does not turn those putative explanations into genuine ones. At any given stage, an explanation depends on prior explanations, and by completing the series one does not tie things off, for one does not come to an explanation that does not depend on prior ones. By completing the series, one has merely given all the putative explanations. One has not eliminated reference to *F* in the explanation of the *F* of *a*. Thus, in the explanation of the *F* of *a*, one has failed to instantiate a general account of *F*. So an essentially repetitive explanation is not an explanation at all in the sense of a general account.

By contrast, in the case of an accidentally repetitive series, the explanation of the *F* of *b* is not part of the explanation of the *F* of *a*. The explanation of the *F* of *a* is, in this case, not merely putative, prior to that of the *F* of *b*. Of course, even in this case, if *F* were inexplicable somewhere in the series, the explanation of the *F* of *a* would not be an instance of a general account of *F*. Still, the one is not part of the other, as in the case where *F* is essential to an explanation of *F*. Since essentially repetitive explanations require explanations within explanations and since none of the contained explanations can ever be more than putative since they too require explanations within them, essentially repetitive explanations are viciously regressive. Therefore, they are not explanations at all.

I wish now to show that the scientific realist's account of necessity by fine structure is essentially repetitive. It thus involves a vicious regress. Suppose $\Box a(Fa)$ is true. The scientific realist accounts for the modality involved by the fine structure of *a*. The relevant component of fine structure is, say, *G*. The following condition must be met. If *G* acccunts for the modality, then the connection between *G* and *F* must itself be modal. So since necessity is an essential feature in the account of necessity, the explanation is essentially repetitive. The explanation of necessity in the series that leads down through deeper layers of fine structure requires at each level a necessary connection between fine structure and some condition that ultimately involves surface level behavior.

At the first level, the modal connection is $\Box a(Ga \rightarrow Fa)$. If the conditional were only contingent, it would be possible for *a* to have *G* but not *F*. Hence it would be possible that *a* is not *F*, which contradicts our assumption that *a* is necessarily *F*. The necessary connection, then, does not just happen to accompany the appeal to fine structure, as would be the case in an accidentally repetitive explanation. The repetition of necessity is essential, and thus the account is viciously regressive.

The scientific realist's position lacks any advantage over the instrumentalist's in regard to the crucial issue of modal connections. The former fails to provide a general account of necessity that can explain even the modality of the latter's stimulus-response conditional. Moreover, since capacities involve necessities, this failure sounds the knell for Quine's optimistic neo-Lockean view that "one can redefine water-solubility by simply describing the structural conditions" of the mechanism of solution.[30] Structural conditions—elements of fine structure—fail to account for the necessities involved.

How are we to get beyond the fine structure model of capacities, which is only a half-way house since it fails to deal with modalities? The scientific realist's ontology needs to be supplemented with natures. There must be a source, which is not itself another property, part, or action, of the modal conditional properties needed in both the explanation of regularities and in the grounding of capacities. Having these conditional properties is to be implied by having natures, in the manner of (2) of Chapter II, §4. Even if there is no end to the levels of fine structure of an entity, it is the nature of the entity that is the basis for the modal connections that the fine structure is involved in at any level.

Salt has an ionic crystal structure with a crystal energy of 183 kcal./mole. It is soluble in water precisely because the attraction between the negative and positive poles of the dipolar water molecule and, respectively, the positive sodium and negative chlorine ions releases enough energy to overcome the 183 kcal./mole ionic attraction in the crystal.[31] Salt's ionic structure is a causal feature in its dissolution, but it is not the ground of the necessity of the causal connection just stated between this feature and its dissolving. Indeed, its ionic structure may be by nature, but it is its nature that gives it the properties and connections it has by nature.

Yet is not an account of necessity by natures essentially repetitive also? We saw in Chapter II, §4, that an entity will have its nature of necessity. Otherwise, it could have different necessities than it has. So natures account for necessities only because they are themselves necessary. This seems to raise the suspicion of an essentially repetitive account. However, the account for the necessity of a nature need not send us in search of a nature at a deeper level. For, as we saw, the nature of an entity accounts for all of its necessities, including the necessity with which it has its nature. There is no series to accommodate an essentially repetitive account, for we stop with the nature of an entity and do not go further to the nature of its nature, and so on.

Perhaps we can stop the series for fine structure as well as for natures. Then the fine structure account of necessity would not be regressive. When G accounts for the modality of $\Box\, a(Fa)$, there always remains the modality of $\Box a(Ga \rightarrow Fa)$ to account for. Instead of going to a deeper level of fine structure, might one not stop the series altogether and account for this second modality by G itself? On the one hand, to employ this device would be to give up the idea of scientific realism according to which one proceeds to deeper and deeper levels of fine structure to explain necessary connections at more superficial levels.

On the other hand, there is a fatal internal flaw in this view. Component G may, unlike a nature, belong to a contingently, even though it implies the necessary property F. For in different possible circumstances, a could have F on the basis of different fine structures. Now, for G to explain the necessity of F, the conditional $(Ga \rightarrow Fa)$ must be necessary, and for this to be the case Ga must itself imply this conditional. In this way the series is stopped. But then, since being implied by fine structure means here being necessary, Ga will itself be necessary since it obviously implies itself. This contradicts the evident fact that a may have the component of fine structure G contingently. A non-repetitive account of necessity by fine structure is then excluded.

In blending the fine-structure model with the view that natures are needed in the truth conditions for necessary truths, we get the nature model for capacities:

(6) $C\phi a$ if and only if $(\exists \theta, K)(\theta a$ · (either circumstances of type K contain an action or θ is itself an action that has B as a result) · $(\exists n)(a$ has the nature n · (a has the nature $n \rightarrow (\phi a \rightarrow (\theta a$ in circumstances of type $K \rightarrow B$ obtains))))).

Here as before 'B' abbreviates 'the condition that is a's having ϕ'. The fine-structure component θ need not be by nature. C. D. Broad calls those capacities that belong to a thing's nature "supreme" capacities. If an iron bar acquires the component θ that it needs to attract another iron bar only after being placed in a magnetic field, then its capacity to attract iron is not supreme. Still it might acquire this capacity to attract iron when placed in a magnetic field only if it has some other capacity that is supreme.[32]

However, Broad's general position that the nature of an entity is a collection of certain of its capacities—the supreme capacities—is not one that can be accepted here. For, according to (6), the required ontology contains no capacities. The role of capacities is played by a complex coordination of natures and other components of entities. The common error of supposing that natures are collections of capacities[33] is readily explained. It results from supposing that the content of our concept of a natural kind is the nature of things of that kind. Indeed, we do include, as Locke noted, the concepts of many capacities in the concept we have of a natural kind. But this provides us only with the "nominal essence" of any entity falling under that kind. The nature or "real essence" of any such entity is the basis for any of those features of the nominal essence that are genuinely—not just nominally—necessary.

The basic limitation resulting from such a confusion of nominal essence with nature is that it makes it impossible to offer any account of necessity. How does one account for the necessity of those capacities in the nominal essence that are in fact supreme? Since these capacities constitute the nature, we cannot appeal to anything more fundamental. It would appear then that these capacities would account for their own necessity. Yet to allow this, without further distinguishing supreme capacities, is to allow that any capacity is the basis for its own necessity, even though we have just emphasized that not all capacities are necessary. Thus, if collections of capacities are natures, the ontological basis for the distinction between supreme and contingent capacities, and indeed between the necessary and the contingent generally, disappears.

CHAPTER XI

Things and Conditions

§1. *The Incompatibility of Necessary Connections with an Ontology of Conditions.* The concept of an entity that has components but is not itself a component has played a role at numerous stages in our discussion. The natures required by necessity were components of entities of such a kind, as were the actions required by time and the elements of fine structure required by capacities. But so far, little has been said that would tie the concept of an entity that has components but is not itself a component together with the concept of a thing. Since individuals and conditions are the same particulars as their components, components are like individuals and conditions in being particulars. But individuals and conditions are "complex" particulars since they have components, whereas properties, parts, and actions are "simple" particulars. Conditions, unlike individuals, are themselves the havings of components. Thus an "individual" is a particular that has components though it is not itself the having of any component. In this catalogue of kinds of entities, things fall under the heading of individuals. Traditionally, the concept of a thing has contained the concept of an enduring individual. But since we have carried the idea of time back to that of action, it will turn out to be more natural for us to analyze the concept so that a "thing" is an individual with a capacity to act. Things will, then, be different from simple particulars, which have no components and hence no capacities. They will also be different from non-physical individuals such as numbers, in that non-physical individuals cannot act.

Finally, things are different from conditions both by being individuals, which have conditions but are not conditions, and by having capacities, which, as we shall see, conditions have only derivatively.

The question to be raised here is whether there is any call to add a further dimension—that of the ability to act—to the concept of an individual. Do we really need things in the required ontology? I shall argue that unless there are entities with capacities to act there can be no necessities across time. An ontology coherent with the practice of acting on prior experience must contain things. It was pointed out at the beginning of Chapter I that denials of necessary connections do not come from ontologies that admit things. In this section, I shall attempt to show that ontologies that admit conditions yet reject not just things but any kind of physical individual inevitably deny real necessities of any kind. In this attempt, and in the remainder of the chapter, the arguments will rely almost exclusively on principles established earlier. The point will be to draw consequences from heretofore isolated claims.

By an ontology of conditions I shall mean an ontology that admits conditions but not individuals and hence no things. As we noted in Chapter III, §1, conditions are sometimes called facts-of and sometimes events. For us a condition, fact-of, or event is the having of a component by a particular that need not be a condition itself. Within an ontology of conditions a different view of conditions is required since there are no individuals, and hence no things, to have components. Nonetheless, the competing ontologies will refer to the same entities when they employ expressions such as 'doing running' and 'having tallness'. The difference lies in the analysis of the entities referred to.

The ontology of conditions has received support from rather different quarters. On the one hand, the emphasis on the unceasing transformation of institutions and ideas in the dialectical conception of history has led some to suppose that belief in enduring particulars is incompatible with this conception of history.[1] Since things are one kind of enduring particular, they seem too static to merit inclusion in an ontology that gives history its due. If things are conceived of as inert and as making no contribution to their own endurance, then indeed things are incompatible with the universal striving toward quantitative and, ultimately, qualitative difference recognized by the dialectical conception of history. Once it is pointed out, however, that things are centers of action and that actions are components of things rather than entities distinct from things, there is no longer even an appearance of incompatibility between the relative permanence of things and their striving toward novelty. For then things endure precisely because they are active.

On the other hand, the substitution of space-time for space and time by special relativity theory has been thought to render an ontology of conditions "more natural" than an ontology including things.[2] Somehow the fact that, in the space-time view, spatial points are no longer enduring is supposed to confirm the theory that there are no enduring particulars. At best, however, there is only an analogy between that fact and this theory. From the perspective of our action view of time and hence, through simultaneity, of space, the analogy is used to argue in precisely the wrong way. It is used to argue from space to the content of space, rather than from the content to space. When we start with a consideration of enduring particulars, we find no incompatibility between them and the rejection of enduring spatial points.

The ontology of conditions is thus associated with two of our strongest cultural traditions. So to argue for things easily admits of misinterpretation as a manifestation of both an antihistorical and an antiscientific attitude. But I have just indicated, if only briefly, the faulty logic involved in attempts to reject an ontology including things by reference to the dialectical theory of history and the theory of special relativity. I wish now to show, first, that conditions without individuals can account for no necessities and, second, that conditions without things can account for no necessities across time. Thus, attempts like the above to reject things are incoherent with the practice of action on prior experience.

For the ontologist of conditions, the natures of individuals cannot be the bases of necessities, since individuals are rejected. The fundamental role played by individuals having components is taken over by conditions obtaining or having existence. This suggests that necessities will be necessities of conditions rather than of individuals. And so it will be the "natures" of conditions that base necessities. The view that a feature had by an entity is the nature of the condition that is the having of that feature is the only reasonable one to adopt, if conditions are to have natures at all. For a condition is nothing but the having of a component. If the having itself is its nature, conditions would all have similar natures.

Moreover, it seems clear that distinct conditions of having similar features will have similar natures. This requirement is easily satisfied if the features are the natures. It is important that conditions do not generally have the features of which they are the having. Otherwise, a problem arises about what grounds the necessity with which a condition has the feature that is its nature. (I speak here about features rather than components since there are now on individuals to have components.)

The counterpart of the claim in an ontology including individuals that $\Box\, a(Fa)$ will be the claim in the ontology of conditions that $\Box$ (*a*'s *F*ing)[*a*'s *F*ing obtains]. This is not to say that the claims are synonymous but only that they are paired between the ontologies. The counterpart of $\Box\, a(Fa \rightarrow Gb)$ will likewise be $\Box$ (*a*'s *F*ing)[*a*'s *F*ing obtains $\rightarrow$ *b*'s *G*ing obtains]. Just as, when $\Box\, a(Fa)$, Fa follows from *a*'s having a certain nature, *N*, so too, when $\Box$ (*a*'s *F*ing)[*a*'s *F*ing obtains], the obtaining of *a*'s *F*ing follows from *a*'s *F*ing having a certain nature, *F*. Now given these interpretations, there are three important failures of the attempt to account for necessity in the ontology of conditions, each more general than the preceding one.

First, there are cases where *a* is necessarily *F*, though *b* has *F* with a different modality. In the ontology that includes individuals, this happens because of dissimilarities in the natures of the individuals *a* and *b*. But in the ontology of conditions, the natures involved must be similar, since the conditions are havings of similar features. Thus if $\Box$ (*a*'s *F*ing)[*a*'s *F*ing obtains], then it cannot be contingently true or impossible that *b*'s *F*ing obtains, since the nature of *a*'s *F*ing and of *b*'s *F*ing is simply *F*. If a sodium atom necessarily combines with a chlorine atom to form a molecule, then rather than its being impossible (as it in fact is), it would have to be necessary that a fluorine atom combines with a chlorine atom to form a molecule. Moreover, if some atoms are naturally unstable, then all would have to be, even though we know some break apart only when subjected to high energies. So the ontology of conditions is committed to the view that similar features are had with the same modality. And this conflicts with evident modal differences among instances of similar features.

In view of this criticism, the ontologist of conditions will retreat to a view of necessity that requires universality. He will reject the view that there are necessities of some or many particulars that are not equally necessities of all particulars. A necessity that holds for a single particular will hold for all. This view has been widely held since Locke claimed that necessities are relative to classifications. But what are the consequences of joining it to the only account we found possible to give of induction? It undercuts the desired effect of principle (II) of Chapter V, §1, the principle of necessary basic properties. That principle leads to the conclusion that we must regard some basic properties of individuals as necessary if induction is to be a reasonable practice. Thus the antecedents of supportable hypotheses must stand a chance of signifying a property that is necessary for some individual. But suppose we impose the condition that all singular necessities can be universalized. Then the antecedent of any supportable hypothesis must stand a chance of signifying a property with universal application. Otherwise, it would not stand a chance of signifying a property that is necessary for some individual. The imposed requirement would have the effect of limiting supportable hypotheses to ones that are mostly irrelevant to the practice of action on prior experience, considered as a fundamental practice. For practice deals largely with connections among properties known to have limited application. Thus inductive practice is incoherent with the theory of necessity based on universalizability. But let us see if the ontologist of conditions can even make sense of his own universalizable necessities.

Second, there is a difficulty for necessities across time. The action view of time was possible since things had progressive actions that did not themselves have durations. By going back to progressive actions, it was possible to ground the time of and between conditions (Chapter VIII, §3). Yet conditions, as opposed to progressive actions, are of themselves temporally extended. In an ontology of conditions, a progressive action is not had by an individual, nor is it had by the condition of having it. Yet apart from being had by some entity it is not a source of time, since if it is not had by some entity it is in no way particularized. Thus it cannot be the source of the time of any particular condition or of the time between any two particular conditions. However, in an ontology containing physical individuals, progressive actions are components of individuals and can thus be the basis for the extended conditions of having those actions as well as for times between conditions. In short, an ontology of conditions will have to assume temporal and spatial relations as entities. Conditions will have positions in a network of such relations, as will their stages. But the result of having temporal relations as entities was seen to be that necessities across time were excluded (Chapter VII, §1). Thus the ontology of conditions can admit no necessary connections across time, universalizable or otherwise; it is a natural basis for a Humean denial of necessities across time. But we saw that denying such connections is incoherent with the practice of action on prior experience.

Finally, it is even difficult to account for any necessity within the ontology of conditions. What is the status of the features of which conditions are the having? It is customary to say that they are the "constituents" or the "components" of conditions.[3] But this is usually explained by saying merely that *F* is a constituent of condition *e* when *e* is, at least in part, the having of *F*. In any event, for the ontology of conditions, these features are not, in our sense, components of individuals or even of conditions. They are not the same particulars as individuals—there being no individuals—and they are not the same particulars as conditions—conditions not, in general, having the features of which they are the having. So for the ontology of conditions, *F* is related to the having of *F* in either of two ways. Either *F* is no entity at all or *F* is an entity distinct from the having of *F*. If it is no entity at all, it cannot be used to account for the necessity of a condition by being its nature. If, however, *F* is distinct from, say, *a*'s *F*ing, the ontology of conditions accepts features as a category of entities distinct from conditions. This is not its first admission of entities distinct from conditions. This ontology must also countenance temporal relations as entities distinct from conditions. We thus arrive at a physical ontology similar to that of the *Timaeus,* in which Plato treated physical appearances as conditions—the havings of distinct entities called forms—in the relations collectively called the receptacle.[4]

The difficulty now encountered by the ontology of conditions is that only an entity that a necessity is of can account for this necessity. For, as we saw in Chapter III, §2, if *F* is the nature associated with, but distinct from, *a*'s having *F,* then it will be a necessity of *F* itself that if the nature *F* does support an implication to the feature *G,* then, indeed, the condition of *a*'s having *F* will imply *b*'s having *G.* Otherwise, *a*'s condition of having *F* could fail to have connections its nature, *F,* requires it to have, which would be absurd. When, however, the nature is not distinct from an individual that has it, the association between the nature and the individual is a necessity of the individual, and does not depend on the nature of the nature of the individual. But here the condition and its nature are distinct, and, thus, to ground the association of the two, a nature of this nature is needed, and so on endlessly. We saw that this was a harmful regress.

So unless necessities of physical conditions can be based on the natures of complex particulars other than conditions—hence, on the natures of individuals—there can be no necessities of physical conditions. This requires abandoning the ontology of conditions. The whole idea of natures of conditions is seen to be useless, for all necessities are ultimately grounded on the natures of individuals, that is, on the natures of things or of other individuals if there are any. Moreover, since the ontology of conditions fails to allow even for necessities that can be universalized, it has no basis —other than its general inability to handle necessities—for rejecting restricted necessities of particulars.

As we have seen, our version of the limited-independent-variety account of necessities needed by induction requires non-universalizable singular necessities for some basic properties. Conditions belong to the surfaces of individuals, and necessities utilize the depths of the natures of individuals. It is no surprise, then, that when one tries to have the surfaces without the depths one loses necessities, and thus settles for an ontology that is incoherent with the presuppositions of any human practice.

§2. *Things as Individuals with the Capacity to Act.* Conditions without individuals yield an impoverished ontology. There must then be individuals in order to provide conditions with a locus for occurrence. But a further step is needed to require that there be individuals with a capacity to act, that is, that there be things.[5]

As we saw in Chapter VIII, there must be entities that act if there are to be necessities across time. Since conditions and nonphysical individuals do not act, it is clear that the required entities must be physical individuals. However, it does not follow that an individual has a capacity to act simply because it acts. According to Chapter X, two requirements must be met if there is to be a capacity. There must be an appropriate fine structure, the having of which is a causal factor in realizing the behavior the capacity is for. There must also be a necessary connection involved in the causal relationship from the fine structure to the behavior. If either of these requirements fails, the behavior in question is not the realization of a capacity but is a caprice. However, the actions involved in necessities across time cannot be mere caprices of nature, so the individuals having these actions will have capacities to act and, hence, will be things.

Consider the consequence of saying that, though individuals act, they have no capacity to act. Can it be necessary that if *Fa* then at a subsequent time *Gb?* If, where *F* itself is not an action, neither *a* nor *b* nor a third individual has the capacity to act, then it is a contingent matter that, when *Fa* holds, either *a* or *b* or a third individual will act. For if it were necessary, then some component of *a* or *b* or a third individual would insure that, when *Fa* holds, one of the three individuals would act. And this would amount to one of them having the capacity to act. But if it is contingent that, when *Fa* holds, either *a* or *b* or a third individual will act, then it cannot be necessary that if *Fa* then at a subsequent time *Gb,* for there can be no subsequent time unless one of the relevant entities acts.

Where *F* is itself an action of *a,* it cannot be supposed automatically that something has the capacity to *F*. What needs to be shown is that, whether or not *F* is the actualization of a capacity, there is some action involved that is. For there to be a necessity of the above kind, there must be a condition that is a result. Otherwise, there would be a time subsequent to *a*'s being *F* only contingently. The result need not be *b*'s being *G*, but it will be like *b*'s being *G* in being after *a*'s being *F*. A condition that is a result comes about as a change in the way things are, and a change is an action, in our broad sense. There must be such a change when *a F*'s or else what follows *a*'s being *F* follows it only contingently. So there will be a component, a nature, that functions as fine structure in bringing about the change. Either *a* or some other involved individual will, then, have a capacity to act. If one rejects such a capacity, one must reject the necessity across time.[6]

In §1, I showed that the necessities required for induction require individuals. Given our account of necessity, the required individuals will have natures, since the necessities are necessities of the individuals. I have now shown that necessities across time require individuals with capacities to act. There is the possibility that some of the individuals required by the former argument lack capacities. They may have natures but no natural actions. If these individuals had natural actions, their natures would provide a basis for their having capacities for these actions. (There is no obstacle to expanding the notion of fine structure to include natures.) We cannot then say that the individuals required by induction are all things. But we have just shown that at least some of them must be things and hence that the required ontology will contain things.

The differentia in the definition of things is the having of a capacity to act. It turns out that having the capacity to act is not characteristic of any entities other than things. Thus, having the capacity to act implies being an individual, which was the genus in our definition. And so the seemingly more general predicates 'particular with the capacity to act' and 'entity with the capacity to act' have in fact the same extension as the definition 'individual with the capacity to act'. To justify this claim, I shall examine the relation of non-individuals, such as components and conditions, to capacities. I wish to establish the general position that the claim that a component or a condition has a capacity is true only because an individual has a capacity.

§3. *Capacities, Conditions, and Components.* First, consider the question of whether conditions have capacities. The condition of being sharp, we might say, is capable of causing a cut. But to what entity does the required fine structure belong? The fine structure will be, say, the component of sharpness belonging to the knife. And the basis of the causal necessity required for the capacity will be the nature of this sharp individual. The fine-structure factor and the factor behind the causal necessity are not then factors of the condition of being sharp but of the individual with this condition.

Admittedly, the fine-structure factor is a "constituent" of the condition of being sharp, but this means only that sharpness is a component of the individual with this condition. Moreover, the causal necessity is not of the condition since, in view of §1, the nature of the condition would be distinct from the condition and could not ground the causal necessity. So the causal necessity is of the individual, and hence the nature needed to support this necessity is the nature of the sharp individual. In brief, conditions do not themselves have capacities; whenever a statement that a condition has a capacity is accepted, it is accepted only because individuals with these conditions have the corresponding capacities.

Second, consider the question of whether components have capacities. The attribution of capacities to components demands reinterpretation to avoid sheer absurdity. The component redness that an individual has does not have the capacity to be or to become some other component. A component is always precisely what it is and does not change, since we employ components to explain just what change is. In addition, a component does not have the capacity to make something happen or to be the object of some act, such as seeing. Yet why not?

A component by itself is not a cause, though an individual's having a component can be a cause. Otherwise, two causes might be different components without being distinct particulars; the heat of a fire that causes a burn and the brightness of the same fire that causes a shadow would not be distinct causes, being components of the same fire. Causal claims could then change truth value by the replacement, at the point of the term for the cause, of a reference to one component with a reference to a different one, even though the reference does not change to a distinct particular. On the surface, at least, this is a difficulty.

But what if one allows the distinction between the transparent and the opaque to apply to the context of the term for the cause as well as to that of the term for the effect (cf. Chapter X, §4)? Thus:

(1) A crisis is caused by Wilson's speaking about war

might be true, when:

(2) A crisis is caused by Wilson's speaking 200 words

is false, since, though Wilson's speaking about war and his speaking 200 words were the same event, the context is opaque for terms for causes. However:

(3) A crisis is caused by the condition that is Wilson's speaking 200 words

would be true, given the truth of (1) and the sameness of the conditions, since the context is transparent for terms for causes.

Still, the above-mentioned difficulty remains. The heat and the brightness of the fire have distinct effects. Thus the replacement of a term for heat by a term for brightness in a transparent context like (3) would affect a change of truth value. To allow for this, one would be forced to the conclusion that the heat and the brightness are, in fact, distinct particulars. Then the terms for them could not be interchanged in a transparent context. But since we have strong reasons for thinking that components of this kind are not distinct, we should rather conclude that components are simply not causes at all. Then all attempts to insert terms for them in the place for causal terms in affirmative causal claims are misguided. (Similarly, since conditions, not components, are extended, we avoid the difficulty that if 'the sharpness of *a* lasts one year' is true then, since components of *a* are all the same, 'the hotness of *a* lasts one year' would be true.)

But perhaps components can be objects of acts. If a component were the object of an act, a different component of the same individual should not have to be an object of such an act. I do not see the red of an object's back when I inspect the green of its front. But normally, if one sees an entity, then one sees any entity that is the same particular it is. Here I am taking the object of the act to be a real and not just an intentional object. This assumption is perfectly natural where we are speaking of real components and not of the contents of perceivers' beliefs about what they perceive. Thus 'Hugo sees green' implies 'There is green that Hugo sees'. So we arrive at the objectionable result that if the green individual is red in back, Hugo's seeing red is implied by his seeing green, even though Hugo may not have noticed the individual's back. It is not open to us to avoid this absurdity by claiming that the green and the red of the same individual are distinct. For then we would be faced with the vicious regress of Chapter VII, §1.

Now if components do not change and if they neither act nor are acted on, they lack capacities. Ascribing capacities to them is at best a way of saying that individuals with these components have certain capacities, and that these components are themselves parts of the fine-structure factor in these capacities.

It suffices, then, to characterize things as entities with capacities to act in order to distinguish them from conditions and components. But this characterization would also distinguish things from physical individuals that, despite our definition of them, are simple and from any kind of momentary entity. Simple physical individuals have no components and are thus propertyless foci for external relations to properties. Now perhaps the properties externally related to physical simples could do the work of those components of complex individuals that ground the capacities of these individuals. But externally related natures will not, without the unpalatable regress discussed in Chapter III, §2, do the work of grounding the necessity involved in the causal connection required by capacities. Thus simple physical individuals, sometimes referred to as bare particulars, have no capacities and *a fortiori* no capacities to act.[7] They cannot do the job that things do in the required ontology.

Momentary entities, conceived of not as instantaneous events but as instantaneous slices of enduring individuals, can have capacities, though not capacities to act. A momentary entity could still have the capacity to be a factor in influencing other entities. Its momentary presence could, in the context of the action of some other entity, be a causal factor in influencing the outcome of that action. But beyond this, it lacks even the capacity to be in certain ways corresponding to non-relational features. It does not have the capacity to be red just by being red, since its having red would then have to cause it to be red, which it clearly does not do. And when it is red it does not have the capacity to be red because of a component other than red. For if it has the capacity because of another component, then either this other component would have to have functioned earlier as the cause of this red now, or it would have to function now to cause a later and hence a different redness in this individual. But in neither case is the individual momentary; it becomes an enduring individual. Finally, a momentary entity does not have the capacity to be what it is not, for then some feature of its fine structure would have to have, in conjunction with some act, a certain outcome that makes a difference to the momentary entity. Such an outcome would, in view of the intervening act, occur later on, and hence too late to be a condition of the momentary entity.

How does this relate to having the capacity to act? Since actions are components, they belong to a kind of being. So if momentary entities are barred from having capacities to be certain ways, they are equally barred from having the capacity to act. In other words, the above argument can be transferred point by point to capacities to act. If a momentary entity is acting, it can have a result only in another entity, for otherwise it could have a condition—the result of the action—that is later than this action. But momentary entities do not, in view of the above argument, have capacities for actions that have results in other entities. Since this is the only kind of action possible for them, they do not have the capacity to act in any way. This action with results in other entities could well establish momentary entities in time, but, without capacities to act, momentary entities would stand only in contingent connections.[8]

The futility of upholding the physical necessity needed for human practice while maintaining an ontology of conditions, an ontology of simple individuals, or an ontology of momentary individuals should be apparent. Conversely, it is not surprising that devastating critiques of necessities across time should have come from philosophers for whom one or another of these ontologies was ascendent. Since momentary individuals could have natures, there can be necessities of these individuals, though none of these necessities would be across time. However, since conditions and simple individuals could have no natures, they are the subjects of no necessities at all. Given the strong reasons we have for necessities across time, it becomes impossible for us to allow either events, simple individuals, or momentary entities to have the exclusive title of physical particulars. Of course, entities of any one of these kinds may exist; we are only denying that without things they can constitute an adequate ontology.

Consider, finally, the relation of capacities to time and space. From where I am seated, I am able with my hands to move individuals on my desk but not individuals on the moon. Capacities to act on individuals thus seem conditioned by their proximity. Perhaps then spatial and temporal relations must be assumed as entities if there are to be capacities to act on distinct individuals. However, capacities for actions, but not for actions on other individuals, do not seem to suppose a temporal and spatial network. I have the capacity to run even when denied the space to run in.

According to the view described in Chapter IX, §4, actions between distinct individuals are possible either because they ultimately occur and then provide their own temporal basis or because other actions occur between those individuals and provide what we called a temporal triangle. Independently of actual actions, there are no possible actions between distinct individuals. There is a perfectly analogous situation for potential actions between distinct individuals. Independently of actual actions there are no capacities for actions between distinct individuals. This means that actions must in some way be included among the components of fine structure when our analysis of capacities is applied to capacities to act on distinct individuals. Part of the fine structure will be the non-specific feature of there being some action, of the entity with the capacity, on the distinct entity that is potentially acted on.

Thus *a*'s having the capacity to act in the manner *F* on the distinct entity *b* requires, first, that some action occur from *a* to *b*, either directly or through intermediaries, and, second, that *F* be causally explained by other features of the fine structure of *a*. (The only action there is between *a* and *b* may turn out to be *F* itself.) This is not to say that actions for which there are capacities will end up requiring actions for which there are no capacities. This account allows that, for every action between *a* and *b*, there can be a capacity. There is neither regress nor circularity, and no need for spatial or temporal relations.

§4. *Sameness and Existence for Conditions.* By establishing that things are indispensable we have in no way undercut the need for conditions. In fact, there must be conditions, for things must have components in order to have capacities. Even if there were only one individual in the physical universe—and nothing I have said implies there must be many—there would still have to be many particulars—at least one individual and at least one condition. So monism, as the view that there is only one particular, is incompatible with the required ontology. Recall that, unless conditions are particulars distinct from things, they too will be components, and there will be a regress of conditions required for the having of any property (Chapter VIII, §4). But if things are distinct from conditions, something more needs to be said about their relation to one another. I shall argue that, though conditions are unlike components in that they are distinct from things, they are like components in having the status of secondary entities, whereas things are primary entities.

By a "primary entity" I shall mean an entity that satisfies two requirements. The first is that it is "independent as regards sameness." An entity satisfies this requirement when it is not a component of any other entity. Otherwise, what entities it is the same as would depend on what entity it is a component of. Whether this redness is the same particular as this circularity depends on whether there is an individual both are components of. But whether this penny is the same particular as this redness does not depend on what this penny is a component of, since it is not a component at all.

The second requirement is that it is "independent as regards existence." An entity satisfies this requirement when the associated component called existence does not depend on any entity other than this entity. In other words, there being the component of existence associated with an entity depends on nothing other than there being this entity. I say the component of existence "associated with" an entity rather than the entity's component of existence since, for example, the dependent existence of a component like redness is not a component in redness. Since components do not have components, the dependent existence of the color is ultimately the existence of the individual with the color.

It is important to emphasize that independence as regards the feature existence need not imply independence as regards the condition of having existence. For a primary entity will have existential independence even when its coming into existence and its having existence are dependent conditions.[9] A thing, for example, might be brought to exist or caused to be in the condition of having existence by some other thing's condition. Still, once its having existence is caused, it has a component of existence and this component is not thereby caused; indeed this component, as the existence of a thing, does not depend on any condition.

I have had to rely on the notion of component here; an entity is independent as regards sameness when what it is the same as does not depend on what it is a *component* of, and an entity is independent as regards existence when the associated *component* of existence does not depend on any entity other than it. But with some sacrifice in definiteness, the reliance on the notion of component can be avoided. Then we say an entity is independent as regards sameness when what it is the same as does not depend on its belonging to any whole; an entity is independent as regards existence when, over and above any dependency it might have for its coming to exist and for its being sustained in existence, there is no other way that involves existence in which the entity is dependent.

Thus the phenomenalist treats impressions as primary and things as secondary. For the existence of things depends on impressions in a way that implies neither that things come to be nor that they are sustained because of impressions. In short, the dependency involves existence but is not causal. The historical materialist treats economic roles as primary and a juridical system, say, as secondary. For the existence of a juridical system depends on roles in the process of production in a way that is compatible with its being a cause of the coming into existence of some modifications of economic roles. The scientific realist treats microentities as primary, and trees and birds as secondary. For him, the existence of trees and birds depends on microentities in a way that does not imply that they are caused by microentities to come to be and to endure.

Here then are ontologies in which the notion of component is either rejected—because of a commitment to simples—or not well worked out. Yet in regard to them the notion of ontological independence, that is, of independence as regards existence, has application. (The same point could be made for independence as regards sameness.) But in what follows I shall keep to my characterization in terms of components. In any ontology the connections between entities will include dependencies as regards sameness and existence. The justification of these dependencies will be one of its main problems. In my ontology, this justification will quite naturally rely on the notions of component and individual.

The general notion of dependency was explained in Chapter IX, §3, with the help of the notion of the factive conditional. Thus, to say that the existence of an entity *a* depends on *a* but not on any other entity is to say that:

(4) There is the entity *a* > there is the component of existence that is associated with *a*

is true, but the following is false for any *b* other than *a:*

(5) There is an entity *b* > there is the component of existence that is associated with *a*.

Of course, the component existence is a sufficient condition for there being the entity associated with it; conversely, there being the entity associated with it will be a sufficient condition for this component. So the general notion of sufficient condition will not explain the asymmetrical notion of dependency needed here. This notion of dependency is, however, illuminated by the notion of making something true which was built into the notion of the factive conditional. When *a*'s existence depends on *a,* there being an entity *a* makes it true or is the ground for the fact that there is the component of existence that is associated with *a.* But there being the component of existence does not make it true and does not ground the fact that there is the entity *a.* In short, the part does not imply the whole. There being the component is at best a sign of there being the entity.

Further, if properties and conditions are dependent, as regards existence, on things with them, then that there are these things factively implies that there are the components of existence that are associated with their properties and conditions.[10] That there is existence that is associated with the yellowness of a thing *a* is made true or grounded by there being the thing *a,* but not conversely. Of course, *a* might change color, but as was emphasized earlier, the factive conditional is contextual.

Which entities in the required ontology are primary, if any are? Things, but neither components nor conditions, qualify as primary. (Moreover, if there are physical individuals that are not things, they too would be primary, but I shall limit attention to things.) Things are independent as regards sameness since they do not have the status of components, and for the same reason conditions are independent as regards sameness. But though things are independent as regards existence, conditions of things depend on things for their existence. Similarly, components are not independent as regards existence; they are dependent as regards their existence on the things that have them. Let us look now at the justification for the claims that conditions and components are dependent as regards existence.

As for the primacy of things, I shall consider only the question of whether things, if they have independence as regards existence, are necessary beings. If existence is a component that an entity has only because it has the nature it does, then the entity is said to be a necessary being. It does not logically follow from the fact that an entity is a necessary being that it always exists or that it exists in all possible circumstances. All that logically follows is that, when it exists, its having the component of existence will not be due to the condition of any entity playing the role of its cause, but will flow from its having the nature it does.

Even so, primary entities need not be necessary beings. What follows from a primary entity's having the nature it does is not its having existence, but at most its having the conditional property that it has when it is true that there being this entity factively implies there being its existence. Thus, ontological independence means that there being the component of existence depends only on there being the entity with it. It does not mean that having the component of existence depends on either there being the entity or on its having the nature it does. The necessity of an entity concerns its condition of having existence, whereas its primacy concerns its component of existence.

Let us inspect this distinction simply from the perspective of causation. A necessary being could neither be caused to come to have existence nor sustained causally in its having existence. Otherwise, its having existence would not be due simply to its having the nature it does. The situation is different when the entity is merely a primary entity. Even though the entity's component existence depends only on this entity, there may be a cause of its coming to have this component or of its being sustained in having this component. In a similar manner, the component yellow an old newspaper has is dependent on the molecular structure of the newspaper and hence on the newspaper, even though it is not the newspaper that causes its having yellowness but rather the sunlight to which it was exposed. The component existence of an entity may depend on the entity, even though for the entity to exist—that is, for it to have this component existence—a cause may be needed. In sum, things can be independent as regards existence without having to be necessary beings.

The theological argument from contingency depends on a blurring of this distinction. One goes from the premiss that physical things do not exist by nature to the conclusion that some being exists by nature by way of the premisses that contingent beings are dependent as regards existence and that dependent existence is grounded in independent existence. But, in view of the above, it is simply false that contingent beings must have dependent existence and, hence, it is simply false that independent beings must be necessary beings.

Why are conditions secondary entities? We can approach this

question by examining the foundations of the relation *condition of*. Assume we are dealing with a condition of a thing. The component the condition is the condition of having is the foundation on the part of the thing. But it is not so clear what the foundation is on the part of the condition itself. If the condition is one of having redness, then it is not the case that redness is itself a component of the condition, for then the condition, as well as the thing, would be red. Redness will not, then, be a foundation at both ends of the relation. My proposal is that the unity of the condition is all there is to the foundation of the relation *condition of* in the condition itself. The reason for this is imply that nothing more is required of the condition than that it be, and hence be a unity, for it to stand in this relation to a thing. But a thing must have the relevant component to stand in this relation to a condition.

Now the unity of a thing is the sameness of the thing both with itself and its components (Chapter VII, §5). The unity of the thing is the binding together of the components, including unity, with one another and of the thing with each of its components. That is, if *a* has unity, then any two components of *a* are the same, and *a* is the same as any component of *a*. The unity of a condition is also the binding together of the condition with its components and of these components among themselves.

But the important fact is that the unity of a condition of a thing has its roots elsewhere. This is understandable since the condition concerns a thing and one of its components. The unity binds together since this unity is itself a complexity whose elements are elsewhere. The unity is the complexity there is when there is, on the one side, a thing and, on the other side, a component of that thing. This is not the complexity there is just among the components of the thing, for, since a thing is different from any of its components, the thing is not reflected in this complexity. It is, rather, the complexity there is as a result of there being a thing and one of its components. This complexity does not contain the thing or its component as a component, for, as the unity of a condition, this complexity is itself a component, and thus has no components.

Moreover, even though the condition has this complexity, the thing and its component are not had by the condition as components. If it had them as components, it would be the same particular as the thing and be qualified in the way the thing is qualified by having that component. Since the unity of the condition is this complexity, it cannot be the case that the condition is the ontological ground for either the thing or the component of it. For the complexity of there being a thing and one of its components requires there being a thing and one of its components. Since the existence of a condition requires its unity and since its unity is the complexity of there being a thing and its component, the existence of the condition depends on a thing and its component. Once it is shown that components depend on things for their existence, we can say simply that conditions depend on things as regards existence if they are conditions of things.

To show that a component is existentially dependent on a thing or whatever has the component, it suffices to point out that a component depends on a thing or whatever has the component for sameness. If a component were not dependent on, say, a thing with it for its existence, it would have its own existence or depend on some other entity for its existence. Thus, its existence could not be one shared with the thing. So the component's existence would not be the same particular as the thing. But if its existence is not the same particular as the thing, the component itself is not the same particular as the thing. So a component would not be dependent as regards sameness on the thing with it. In sum, the existence of a component is dependent since it is not a component of this component, but is the existence of the thing with this component.

§5. *The Dialectic of Sameness.* The doctrine that relations are entities was seen to lead to the result that things are really isolated from one another. By contrast, if in place of relations there are relational properties and foundations for them, then there is a togetherness of things (Chapter VII, §4). This togetherness results from the fact that a thing has a relational property, not by it alone having a foundation, but in addition by another thing having a matching foundation. Given the foundations in distinct things, these things will have properties by which they internalize one another, that is, they will have relational properties.

Nonetheless, this togetherness seems to be associated with a rigid distinctness of the things participating in it. And such a rigid distinctness is incompatible with the fact that these things often exist in communities in which their distinctness is modified. The togetherness we have offered, while a step beyond the separateness imposed by relations as in-between entities, still leaves the things participating in it as distinct entities. But at every level—the atomic, the chemical, the biological, and the social—we are faced with phenomena for which the assumption of the distinctness of the key entities provides an inadequate account.

One way to attempt to solve this problem is to call a retreat on the distinctness of things. Things are then reduced to the level of components in order that they might be members of communities, which in turn acquire the role of primary entities.[11] But this solution fails to provide for the fact that things come into and go out of communities. On the one hand, they may become members of a community and before they cease to exist the community dissolves. On the other hand, they may cease to be components in one community and shortly thereafter begin to be components of a distinct community by ceasing to participate actively in the former and beginning to participate actively in the latter. This attempted solution to the problem of community by reducing things to components is a static solution in that it ignores these changes of sameness and traps things once and for all in given communities.

The concept of part elaborated in Chapter X, §2, provides the basis for another approach to reconciling the distinctness of things with their roles in communities. A part is the kind of component that can become a distinct entity by being separated from the entity of which it is a component. So there is a change of sameness involved in the separation. Conversely, if an entity becomes a part, it is no longer the same particular. It becomes the same as the entity of which it is now the component.

Of course, a part is in some sense the same entity as the corresponding separate entity. But we can reconstruct this sense in terms of the materials at hand. First, the part and the corresponding separate entity are similar, in the way the green of this thing is similar to the green of that thing, but both distinct and different. This alone is not enough even to approach closely the intuitive sense of sameness as applied to a part and a corresponding separate entity. What more is involved? Second, a part and a corresponding separate entity are related by becoming. The separate entity becomes a part, or the part becomes the separate entity. So a part and a separate entity are "the same entity" in the sense that they are similar and the one becomes the other.

If, on the other hand, things were simples, there would be nothing describable as a part becoming a separate entity, since in this view parts must already be separate entities. An ontology of simples does not countenance a dialectic of sameness whereby, in time, the many become a complex one. In the ontology of simples, communities must be simples if they exist at all, in which case there are no entities that are components of them. Conversely, in the same ontology, if communities have components playing roles in them, then the communities themselves do not exist. Every community that has component members is a fiction, and the distinctness of things is an inflexible law. Individualism is then an ontological necessity and not just an ideology if there are component members of communities.

One might seem to resolve this dilemma by saying that communities are sets to which individuals stand in the membership relation. In this view, both the community and the individuals in it can be distinct simple individuals. But if communities are sets, then it becomes impossible to explain their changes when their membership remains unaltered, or their sameness when their membership changes. Communities change their form and even dissolve without, in the process, changing members. The only basis for understanding communities is a component ontology, in which the individual-component contrast is radically different from the set-member contrast.

The ontology of components allows us to say simultaneously that things are entities and that communities of things, or of entities that when separated are things, are entities. In addition, given the theory of parts we have associated with the ontology of components, there can be processes whereby entities no longer remain the same since they become components of communities, and whereby, conversely, communities dissolve or lose some of their component members, which then revert to distinct entities.

Such processes are not limited to the physical, chemical, and biological levels, where it seems obvious that bits of matter are appropriated by systems that can, in turn, generate distinct systems from their parts. People are also entities that can exist either as distinct entities or, through genuine participation, as entities that are components of various sorts of communities. Mere formal membership without active participation is never sufficient for a change of sameness from personal to communal sameness. Conversely, mere formal community that depends exclusively on ritual is not an entity for whose sameness members exchange their personal sameness.

Since people are genuine entities, even as components of communities, and since the communities of which they are components are genuine entities, the dichotomy between individualism and holism breaks down. Communities do not, as they do for individualism, contain individuals in the sense of entities that are rigidly distinct. But neither are communitites, as they are for holism, wholes in which the members have lost their entitative status. Communities are distinct entities in which members are components that can still become distinct entities. Insofar as communities are distinct entities, they must have components other than their parts. They will have properties, actions, and natures. Thus it is clear that not all explanations of interaction among communities will be explanations by means of their parts, as the individualist would contend.[12] Of course, it does not follow that the extreme holist would be right in thinking that the parts never serve an explanatory role in regard to the action of the community. He would, nonetheless, be led to say this because of his denial of entitative status to the parts. But if parts are entities, then like properties or natures, they can be appealed to in accounting for what the community does. Further, as parts they may have come to the community from having been entities with the status of distinct entities. And they are not trapped by the community since it is possible for them to return to the status of distinct entities or to participate in distinct communities at distinct times.

NOTES

Notes to Chapter I

1. Cf. David Hume, *A Treatise of Human Nature,* ed. L. A. Selby-Bigge (Oxford: Clarendon Press, 1888), Book I, Part III, Sec. 14, pp. 159–62.

2. L. Frank Baum, *The Wonderful Wizard of Oz* (Chicago: Hall, 1900), Chap. 4.

3. Cf. Nelson Goodman, *Fact, Fiction, and Forecast* (Cambridge, Mass.: Harvard University Press, 1955), p. 38.

4. Cf. Karl Popper, *The Logic of Scientific Discovery* (London: Hutchinson, 1959), pp. 33, 255, 265, 418.

5. Popper, *Scientific Discovery,* p. 61, n. 1.

6. Descartes, *Principles of Philosophy,* Part III, Principle IV, in *Oeuvres de Descartes,* ed. Charles Adams and Paul Tannery, Vol. 9–2 (Paris: Vrin, 1964), p. 104.

7. Plato, *Timaeus* 68D, in F. M. Cornford, *Plato's Cosmology* (London: Kegan Paul, 1937), p. 278.

8. Plato, *Theaetetus* 178E–179B, in F. M. Cornford, *Plato's Theory of Knowledge* (London: Kegan Paul, 1935), p. 91.

9. *Before Philosophy,* ed. Henri and H. A. Frankfort (Baltimore: Penguin, 1949), Chap. 1.

10. C. S. Lewis, *Out of the Silent Planet* (New York: Macmillan, 1965), p. 94.

11. Cf. J. J. C. Smart, *Philosophy and Scientific Realism* (New York: Humanities, 1963), pp. 40–49.

12. "Time and the World Order," *Minnesota Studies in the Philosophy of Science,* ed. Herbert Feigl and Grover Maxwell, Vol. 3 (Minneapolis: University of Minnesota Press, 1962), p. 593.

13. "Counterfactuals, Dispositions, and the Causal Modalities," *Minnesota Studies in the Philosophy of Science,* ed. Herbert Feigl, Michael Scriven, and Grover Maxwell, Vol. 2 (Minneapolis: University of Minnesota Press, 1958), p. 264.

14. "Empiricism and the Philosophy of Mind," *Minnesota Studies in the Philosophy of Science,* ed. Herbert Feigl and Michael Scriven, Vol. 1 (Minneapolis: University of Minnesota Press, 1956), p. 303.

15. Wilfrid Sellars, "Scientific Realism or Irenic Instrumentalism" in his *Philosophical Perspectives* (Springfield, Ill.: C. C. Thomas, 1967), pp. 337–69.

Notes to Chapter II

1. William Kneale, *Probability and Induction* (Oxford: Clarendon Press, 1949), p. 80.
2. Karl Popper, *The Logic of Scientific Discovery* (London: Hutchinson, 1959), pp. 429–30.
3. Cf. R. B. Braithwaite, *Scientific Explanation* (Cambridge: Cambridge University Press, 1955), p. 301.
4. Cf. Nelson Goodman, *Fact, Fiction, and Forecast* (Cambridge, Mass.: Harvard University Press, 1955), Chap. 4.
5. A. R. Anderson and N. D. Belnap, Jr., "The Pure Calculus of Entailment," *Journal of Symbolic Logic* 21 (1962), pp. 19–52. The same authors have conveniently shortened and combined this and another article into "Entailment," in *Logic and Philosophy,* ed. Gary Iseminger (New York: Appleton-Century-Crofts, 1968), pp. 76–110. For the semantical completeness of system R of relevant implication see Robert K. Meyer and Richard Routley, "The Semantics of Entailment, I," *Truth, Syntax, Modality,* ed. Hugues Leblanc (Amsterdam: North Holland, 1972).
6. C. I. Lewis and C. H. Langford, *Symbolic Logic,* 2d ed. (New York: Dover, 1959), pp. 122–47. Appendix II, pp. 492–502, contains a description of the standard systems, S1 through S5, of modal logic, to which I shall refer later.
7. Aristotle, *Metaphysics,* trans. Richard Hope (Ann Arbor: University of Michigan Press, 1960), 1041b30.
8. Aristotle, *Metaphysics* 1038a20.
9. Aristotle, *Metaphysics* 1032a6.
10. John Locke, *An Essay Concerning Human Understanding,* ed. A. C. Fraser, Vol. 1 (Oxford: Clarendon Press, 1894), Book II, Chap. 31, Sec. 6.
11. Cf. Saul A. Kripke, "Sementical Considerations on Modal Logic," *Acta Philosophica Fennica* 16 (1963), pp. 83–94.
12. Cf. William Kneale, "Universality and Necessity," *British Journal for Philosophy of Science* 12 (1961), pp. 89–102.
13. Cf. Nino B. Cocchiarella, "A Completeness Theorem in Second Order Modal Logic," *Theoria* 35 (1969), pp. 81–103.
14. Ruth Barcan Marcus, "Modalities and Intensional Languages," in *Contemporary Readings in Logical Theory,* ed. I. M. Copi and J. A. Gould (New York: Macmillan, 1967), p. 293.
15. Willard Van Orman Quine, "Three Grades of Modal Involvement" in his *The Ways of Paradox* (New York: Random House, 1966), p. 174.
16. Cf. Aristotle, *Metaphysics* 1029b13–22.
17. Aristotle, *Physics,* trans. Richard Hope (Lincoln: University of Nebraska Press, 1961), 192b22.

Notes to Chapter III

1. Cf. G. W. F. Leibniz, Reply to Foucher, August 3, 1693; Letter to deVolder, April, 1702; "Principles of Nature and Grace," 1714, §1, in *Leibniz: Selections,* ed. P. P. Wiener (New York: Scribners, 1951), pp. 99, 176, 522, respectively.

2. David Hume, *A Treatise of Human Nature,* ed. L. A. Selby-Bigge (Oxford: Clarendon Press, 1888), Book I, Part I, Sec. 7 ad fin.

3. Bertrand Russell, "The Philosophy of Logical Atomism" in his *Logic and Knowledge,* ed. R. C. Marsh (New York: Macmillan, 1956), p. 270.

4. Cf. Gustav Bergmann, "Meaning" in his *Logic and Reality* (Madison: University of Wisconsin Press, 1964), pp. 85–97.

5. Cf. P. F. Strawson, *Individuals* (London: Methuen, 1959), p. 175.

6. Cf. Gottlob Frege, "On Concept and Object" in his *Philosophical Writings of Gottlob Frege,* trans. Peter Geach and Max Black (Oxford: Blackwell, 1952), p. 45.

7. This contrast between the two views of predication parallels that in Plato between the blending of the forms and participation in the forms; cf. *Sophist* 253D and F. M. Cornford's comment in his *Plato's Theory of Knowledge* (London: Kegan Paul, 1935), p. 266. For a detailed study of the two views of predication—the sameness and the exemplification views—see John Francis Peterson, "Logical Atomism and the Realism-Nominalism Issue" (Ph.D. diss., Indiana University, 1965).

8. Aristotle, *Physics,* trans. Richard Hope (Lincoln: University of Nebraska Press, 1961), 202b16.

9. Aristotle, *Metaphysics,* trans. Richard Hope (Ann Arbor: University of Michigan Press, 1960), Delta 9.

10. Cf. Jean-Paul Sartre, *L'être et le néant* (Paris: Gallimard, 1943), p. 235: "Mais le jaune du citron n'est pas un mode subjectif d'apprehension du citron: il est le citron . . . . En fait, le citron est étendu tout à travers ses qualités et chacune de ses qualités est étendu tout à travers chacune des autres . . . . En ce sens, toute qualité de l'être est tout l'être."

11. Cf. Fred Feldman, "Leibniz and 'Leibniz' Law'," *Philosophical Review* 79 (1970), pp. 510–22.

12. Leibniz, Fifth Letter to Clarke, 1716, §47, in *Leibniz: Selections,* p. 253.

13. Cf. Henry Margenau, *The Nature of Physical Reality* (New York: McGraw-Hill, 1950), p. 441.

14. Cf. David Wiggins, *Identity and Spatio-Temporal Continuity* (Oxford: Blackwell, 1967), pp. 10–13.

15. Cf. Aristotle, *Metaphysics* 1031a14–18, 1038b10–12, 1071a28; and Rogers Albritton, "Forms of Particular Substances in Aristotle's Metaphysics," *Journal of Philosophy* 54 (1957), pp. 699–708.

16. Cf. Leibniz, "Refutation of Spinoza," c. 1708 in *Leibniz: Selections,* pp. 485–97.

17. Plato, *Timaeus* 29C, 52C in F. M. Cornford, *Plato's Cosmology* (London: Kegan Paul, 1937).

18. Aristotle, *Metaphysics* 1036a2, 1042a17.

19. Cf. Panayot Butchvarov, *Resemblance and Identity* (Bloomington: Indiana University Press, 1966), p. 129.

20. Bertrand Russell, "On the Relations of Universals to Particulars" in his *Logic and Knowledge,* ed. R. C. Marsh (New York: Macmillan, 1956), pp. 111–12.

21. Aristotle, *Metaphysics* 1038a19–35.

22. Cf. John Locke, *An Essay Concerning Human Understanding,* ed. A. C. Fraser (Oxford: Clarendon Press, 1894), Book III, Chap. 6, Sec. 14–19.

23. John Locke, *Essay,* Book III, Chap. 6, Sec. 4.

24. Cf. D. K. Lewis, "Counterpart Theory and Quantified Modal Logic," *Journal of Philosophy* 65 (1968), pp. 113–26.

25. Karl Popper, "Three Views Concerning Human Knowledge" in his *Conjectures and Refutations* (New York: Basic Books, 1963), pp. 103–04.

Notes to Chapter IV

1. Cf. Herbert Feigl, "De Principiis Non Disputandum . . . ?" in *Philosophical Analysis,* ed. Max Black (Englewood, Cliffs, N.J.: Prentice-Hall), p. 143.

2. Cf. Wesley C. Salmon, *The Foundations of Scientific Inference* (Pittsburgh: University of Pittsburgh Press, 1966), pp. 88, 105.

3. Cf. Hans Reichenbach, "The Logical Foundations of the Concept of Probability" in *Readings in Philosophical Analysis,* ed. Herbert Feigl and Wilfrid Sellars (New York: Appleton-Century-Crofts, 1949), p. 321.

4. Cf. Nelson Goodman, *Fact, Fiction, and Forecast* (Cambridge: Harvard University Press, 1955), pp. 67, 96, 108, 117.

5. Isaac Levi, *Gambling With Truth* (New York: Knopf, 1967), pp. 86, 180.

6. Cf. Rudolf Carnap, *Logical Foundations of Probability* (Chicago: University of Chicago Press, 1950), p. 548.

7. Cf. Robert C. Stalnaker, "Probability and Conditionals," *Philosophy of Science* 37 (1970), p. 75.

8. *An Analysis of Knowledge and Valuation* (LaSalle, Ill.: Open Court, 1946), p. 228.

9. Cf. Robert C. Stalnaker, "A Theory of Conditionals," *Studies in Logical Theory: American Philosophical Quarterly,* Monograph 2 (Oxford: Blackwell, 1968), pp. 98–112.

10. H. W. B. Joseph, *An Introduction to Logic,* 2d ed. (Oxford: Clarendon Press, 1916), p. 423.

11. J. M. Keynes, *A Treatise on Probability* (London: Macmillan, 1921), pp. 56–57; cf. Rudolf Carnap, *Logical Foundations,* p. 565.

12. Cf. also William Kneale, *Probability and Induction* (Oxford: Clarendon Press, 1949), p. 171.

13. A. J. Ayer, "Chance," *Scientific American* 213 (October, 1965), p. 52.

14. Cf. G. H. von Wright, *The Logical Problem of Induction* (Oxford: Blackwell, 1957), pp. 102–17.

15. Rudolf Carnap, *The Continuum of Inductive Methods* (Chicago: University of Chicago Press, 1952), pp. 25 and 40 for comments on a rule that makes support insensitive to possibilities.

16. Cf. Salmon, *Foundations*, pp. 83–96.

17. This criticism applies to the argument of Milton Fisk's, "Are There Necessary Connections in Nature?" *Philosophy of Science* 37 (1970), pp. 385–400.

Notes to Chapter V

1. J. M. Keynes, *A Treatise on Probability* (London: Macmillan, 1921), p. 258.

2. Keynes, *Treatise*, p. 251.

3. Jean Nicod, *Le problème logique de l'induction* (Paris: Presses Universitaires de France, 1961), pp. 65–79.

4. Nicod, *Le problème logique*, p. 254.

5. C. D. Broad, "The Relation Between Induction and Probability," Part II, *Mind* 29 (1920), pp. 11–45.

6. Cf. Stephan Barker, *Induction and Hypothesis* (Ithaca, N.Y.: Cornell University Press, 1957), p. 60.

7. David Bohm, *Causality and Chance in Modern Physics* (London: Routledge and Kegan Paul, 1957), Chap. 1, Sec. 10; Chap. 5, Sec. 4.

8. Bohm, *Causality and Chance*, p. 133.

9. Nelson Goodman, *Fact, Fiction, and Forecast* (Cambridge: Harvard University Press, 1955), Chap. 3.

10. Cf. Richard C. Jeffrey, *The Logic of Decision* (New York: McGraw-Hill, 1965), p. 155.

11. Cf. Lawrence Sklar, "Is Probability a Dispositional Property?" *Journal of Philosophy* 67 (1970), pp. 355–67.

12. Antonio Gramsci, *The Modern Prince and Other Writings*, trans. Louis Marks (New York: International Publishers, 1957), p. 95.

Notes to Chapter VI

1. Cf. Willard Van Orman Quine, "The Problem of Interpreting Modal Logic," *Journal of Symbolic Logic* 12 (1947), pp. 42–48.

2. Cf., for example, Wesley Salmon, *The Foundations of Scientific Inference* (Pittsburgh: University of Pittsburgh Press, 1966), pp. 27–40.

3. Cf. Willard Van Orman Quine, "Two Dogmas of Empiricism" in his *From a Logical Point of View* (Cambridge: Harvard University Press, 1953), p. 36.

4. Cf. Alfred Tarski, *Logic, Semantics, Metamathematics,* ed. J. H. Woodger (Oxford: Clarendon Press, 1956), pp. 193–98.

5. Tarski, *Logic, Semantics, Metamathematics,* pp. 31, 34.

6. Willard Van Orman Quine, *Word and Object* (New York: Technology Press and Wiley, 1960), pp. 66–67.

7. Immanuel Kant, *Critique of Pure Reason,* trans. N. K. Smith (London: Macmillan, 1953), A155–B194.

8. Kant, *Critique,* A256–B311.

9. John Henry Newman, *A Grammar of Assent,* 1870, Book I, Chap. 4, Sec. 1, para. 1 (reissued; New York: Doubleday Image, 1955).

10. Edmund Whittaker, *Aether and Electricity,* Vol. 2 (New York: Harper, 1960), p. 13.

11. Cf. Hans Reichenbach, *The Philosophy of Space and Time* (New York: Dover, 1958), pp. 146–47.

12. Kant, *Critique,* A155–B194.

13. Cf., for example, Donald Davidson, "True to the Facts," *Journal of Philosophy* 66 (1969), pp. 748–64.

14. Bertrand Russell, "The Philosophy of Logical Atomism" in his *Logic and Knowledge,* ed. R. C. Marsh (New York: Macmillan, 1956), p. 209.

15. Kant, *Critique,* B3–4.

16. David Hume, *A Treatise of Human Nature,* ed. L. A. Selby-Bigge (Oxford: Clarendon Press, 1888), Book I, Part III, Sec. 14, pp. 161–62.

17. Cf. P. F. Strawson, *Individuals* (London: Methuen, 1959), p. 90.

18. Albert Einstein, Boris Podolsky, and Nathan Rosen, "Can Quantum-Mechanical Description of Physical Reality be Considered Complete?" *Physical Review* 47 (1935), pp. 777–80.

19. Niels Bohr, "Discussion with Einstein on Epistemological Problems in Atomic Physics" in *Albert Einstein: Philosopher-Scientist,* ed. P. A. Schilpp (New York: Tudor, 1949), p. 234.

Notes to Chapter VII

1. Cf. G. W. F. Leibniz, Fifth Letter to Clarke, 1716, §47, in *Leibniz: Selections,* ed. P. P. Wiener (New York, Scribners, 1951), p. 254.

2. David Hume, *A Treatise of Human Nature,* ed. L. A. Selby-Bigge (Oxford: Clarendon Press, 1888), Book I, Chap. 2, Sec. 3.

3. Cf. F. H. Bradley, *Appearance and Reality,* 2d ed. (New York: Macmillan, 1902), p. 142.

4. Bradley, *Appearance,* p. 32.

5. Alfred North Whitehead, *Science and the Modern World* (New York: Mentor, 1949), pp. 52, 106.

6. Cf. the view of Brentano as discussed by Reinhardt Grossmann in "Acts and Relations in Brentano," *Analysis* 21 (1960), pp. 1–5.

7. Aristotle, *Categories* 11a15, in J. L. Ackrill, *Aristotle's Categories and De Interpretatione* (Oxford: Clarendon Press), 1963.

8. Aristotle, *Metaphysics,* trans. Richard Hope (Ann Arbor: University of Michigan Press, 1960), 1020b26–31.

9. Thomas Aquinas, *Commentary on Aristotle's Physics,* trans. R. J. Blackwell, R. J. Spath, and W. E. Thirlkel (New Haven: Yale University Press, 1963), Book III, Lectio 1, Sec. 280.

10. On the problem of how the action can be prior in time to the having of the relational property, see the exhaustive discussion by A. Krempel, *La doctrine de la relation chez saint Thomas* (Paris: Vrin, 1952), pp. 218–25.

11. Bertrand Russell, *The Principles of Mathematics* (Cambridge: Cambridge University Press, 1903), §212.

12. Russell, *Principles,* §214.

13. Cf. Fred Wilson, "Weinberg's Refutation of Nominalism," *Dialogue* 8 (1969), p. 468.

14. Cf. C. I. Lewis and C. H. Langford, *Symbolic Logic,* 2d ed. (New York: Dover, 1959), pp. 387–88.

15. Cf. Willard Van Orman Quine, *Methods of Logic,* rev. ed. (New York: Holt, 1960), p. 192.

16. Cf. R. K. Meyer, "An Undecidability Result in the Theory of Relevant Implication," *Zeitschrift für mathematische Logik und Grundlagen der Mathematik* 14 (1968), pp. 255–62.

17. Cf. Alonzo Church, *Introduction to Mathematical Logic* (Princeton: Princeton University Press, 1956), pp. 125–27.

18. Leibniz, *Discourse on Metaphysics,* §§13–15, in *Leibniz: Selections,* pp. 305–12.

19. Whitehead, *Science and the Modern World,* p. 96.

20. Karl Marx, *Capital,* trans. Samuel Moore and Edward Aveling, Vol. 1, (New York: International Publishers, 1967), Part I, Chap. 1, Sec. 3, Subsec. A(3), p. 57.

21. Thomas Aquinas, *On Truth,* trans. R. W. Mulligan, Vol. 1 (Chicago: Regnery, 1952), Question I, Article 5, *ad* 16.

22. Ludwig Wittgenstein, *Tractatus Logico-Philosophicus* (New York: Humanities Press, 1951), 4.241.

Notes to Chapter VIII

1. Henri Bergson, *Essai sur les données immédiates de la conscience,* 68th ed. (Paris: Presses Universitaires de France, 1948), p. 90.

2. Descartes, *Reply to Objections II,* axiom 2, in *Oeuvres de Descartes,* ed. Charles Adams and Paul Tannery, Vol. 9–1 (Paris: Vrin, 1964), p. 127.

3. Descartes, *Meditation VI;* cf. *Oeuvres,* Vol. 9–1, p. 62.

4. Descartes, *Meditation III;* cf. *Oeuvres,* Vol. 9–1, p. 39.

5. David Hume, *A Treatise of Human Nature,* ed. L. A. Selby-Bigge (Oxford: Clarendon Press, 1888), Book I, Part II, Sec. 3.

6. Alfred North Whitehead, *Process and Reality* (New York: Macmillan, 1929), p. 107.

7. William of Ockham, *Philosophia Naturalis,* Rome, 1637, Part III, Chap. 4; quoted in Herman Shapiro, *Motion, Time and Place According to William Ockham* (St. Bonaventure, N.Y.: Franciscan Institute, 1957), p. 31.

8. William of Ockham, *Philosophia Naturalis,* Part III, Chap. 6, in Shapiro, *Motion, Time and Place,* p. 39.

9. Cf. William of Ockham, *Philosophia Naturalis,* Part IV, Chap. 4, in Shapiro, *Motion, Time and Place,* p. 97, n. 237. Here Ockham feebly attempts to avoid treating the sequential relations as entities.

10. Aristotle, *Physics,* trans. Richard Hope (Lincoln: University of Nebraska Press, 1961), 235b5.

11. Cf. Roderick Chisholm, "Events and Propositions," *Nous* 4 (1970), pp. 15–24.

12. Cf. Donald Davidson, "The Logical Form of Action Sentences," in *The Logic of Decision and Action,* ed. Nicholas Rescher (Pittsburgh: Pittsburgh University Press, 1967), pp. 81–95.

13. Cf. Romane Clark, "Concerning the Logic of Predicate Modifiers," *Nous* 4 (1970), pp. 311–35.

14. Aristotle, *Metaphysics,* trans. Richard Hope (Ann Arbor: University of Michigan Press, 1960), 1033a33.

15. Cf. Plato, *Phaedo* 101C, in *Plato's Phaedo,* trans. R. Hackforth (Indianapolis: Library of Liberal Arts, 1955), p. 135. Also Whitehead, *Process and Reality,* pp. 521–22.

16. Aristotle, *Metaphysics* 1034b19.

17. Aristotle, *Metaphysics* 1048b8–38.

18. Aristotle, *Physics* 193b12.

Notes to Chapter IX

1. Milton Fisk, "A Pragmatic Account of Tenses," *American Philosophical Quarterly* 8 (1971), pp. 93–98.

2. Cf. Eugene P. Wigner, "Violations of Symmetry in Physics," *Scientific American* 213 (December, 1965), pp. 28–36.

3. Adolf Grünbaum, *Philosophical Problems of Space and Time* (New York: Knopf, 1963), p. 213, n. 2.

4. Georges Lechalas, *Étude sur l'espace et le temps* (Paris: Alcan, 1896), p. 174.

5. Lechalas, *Étude sur l'espace,* p. 174.

6. Grünbaum, *Philosophical Problems,* p. 191.

7. Cf. Mario Bunge, *Causality* (Cleveland and New York: Meridian, 1963), p. 162.

8. Bunge, *Causality,* pp. 197–203.

9. Cf. the lucid account of reversibility by Richard Schlegel, *Time and the Physical World* (East Lansing: Michigan State University Press, 1961), Chap. III.

10. A converse description of the sequence *cum* action is not then analogous to a reverse run of a movie reel of the pitch (cf. Wolfgang Büchel, *Philosophische Probleme der Physik* [Freiburg im Breisgau: Herder, 1965], pp. 143–46).

11. Cf. W. D. Ross, *Aristotle's Physics* (Oxford: Clarendon Press, 1936), pp. 71ff.

12. Adolph Grünbaum, "Modern Science and Zeno's Paradoxes of Motion" in *Zeno's Paradoxes,* ed. Wesley Salmon (Indianapolis: Bobbs-Merrill, 1970), pp. 211–18.

13. Cf. James Thompson, "Comments on Professor Benacerraf's Paper" in *Zeno's Paradoxes,* ed. Wesley Salmon, pp. 131–32.

14. G. W. F. Leibniz, "On Nature in Itself; or on the Force Residing in Created Things, and Their Actions," 1698, in *Leibniz: Selections,* ed. P. P. Weiner (New York: Scribners, 1951), p. 151.

15. Cf. Grünbaum, *Philosophical Problems,* pp. 187–88.

16. Cf. Büchel, *Philosophische Probleme,* pp. 458–64.

17. Cf. Gerald Feinberg, "Particles that Go Faster than Light," *Scientific American* 222 (February, 1970), pp. 69–77.

18. Mary Hesse, *Forces and Fields* (Edinburgh: Nelson, 1961), pp. 279–89.

19. Cf. Rudolf Carnap, "Über die Abhängigkeit der Eigenschaften des Raumes von denen der Zeit," *Kant Studien* 30 (1925), pp. 331–45.

20. Cf. Paul Fitzgerald, "Tachyons, Backwards Causation, and Freedom," *Boston Studies in Philosophy of Science,* ed. R. C. Buck and R. S. Cohen, Vol. 8 (Dordrecht: Reidel, 1972), pp. 415–36.

21. Cf. J. D. van der Waals, Jr., "Über die Erklärung der Naturgesetze auf statistisch-mechanischer Grundlage," *Physicalisches Zeitschrift* 12 (1911), pp. 547–49; for the calculation see Büchel, *Philosophische Probleme,* pp. 100–06.

22. Cf. Grünbaum, *Philosophical Problems,* pp. 255–56.

23. Cf. Satosi Watanabe, "Time and the Probabilistic View of the World" in *The Voices of Time,* ed. J. T. Fraser (New York: Braziller, 1966), p. 534.

24. Cf. Hans Reichenbach, *The Direction of Time* (Berkeley and Los Angeles: University of California Press, 1956), §14.

25. Reichenbach distinguishes points of branching from points of merging by saying the latter are, whereas the former are not, equilibrium points (*The Direction of Time,* p. 138). Here I have followed Grünbaum (*Philosophical Problems,* p. 258) in allowing the possibility of branchings at equilibrium points as well.

26. Cf. Reichenbach, *The Direction of Time,* pp. 139–40.

Notes to Chapter X

1. Cf. Aristotle, *Physics,* trans. Richard Hope (Lincoln: University of Nebraska Press, 1961), 201a10.

2. Cf., for example, Gilbert Ryle, *The Concept of Mind* (London: Hutchinson, 1949), pp. 117–25.

3. Cf., for example, Willard Van Orman Quine, *Word and Object* (New York: Technology Press and Wiley, 1960), pp. 222–25.

4. Cf. Bruce Aune, "Fisk on Capacities and Natures," *Boston Studies in Philosophy of Science,* ed. R. C. Buck and R. S. Cohen, Vol. 8 (Dordrecht: Reidel, 1972), pp. 83–87. In light of Aune's criticisms, I have been able to formulate the issue concerning modality and these two models for capacities more accurately.

5. John Locke, *An Essay Concerning Human Understanding,* ed. A. C. Fraser (Oxford: Clarendon Press, 1894), Book III, Chap. VI, Sec. 3.

6. Locke, *Essay,* Book III, Chap. VI, Sec. 6.

7. Locke, *Essay,* Book II, Chap. VIII, Sec. 9.

8. Locke, *Essay,* Book II, Chap. XXV, Sec. 8.

9. Cf. Ernan McMullin, "Capacities and Natures: an Exercise in Ontology," *Boston Studies in Philosophy of Science,* ed. R. C. Buck and R. S. Cohen, Vol. 8 (Dordrecht: Reidel, 1972), pp. 63–82.

10. Isaac Newton, *Mathematical Principles of Natural Philosophy,* trans. Andrew Motte, Vol. 1 (Berkeley and Los Angeles: University of California Press, 1962), Definition III, p. 2.

11. Hermann Weyl, *Space, Time, Matter,* trans. H. L. Brose (New York: Dover, 1950), §25.

12. Cf. James Clerk Maxwell, *Matter and Motion,* 1877 (reissue; New York: Dover, n.d.), §83.

13. Cf. Roger Squires, "Are Dispositions Causes?" *Analysis* 29 (1968), pp. 45–47.

14. Alfred North Whitehead, *Process and Reality* (New York: Macmillan, 1929), p. 34.

15. Cf. D. M. Armstrong, "Dispositions and Causes," *Analysis* 30 (1969), pp. 23–26.

16. Cf. Aristotle, *Metaphysics,* trans. Richard Hope (Ann Arbor: University of Michigan Press, 1960), 1046b28–1047a23.

17. Cf. David Weissman, *Dispositional Properties* (Carbondale: Southern Illinois University Press, 1965), p. 62.

18. Cf. Nelson Goodman, *Fact, Fiction, and Forecast* (Cambridge: Harvard University Press, 1955), p. 45; Karl Popper, *The Logic of Scientific Discovery* (London: Hutchinson, 1959), p. 424.

19. Cf. Isaac Levi, *Gambling with Truth* (New York: Knopf, 1967), p. 196.

20. Cf. Karl Marx, *Capital,* trans. Samuel Moore and Edward Aveling, Vol. 1 (New York: International Publishers, 1967), Part II, Chap. 6, p. 172.

21. Cf. Milton Fisk, "A Defence of the Principle of Event Causality," *British Journal for Philosophy of Science* 18 (1967), pp. 89–108.

22. Cf. David Bohm, *Quantum Theory* (New York: Prentice-Hall, 1951), pp. 175, 225.

23. Werner Heisenberg, *Physics and Philosophy* (New York: Harper Torchbook, 1962), p. 185.

24. Cf. Wilfrid Sellars, "The Language of Theories" in his *Science, Perception, and Reality* (New York: Humanities Press, 1963), pp. 106–26.

25. Cf. V. I. Lenin, *Materialism and Empirio-Criticism* (New York: International Publishers, 1927), Chap. 3, Sec. 3, p. 155.

26. Rom Harré notes in regard to his fine structure model for capacities that "There are further issues here, namely, the force of the modal operation . . ." ("Powers," *British Journal for Philosophy of Science* 21 [1970], p. 101). See also Rom Harré, *The Principles of Scientific Thinking* (Chicago: University of Chicago Press, 1970), p. 273.

27. Norwood Russell Hanson, "Logical Positivism and the Interpretation of Scientific Theories," mimeographed (New Haven, Yale University, 1967).

28. Angus Ross, "Natural Kinds and Necessity," typescript (Norwich, East Anglia University, 1969).

29. Thomas Aquinas, *Summa Theologica,* Part I, Question 46, Article 2, *ad* 7, in *The Basic Writings of Saint Thomas Aquinas,* ed. Anton C. Pegis, Vol. 1 (New York: Random House, 1945), p. 455.

30. Willard Van Orman Quine, "Natural Kinds" in his *Ontological Relativity* (New York: Columbia University Press, 1969), p. 136.

31. Cf. Linus Pauling, *The Nature of the Chemical Bond,* 2d ed. (Ithaca: Cornell University Press, 1948), §43.

32. C. D. Broad, "The 'Nature' of a Continuant," in *Readings in Philosophical Analysis,* ed. Herbert Feigl and Wilfrid Sellars (New York: Appleton-Century-Crofts, 1949), pp. 472–81.

33. Cf. also M. R. Ayers, *The Refutation of Determinism* (London: Methuen, 1968), p. 86.

Notes to Chapter XI

1. Frederick Engels' view of motion as "the mode of existence . . . of matter" might be construed as an ontology of conditions (*Dialectics of Nature,* trans. Clemens Dutt [New York: International Publishers, 1940], p. 35). Lenin, however, says: "Whether we say the world is moving matter, or that the world is material motion, makes no difference whatsoever" (*Materialism and Empirio-Criticism* [New York: International Publishers, 1927], Chap. 5, Sec. 3, pp. 277–78). Since Lenin recognizes necessities, whether the world is moving matter or material motion should be a question of first importance.

2. Bertrand Russell, *The Analysis of Matter* (New York: Dover, 1954), pp. 244, 284, 286.

3. Cf. Bertrand Russell, "The Philosophy of Logical Atomism" in his *Logic and Knowledge,* ed. R. C. Marsh (New York: Macmillan, 1956), Secs. I–II.

4. Plato, *Timaeus* 49D-E in F. M. Cornford, *Plato's Cosmology* (London: Kegan Paul, 1937), p. 278.

5. "Substance is a being capable of action" (G. W. F. Leibniz, "The Principles of Nature and Grace," §1, in *Leibniz: Selections,* ed. P. P. Wiener (New York: Scribners, 1951), p. 522.

6. Cf. Nicholas Maxwell, "Can There be Necessary Connections Between Successive Events?" *British Journal for Philosophy of Science* 19 (1967), pp. 1–25.

7. Cf. Gustav Bergmann, "Russell's Examination of Leibniz Examined," in his *Meaning and Existence* (Madison: University of Wisconsin Press, 1960), p. 155–88.

8. Cf. Nelson Goodman, *The Structure of Appearance* (Indianapolis: Bobbs-Merrill, 1966), p. 128.

9. Cf. Aquinas, *Summa Theologica,* Part I, Question 104, Article 1, in *The Basic Writings of Saint Thomas Aquinas,* ed. Anton C. Pegis, Vol. 1 (New York: Random House, 1945).

10. Cf. Aristotle, *Categories* 1a23, in J. L. Ackrill, *Aristotle's Categories and De Interpretatione* (Oxford: Clarendon Press), 1963; and *Physics,* trans. Richard Hope (Lincoln: University of Nebraska Press, 1961), 185a32.

11. Cf. Herbert Marcuse, *Reason and Revolution* (Boston: Beacon Press, 1960) pp. 44–47.

12. Cf. Karl Popper, *The Open Society and Its Enemies,* Vol. 2 (New York: Harper Torchbook, 1963), pp. 91, 245.

INDEX

Italic page references are to passages that explain the meanings of terms or phrases with those references.